# DÖNITZ AND THE WOLF PACKS

Like one that on a lonesome road
　　Doth walk in fear and dread,
And having once turn'd round, walks on,
　　And turns no more his head;
Because he knows a frightful fiend
　　Doth close behind him tread.

— Samuel Taylor Coleridge

By the same author

*Masters Next to God*
*They Sank the Red Dragon*
*The Fighting Tramps*
*The Grey Widow Maker*
*Blood and Bushido*
*SOS – Men Against the Sea*
*Salvo!*
*Attack and Sink*

# DÖNITZ AND THE WOLF PACKS

## BERNARD EDWARDS

ARMS AND
ARMOUR

*This book is for the merchant seamen,*
*the PBI of the Battle of the Atlantic.*

Arms and Armour Press
An Imprint of the Cassell Group
Wellington House, 125 Strand, London WC2R 0BB

Distributed in the USA by Sterling Publishing Co. Inc.,
387 Park Avenue South, New York, NY 10016-8810.

Distributed in Australia by Capricorn Link (Australia) Pty.
Ltd, 2/13 Carrington Road, Castle Hill, NSW 2154.

British Library Cataloguing-in-Publication Data:
a catalogue record for this book is available from the
British Library

ISBN 1-85409-256-1

Designed and edited by DAG Publications Ltd. Designed
by David Gibbons; edited by Philip Jarrett;
Printed and bound in Great Britain by
Hartnolls Limited, Bodmin, Cornwall

*The author wishes to acknowledge*
*the valuable co-operation of the Public Record Office, Kew.*

# Contents

# Introduction

Of the war at sea, Winston Churchill wrote:

> Amid the torrent of violent events one anxiety reigned supreme. Battles might be won or lost, enterprises might succeed or miscarry, territories might be gained or quitted, but dominating all our power to carry on the war, or even keep ourselves alive, lay our mastery of the ocean routes and the free approach and entry to our ports.

Nowhere was the battle harder fought than on the trade routes of the North Atlantic, where vast convoys of Allied and neutral ships shuttled back and forth with food and the necessities of war, upon which the fate of Britain – and therefore that of all the other nations of the free world – depended.

This was a cruel, brutish struggle in which no quarter was asked or given. Both sides faced two enemies simultaneously; the thunder of the guns ranged against them, and the awesome might of a perpetually hostile ocean. Consequent on this, to survive the destruction of a ship or submarine was not the end, but only the beginning of an ordeal which all too often culminated in a lingering death by drowning or exposure. It is on record that many more men died silently in lifeboats, on rafts or in the icy water, than in the violence of the sinking of their ship.

The adoption of the wolf pack tactic by the C-in-C U-boats, Admiral Karl Dönitz, was a master stroke. It might be said that he drew his inspiration from the dark forests of Europe, where once the predatory wolves roamed in packs and the frightened deer ran in herds. And so, when the merchantmen of the Battle of the Atlantic gathered in convoys for protection, the U-boats – the 'grey wolves' of the sea – hunted in packs. When a convoy was signalled, Dönitz formed a pack from U-boats in the immediate area, dispersing it again after the attack and then forming another pack when the next convoy came along. Thus, in the course of one war patrol, a U-boat could be involved in a number of packs, each of which Dönitz named in much the way that Atlantic hurricanes are now identified as they form.

Dönitz's wolf packs came within an ace of winning the Battle of the Atlantic, and so the war, for Germany. They failed only because the U-boats were not true submarines, and were too often forced to fight on the surface; the *Schnorkel*, which could have tipped the balance, came too late. Even so, every convoy successfully attacked by the packs was considered by the Allies to be the equivalent of a battle lost on land, such was the need for the cargoes to get through.

The men who manned the U-boats suffered dreadful privations and faced intolerable dangers, but in recompense they were fêted by a grateful nation as heroes, showered with medals and promised immortality. That they were responsible for the wanton slaughter of so many thousands of their brother sea-men, for all men of the sea are brothers, did not concern them. Yet, nefarious though their trade may have been, they were not, for the most, evil men. Certainly they saw themselves not as ruthless killers, but more as 20th-century reincarnations of the swashbuckling pirates of the Spanish Main. Those who gave their lives in the conflict, more than 28,000 of them, found their immortality in a magnificent shrine at Möltenort, overlooking the waters of Kiel Bay. Those who survived the bombs and depth charges to live into old age still dream of glory and harbour no regrets for their past deeds.

# 1

# The Birth Pangs

On the afternoon of 5 September 1914 the German submarine *U21* lay hidden just below the surface off the entrance to the Firth of Forth on Scotland's east coast. The weather was fine, but the white horses were running in a fresh breeze, and spray sometimes obscured the view through the raised periscope. However, the U-boat's commander, Kapitänleutnant Otto Hersing, was a patient man, and eventually the target he was awaiting hove in sight.

She was the British Scout-class light cruiser HMS *Pathfinder*, 2,940 tons, armed with ten 12-pounder guns. Black smoke rolled back from the cruiser's three tall funnels and her bow-wave foamed white as she headed for the open sea at a smart pace.

Hersing computed the approaching ship's course and speed, carefully manoeuvred the U-boat into a position to intercept, and waited for the range to close. The minutes passed like hours, and the tension in the control room of the small submarine mounted to fever pitch. Then, at last, the British ship filled the periscope's lens and Hersing rapped out 'Fire one!'

There was a rush of compressed air as the torpedo left the tube and the U-boat suddenly lost her trim, bucking and rearing like a skittish horse. For a moment it seemed that she would shoot to the surface out of control, then water flooding into her forward ballast tanks brought her back on to an even keel.

Hersing bent to the periscope again, and when the lens cleared he saw the target ship still coming on, blissfully unaware of her peril. A minute passed with U-boat commander counting off the seconds silently, and then, when it seemed certain that the torpedo had missed or failed to explode, the enemy cruiser suddenly staggered and stopped dead in her tracks, a tall column of water and debris shooting skywards from abaft her bridge. Seconds later she blew apart as her main magazine went up, and within four minutes HMS *Pathfinder* had gone to the bottom, taking with her 259 of her crew of 360.

Before the first of the rescue ships racing to *Pathfinder*'s aid reached the scene, *U21* slipped silently away. With one well-placed torpedo, Otto Hersing had signalled the arrival of the deadliest weapon yet seen in naval warfare, the diesel and electric powered submarine. Its coming marked the end of centuries of dominance by the large surface warship. Unfortunately for those who would lose their lives over the coming decades, it would take a long time for the message to reach the British naval hierarchy of the day.

There is a strongly-held belief that man's origins lie deep in the oceans. Assuming this to be true, it could account for his unflagging efforts down through the centuries to conquer the dark waters beneath the waves. Legend has it that it all started more than two thousand years ago, in 332 BC, with Alexander III, King of Macedon. In one of his punitive expeditions against the Persians, the young king is said to have gone underwater in the Mediterranean in a crude diving vessel consisting of an iron frame covered with animal skins. This story may be no more than a flight of fancy; we are unlikely ever to know the truth. Certainly the first recorded design for a workable submarine did not appear for many centuries.

William Bourne, a carpenter, gunmaker and writer, was a contemporary of Drake and Raleigh, but unlike these great Elizabethan voyagers his vision lay beneath the sea. In 1578 Bourne produced plans for a submersible ship with a double hull and ballast tanks, much like the modern submarine. Perhaps fortunately for Bourne and anyone tempted to sail with him, the inventor died before his underwater craft could be built. The flexible inner hull of the ship would almost certainly have collapsed underwater with disastrous results.

Bourne's submarine remained on the drawing board until a Dutch physician, Cornelis Drebble, moved to England and became tutor to the children of James I. Drebble was another prodigious scientific explorer, sometimes credited with the invention of the microscope, telescope and thermometer, and in 1620 he obtained the King's backing for a submersible craft. Using Bourne's plans, Drebble built a wooden hull, covered it with a leather canopy smeared with tallow to make it waterproof, and succeeded in travelling underwater in the River Thames for a short distance at a depth of twelve feet. Drebble and his twelve oarsmen no doubt had an uncomfortable and perilous voyage, but they spent long enough below the surface to earn an important place in the record books.

The theory having been tested and found feasible, experiments with underwater craft continued in earnest, but it was not until the internal combustion engine and the electrical storage battery came along in the 1890s that the true submarine, a vessel capable of navigating under the sea, was born. When Europe went to war in 1914 the submarine was well on the way to becoming a sophisticated weapon. The British Admiralty, however, was not ready for this new approach to naval warfare. Its answer to the submarine was to build the largest fighting ships yet known, the huge, big-gun Dreadnought battleships, each costing £2 million and capable of hurling ten tons of shells at an enemy every eight minutes. Wiser heads across the North Sea in Germany saw the potential of the threat from beneath the sea and put their money into the *Unterseeboot*.

When war broke out in early August 1914, the British Grand Fleet consisted of 21 Dreadnought battleships, eight pre-Dreadnoughts, four battlecruisers and their attendant cruisers and destroyers. The German High Seas Fleet was heavily outnumbered, and immediately retired behind the defences of the Heligoland Bight, leaving the huge British fleet to steam majestically up and down the North Sea, showing the flag but achieving little beyond putting the fear of God into German and neutral merchant ships.

Germany's answer, the '*kleinkrieg*', a war of stealth by U-boat, began at dawn on 6 August, when ten U-boats left Wilhelmshaven and threaded their way through the minefields into the North Sea. The start of their voyage was not auspicious: they first ran into dense fog, in the midst of which *U9*, commanded by Kapitänleutnant Otto Weddigen, experienced engine trouble and was forced to turn back. The other boats carried on to the north, anxious to come to grips with the enemy's big ships. These were found off the Orkneys by *U13* and *U15* on the morning of the 8th; three 22,500-ton Dreadnoughts unconcernedly carrying out a practice shoot with their 13.5in guns while a number of destroyers and torpedo boats idled nearby.

The U-boats dived and moved in, *U15* leading. When within range of the nearest Dreadnought she fired one torpedo. Unfortunately for the German submariners, lookouts aboard HMS *Monarch* saw the track of the missile and the battleship heeled under full helm, swinging her stern away from the danger. The torpedo passed harmlessly by, but it stirred up a veritable hornets' nest for the U-boats. The battleships scattered, but the destroyers and torpedo boats came tearing in, their guns firing wildly at the unseen enemy.

When the furore had died down, the two U-boats surfaced and set course for home. They had not gone far when they ran into the fog again and became separated. The fog gave way to a half gale, and *U15*'s diesels broke down. While she lay hove-to, rolling in the rough seas, she was found by the light cruiser HMS *Birmingham*, which promptly rammed her, sending her to the bottom with all hands. *U13* also failed to return to Wilhelmshaven, and was presumed to have hit a mine.

It might have been supposed that this incident, followed by the sinking of *Pathfinder* on 2 September, would have alerted the Admiralty to the very real threat the U-boat posed to the big ships, but the message failed to get home. The Grand Fleet, sometimes stretching from horizon to horizon, continued to parade majestically up and down the North Sea, demonstrating the awesome power of the Royal Navy and daring the Kaiser's High Seas Fleet to come out and do battle. It proved to be a pointless exercise, for Germany's big ships were content to lie snug in their anchorages behind the guns of Heligoland, while the U-boats cruised unseen looking for soft targets.

Meanwhile, British submarines were also sweeping the North Sea, anxious to avenge *Pathfinder*. On 13 September *E9*, commanded by Lieutenant-Commander Max Horton, an officer destined for great things, penetrated the Heligoland Bight and sank the German light cruiser *Hela*.

On 22 September Otto Weddigen was back at sea with *U9*, her diesels repaired and functioning smoothly. As dawn broke he was cruising on the surface off the Dutch coast, some 30 miles west of Ymuiden, when he sighted the three 12,000-ton cruisers *Aboukir*, *Hogue* and *Cressy* steaming in company. Built at the turn of the century, the ageing warships, manned largely by reservists, were on guard against possible hit-and-run attacks on shipping in the Straits of Dover by German torpedo boats. They seemed oblivious to the threat posed by U-boats, for they were making a leisurely 10 knots and were not zig-zagging.

Weddigen took *U9* below the waves as soon as the British ships were sighted, and such was his luck that he only had to bide his time as they steamed straight towards him. HMS *Aboukir* was first to come within range, and Weddigen's torpedo caught her squarely amidships. She blew up and sank immediately. A few minutes later, before the British had time to recover from the shock, a second torpedo ripped open the hull of the *Hogue*. She went down in five minutes, her guns firing a few ineffectual shots at *U9* as the submarine lost trim and surfaced briefly.

It was by now obvious to the captain of the *Cressy* that an enemy submarine was responsible for the loss of the other ships, not mines, as he had first thought. But instead of seeking to save his own ship, he raced in to pick up the survivors struggling in the water. His action was in the best traditions of the Royal Navy, but under the circumstances it was suicidal. Otto Weddigen, who had by now reloaded his tubes, was not about to throw away the chance of a hat-trick in the interests of chivalry. It required only the minimum of movements to bring the enemy cruiser into his sights.

Only at the last minute did the *Cressy's* lookouts sight *U9's* periscope, and by then it was too late. The cruiser sheered away and tried to run for it, but as she did so two torpedoes streaked through the water and slammed into her hull. The *Cressy* staggered under the shock of the double explosion, listed heavily to starboard, then rolled over.

That early autumn day in 1914 had become a day of shame that would live in the memory of the Royal Navy for ever more. In the space of one hour, as the sun lifted over the horizon in the North Sea, one small German submarine, manned by only 40 men, had disposed of three formidable British warships totalling 36,000 tons. These great ships, *Aboukir*, *Hogue* and *Cressy*, named for famous British victories on land and sea, took 1,460 men to the bottom with them.

There was panic at the Admiralty, and as the only two bases on the East Coast capable of sheltering the Grand Fleet, Scapa Flow and Rosyth, offered no protection against submarines, the fleet was temporarily withdrawn to Loch Ewe, on the west coast of Scotland. At the same time, as a result of the sinking of the *Hela* by *E9*, the bulk of the German High Seas Fleet retired through the Kiel Canal into the Baltic.

The situation at sea was now ludicrous. The world's two most powerful fleets, mustering between them no fewer than 55 battleships and 28 armoured cruisers, had been sent scurrying for shelter by the actions of two tiny underwater craft. The big ships would return, but because of the threat posed by marauding submarines the power of their guns would never be the same again. A month later came an incident which was to change the nature of war at sea for all time.

On 20 October *U17*, commanded by Korvettenkapitän Feldkirchner, was off the coast of Norway, returning to Wilhelmshaven after an unfruitful patrol. When 14 miles west-south-west of Skudesnaes she sighted the 866-ton British steamer *Glitra*, bound from Grangemouth to Stavanger with a cargo of coal, coke, iron plate and drums of oil. Feldkirchner had no specific orders to attack merchant ships, but neither had he any orders to the contrary, and as he was returning to port empty handed he decided to take action against what was, after all, an enemy ship.

The destruction of the *Glitra* was carried out in a most gentlemanly manner, Feldkirchner adhering strictly to the 'International Cruiser Rules', which stipulated that a merchant ship must not be sunk until her crew and passengers had taken to the boats. The steamer was stopped and boarded, and, when her crew were safely in the boats, scuttling charges were laid and the *Glitra* and her valuable cargo went to the bottom. Feldkirchner then towed the lifeboats within easy reach of land before leaving the British seamen to their own devices. The weather was fair, and the *Glitra's* crew reached the shore, indignant at the loss of their ship but none the worse for their experience.

Thus *U17* earned the distinction of being the first submarine to sink a merchant ship, an action not illegal under international law, but one that had hitherto been regarded on both sides of the North Sea as somewhat uncivilised. Feldkirchner half expected to face a court martial on his return to Wilhelmshaven, but to his great relief received only a mild reprimand. Admiral von Ingenohl, Commander-in-Chief of the High Seas Fleet, was opposed to attacks on unarmed merchantmen, but there were others nearer the Kaiser who thought the end justified the means. When, a week later, *U24* (Kapitänleutnant Schneider) torpedoed and sank the French steamer *Ganteaume* without warning, resulting in the loss of 40 lives, there was uproar in Britain and France. In Germany the reaction was muted, for the submarine was now being seen as the answer to Britain's overwhelming superiority in surface warships. Her vital maritime supply lines suddenly seemed very vulnerable.

On 4 February 1915 the German Admiralstab announced: 'The waters around Great Britain and Ireland, including the whole of the English Channel, are herewith declared to be in the War Zone. From February 18 onwards, every merchant ship met with in this zone will be destroyed.'

The dogs of war were unleashed upon the wide oceans, and by the end of the year the U-boats had sunk 1,307,996 tons of Allied and neutral merchant shipping, 855,721 tons of this being under the British flag. As the months passed and the opposing armies became bogged down in the mud of Flanders, so the toll of sunken ships rose relentlessly. It reached a peak in April 1917, 395 ships of 881,027 tons falling to the U-boats in that month alone.

The situation was critical for Britain, for she could not survive for long if cargoes ceased to flow into her ports. In desperation, the Admiralty looked back to Nelson for inspiration and gathered the scattered merchantmen into convoys, where they would be safer under the wing of the Royal Navy. The sinkings continued, but they were on a steep downward curve. By the end of the year more than 98 per cent of ships in convoy were getting through to their destinations unharmed. It became evident to the German Admirals that their hopes of starving the British into submission were doomed to failure unless they found an answer to the convoys. Kommodore Hermann Bauer, Commander-in-Chief, U-boats, put forward a plan to counter the effect of the convoys by similarly grouping U-boats to attack in organised bands. His plan was not taken up, however, and he was transferred out of U-boats shortly afterwards. It was left to Bauer's successor, Kommodore Andreas Michelsen, to resurrect the idea, but he did not do this until May 1918, by which time it had become patently obvious that Germany would lose the war.

Before daylight on 8 May 1918, nine U-boats sailing in company slipped out of Jade Bay and headed north–about the British Isles. Three days later they were drawn up in a north-south line across the Western Approaches, awaiting the prey that must sooner or later steam unsuspectingly into their trap. Unfortunately, although the plan was sound in conception, there appears to have been little communication and no co-ordination between the boats. Over the next fourteen or fifteen days no fewer than 293 ships passed through the net and only three were sunk, and this for the loss of two U-boats, one rammed by a merchantman and another torpedoed by a British submarine. So the first attempt at concerted action by a pack of U-boats ended in dismal failure.

A few months later a similar experiment was proposed in the Mediterranean, but on a much smaller scale. Only two U-boats were to be involved. Korvettenkapitän Steinbauer in *U48*, refuelling in the Austrian port of Pola, devised a plan to wreak havoc among the British convoys westbound from the

Suez Canal. Steinbauer's proposal was for two boats in company to lie in wait off Malta, and attack on the surface at night, slipping through the destroyer screen and into the heart of a convoy before loosing their torpedoes at the unsuspecting merchant ships. It was a bold plan that would end either in brilliant success or disaster for the U-boats. Steinbauer's accomplice on the first attack was to be Oberleutnant-zur-See Dönitz, then commanding *UB68*, also lying in Pola.

At 27 years of age Karl Dönitz was already a seasoned officer, having entered the German Navy as a young cadet in 1910. He had seen service in the Dardanelles as signals officer in the cruiser *Breslau*, and in 1916 had been transferred to the U-boat arm. This move was not of his own choosing, but Dönitz accepted it with good grace and carried on with the business of learning his new trade. This he did well, as was his style, and his first command, the minelayer *UC25*, came at the end of 1917. In two successful cruises in *UC25* Döntiz earned the Knight's Cross and promotion to oberleutnant. He was then given command of the larger *UB68*.

Dönitz was eager to put Steinbauer's plan to the test, but when the time came to leave Pola, *U48* was delayed by engine trouble, and *UB68* sailed alone. She arrived at the prearranged spot, 150 miles east of Malta, on 3 October. Dönitz lay hove-to on the surface, and that night, in the faint light of the new moon, he found himself directly in the path of the expected convoy.

With *UB68* trimmed down so that only the conning tower was above the waves, Dönitz had no difficulty in penetrating the escort screen. However, as he was on the point of aiming his bow tubes, the convoy made a sudden, bold alteration of course. The change of course may have been scheduled, or because the U-boat had been spotted, but the immediate result was that Dönitz found himself directly in the path of a number of oncoming ships and in imminent danger of being rammed. His reactions were swift and decisive. First loosing off a torpedo at the nearest enemy ship, he swung the boat round under helm and engines, and made off into the night. The torpedo missed its target, but *UB68* retired unharmed.

When Dönitz regained contact with the convoy it was almost dawn, and he was obliged to dive before attacking. Once again sudden disaster threatened. No sooner was the U-boat below the surface than, for no perceptible reason, she went out of control, diving almost vertically, until she reached the unprecedented depth of 300ft, far below her safe depth. All lights failed, acid spilled from the banks of batteries below the plates, and panic swept through the boat. Only when all ballast tanks had been blown was the crazy descent checked; then, with maximum buoyancy, *UB68* shot to the surface, once more out of control. Seconds later Dönitz emerged from the conning tower hatch to find that it was now full daylight and he was in the middle of the convoy and under fire from all sides. Escape was impossible, for the submarine's compressed-air tanks were exhausted, and if she dived she would never rise again. The matter was decided when the hull began to fill with choking fumes from spilt battery acid. Dönitz had no choice but to surrender. This was a bitter pill for any commander to swallow, and the twelve months Karl Dönitz spent in a British prisoner-of-war camp added to his resentment.

When Dönitz and his men went into captivity, the war had only a month or so to go. Mutiny had already broken out in the German surface fleet, and although some U-boat crews were willing to continue the fight, their vessels could find no sanctuary in any German naval base. On 11 November 1918 the Armistice was signed and the remaining U-boats sailed into British and French ports to surrender. They were received with loathing, for the U-boat was still regarded as a 'dirty' weapon, unworthy of a page in the history of sea warfare. But the fact that the U-boat was a formidable weapon could not be disputed. In four years of war about 150 of these small craft, each manned by no more than 40 men, had sunk 5,700 Allied and neutral merchant ships totalling over 11 million tons. They had challenged and, in the end, humiliated the mighty British surface fleet. In 1918 it was clear to even the most hidebound of the Admirals that in any future war the submarine would be a major factor in deciding which side won or lost – and that war was not far over the horizon.

Shortly after 1100 on the morning of 3 September 1939, Karl Dönitz, now 48 years old and holding flag rank, sat at his desk in the headquarters of U-boat Command West on the outskirts of Wilhelmshaven, holding a slip of paper. The signal, originated by the Admiralty and addressed to the British Fleet, was uncoded and unequivocal. It read simply: 'TOTAL GERMANY'. Twenty years and ten months after the signing of the Armistice in November 1918, Germany and Britain were again at war. This was a momentous hour for Admiral Karl Dönitz, for, having suffered the humiliation of a British prisoner-of-war camp and then witnessed the slow ruination of his country, the opportunity for revenge was at hand, and he was resolved to take it.

Upon his return to Germany in July 1919, Dönitz had found the nation on its knees. All semblance of discipline had succumbed to the fever of revolution, and anarchy walked hand in hand with hunger and starvation across the land. There was much worse to come. The Treaty of Versailles, signed only a few weeks before Dönitz returned, was a savage instrument, designed to punish Germany and strip her of all of her assets. Her colonies were seized, her heavy industries demolished, and she was ordered to pay £6,000 million in reparations to the Allies. Such a colossal debt could not be borne by a country in ruins, and eventually resulted in catastrophic inflation. At the height of this inflation the exchange rate for the mark was an incredible 43,000,000,000,000 to the pound sterling; it was worthless.

By 1930 there were some signs of economic recovery, but these were swept aside when the world tumbled headlong into depression. As 1931 drew to a close Germany had nine million unemployed and was again on the verge of bankruptcy. The desperate need for a strong hand on the wheel opened all doors to Adolf Hitler and his National Socialist Party; they took complete control of the country in 1933. From then on Germany, transformed into a nation vibrating with strength and confidence, and chanting for *Lebensraum*, moved inexorably towards war with her neighbours. Marshal Foch's comment on the Treaty of Versailles when it was signed, 'This is not peace. It is an Armistice for twenty years,' was about to be proved true.

Karl Dönitz became a committed Nazi and a fervent admirer of Hitler, which may in part account for his appointment in 1935 to command the U-boat Arm at the early age of 44. He immediately set about rebuilding his new command.

The Treaty of Versailles had allowed Germany to build, for defence purposes only, six small battleships, six cruisers, twelve destroyers and twelve torpedo boats, but, with painful memories of the war in mind, she was forbidden submarines. When Hitler came to power he demanded that these restrictions be relaxed, and in June 1935 the Anglo-German Naval Agreement was signed in London. Under the terms of this agreement Germany would be allowed a navy equal to 35 per cent of the Royal Navy. In the case of submarines the figure was 45 per cent, with the option, should both sides agree, of increasing to 100 per cent. For Britain this was a suicidal agreement to make, but the Admirals, complacent to a man and confident in the infallibility of the depth-charge-carrying, asdic-equipped destroyer, saw no threat to the sea lanes. They had not learned the lessons of the First World War.

In 1939 Britain was a nation of 48 million people, her economy geared to the manufacture of goods which she exported to the four corners of the globe. Her annual imports ran to 55 million tons, much of this comprising essential raw materials for her factories and food for her masses. This being so, it is not surprising that the world's largest merchant fleet sailed under the British flag, being made up of more than 5,000 ocean-going ships of nearly 20 million tons gross. The Royal Navy, on the other hand, owing to the politicians' preoccupation with disarmament, had been run down.

On the outbreak of war Dönitz had 56 U-boats in commission. This was not as many as he would have liked, but they were all new, the majority being the larger Type VII boats of 700 tons displacement. The Type VII was unmatched as an attack submarine, having a top speed on the surface of 17 knots and a range of 8,500 miles at 10 knots. It was capable of submerging in 20 seconds, and had a maximum speed underwater of 7.6 knots, a safe diving depth of 250m and a range of 40 miles at 4 knots when submerged.

Its armament consisted of four bow tubes and one stern tube with fourteen torpedoes, an 88mm deck gun with 250 rounds and one 20mm anti-aircraft cannon with 4,380 rounds. On 30 August 1939, four days before war broke out, Dönitz had 39 of his U-boats at sea in the North Sea and Atlantic, strategically placed to attack British shipping when the signal was given. They were bound by the 'Cruiser Rules', which still held good and authorised them to sink enemy merchantmen only after giving due warning and taking steps to ensure the safety of those on board.

At 2100 on 3 September the 13,581-ton Donaldson liner *Athenia* was two days out from Glasgow and 60 miles south-south-west of Rockall, moving out into the open Atlantic. Bound for Montreal, she carried 1,103 passengers, 300 of whom were American, and 305 crew. The war was then only ten hours old, and the possibility of danger seemed remote. Children were being put to bed and their parents were changing for dinner when the torpedo came streaking in from the darkness.

The *Athenia* was hit on the port side abaft the bridge, the massive explosion of the torpedo's warhead cruelly laying her open to the sea, demolishing the forward engine-room watertight bulkhead and wrecking much of the passenger accommodation below decks. The ship developed a 30° list to port and it was difficult to launch the boats, but under the direction of the disciplined British crew the ship was abandoned with the loss of only 112 lives, 28 of them American. The German submarine responsible for sinking the *Athenia*, *U30* (Kapitänleutnant Fritz-Julius Lemp), escaped into the night without rendering assistance to the survivors.

In terms of the rules then governing sea warfare, Lemp's torpedoing of the British liner without warning was an atrocity, and caused a great deal of embarrassment in Germany. In his defence, Lemp claimed that the *Athenia* was zigzagging on an unusual course without lights, and that he assumed she must be an armed merchant cruiser. Hitler, concerned at the possible reaction from America, even accused the Royal Navy of sinking the ship to win American sympathy. It is to the Americans' shame that it took a full year to convince them that the unarmed *Athenia* was really sunk by a German U-boat.

It does seem, however, that the sinking without warning of the *Athenia* was an aberration; a genuine mistake brought about by the over-enthusiasm of men trained to a high pitch of aggression. In the days that followed, by and large, Dönitz's commanders adhered to the 'Cruiser Rules', sometimes to the point of high farce.

At noon on 7 September the 4,060-ton *Olivegrove*, commanded by Captain James Barnetson, was 420 miles west-south-west of Land's End, homeward bound with a cargo of raw sugar from Cuba. The weather was fine, the visibility good, and the ship was making 9½ knots. Barnetson was congratulating himself in having come thus far without meeting the enemy when he sighted a U-boat on the surface. She flew a string of code flags ordering the *Olivegrove* to heave-to, and her signal lamp was flashing the same message in plain language.

Kapitänleutnant Hans-Wilhelm von Dresky, in the conning tower of *U33*, felt a surge of annoyance when the enemy ship suddenly presented her stern and made off with her funnel belching black smoke. But, having in mind the furore caused by the sinking of the *Athenia*, he resisted the temptation to open fire and gave chase. The U-boat, making a good 16 knots on the surface, easily overtook the fleeing tramp and put a shot across her bows. Barnetson, whose ship was unarmed, surrendered without further ado.

As soon as the boats carrying the *Olivegrove's* crew drew clear of the ship, von Dresky put a torpedo into her. He then called the lifeboats alongside the submarine and invited Captain Barnetson aboard. The two commanders shook hands, von Dresky apologised to Barnetson for sinking his ship, and after an amiable conversation lasting some ten minutes the British master returned to his boat. The *U33* then stood by the *Olivegrove's* boats for nine hours until an American passenger ship, which von Dresky had contacted by radio, arrived on the scene to pick up the survivors.

It was soon evident to Dönitz that this gentlemanly conduct of the war by his U-boats would not do, and on 10 October he issued the following instructions:

(a) All merchant ships definitely recognised as enemy can can be torpedoed without warning
(b) Passenger ships in convoy can be torpedoed a short while after notice has been given of the intention to do so.

By this time the convoy system instituted by the Admiralty in the first weeks of the war was beginning to have a noticeable effect. Ships in coastal waters, especially those carrying troops and supplies across the Channel, were heavily escorted, but for the deep-sea ships there were only sufficient destroyers and armed trawlers to convoy them through the Western Approaches as far as 90 miles west of Ireland, in and out. By the end of the year 147 Allied and neutral merchant ships of 510,000 tons, most of them sailing alone and unescorted, had been sunk. In the course of these sinkings nine U-boats had been lost, a rate of loss that Dönitz considered he could not sustain. In consequence, he issued Standing Order No.154, which read:

RESCUE NO ONE AND TAKE NO ONE WITH YOU. HAVE NO CARE FOR THE SHIP'S BOATS. WEATHER CONDITIONS AND THE PROXIMITY OF

LAND ARE OF NO ACCOUNT. CARE ONLY FOR YOUR OWN BOAT AND STRIVE TO ACHIEVE THE NEXT SUCCESS AS SOON AS POSSIBLE. WE MUST BE HARD IN THIS WAR. THE ENEMY STARTED THE WAR IN ORDER TO DESTROY US, THEREFORE NOTHING ELSE MATTERS.

Karl Dönitz had dumped the rule books overside in deep water, and a ruthless, dirty war of attrition against the merchantmen was about to begin.

# 2

# The Wolves Gather

In early September 1940, after twelve months of war, Britain stood alone. France had fallen, Norway was lost, and the battle for supremacy in the air was at its height. On the evening of the 7th a force of 300 German bombers, escorted by 600 fighters, appeared over London's East End and 337 tons of bombs rained down on the population, killing 448 and seriously injuring 1,600. At a little after 2000 that night, as the bombs continued to fall, the code word 'Cromwell' went out to all military bases and church bells rang throughout the land. In the opinion of those reading the signs, invasion from across the Channel was imminent.

The tired remnants of Britain's Expeditionary Force, rescued from the beaches of Dunkirk four months earlier, backed by a Local Defence Volunteer Force of old men and boys, stood-to and awaited the coming of the invasion barges. Fortunately for them, and for Britain, Adolf Hitler, probably influenced by the inability of his Luftwaffe to smash the RAF, turned his attention elsewhere.

At sea, in the deep Atlantic, the fight went on, increasing in ferocity as if to match the approaching winter storms. With the fall of France, German U-boats had gained the vital bases of Brest, Lorient, La Pallice, St Nazaire and Bordeaux on the Biscay coast, bringing them 1,000 miles closer to their main hunting ground. The casualty rate among the merchant ships supplying Britain had risen to more than a quarter of a million tons a month, which was almost three times the replacement rate attained by the hard-pressed British shipyards. Now that the threat of invasion was receding, it was here on the sea that the war would be won or lost. One serving U-boat commander summed up the situation precisely:

We had reason to believe that our hunger blockade against England would soon result in her downfall. On land, moreover, our armies had driven deep into enemy territory. Following our seizure of Poland, Norway had been defeated almost overnight; Holland, Belgium and France were overrun within a few weeks and Denmark occupied. Our capital ships controlled the European waters far into the Arctic region. It seemed to me one thing remained to be done: intensify the U-boat offensive against England, starve the British and force them to surrender. Once we held the British Isles, the war would end.

The acquisition of the French ports, and the consequent reduction in the time required for each patrol, effectively doubled the number of U-boats available. Dönitz now judged that the time was ripe to introduce his *Rudeltaktik*.

The *Rudeltaktik*, or 'pack tactic', was first suggested by Kommodore Hermann Bauer and tried without success in the closing days of the First World War. It was resurrected by Dönitz in 1935 and rehearsed extensively on manoeuvres, but had not yet been seriously tested under war conditions. The method perfected by Dönitz was for a pack of six to ten U-boats to form a patrol line across the expected path of a convoy and wait for the enemy to steam into their net. The first boat to make a sighting did not attack alone, but reported details of ships and escort to U-boat headquarters. She then shadowed the convoy, giving hourly reports by radio on its course and speed. It was then a simple matter for operations control on shore to home the rest of the pack on to the convoy. When all the 'wolves' were in contact they waited for darkness before attacking together on the surface, using the twin advantages of their low silhouette and high speed to create mayhem among the slow-moving ranks of the merchantmen. Such was the theory.

On that day, 7 September 1940, when the bombs rained down on London's dockland and all Britain braced itself for an invasion that would never come, Convoy SC 2 was 325 miles west of the Outer Hebrides, inward bound via the North Channel. Consisting of 53 heavily-laden tramps, most of which had seen better days, SC 2 had sailed from Sydney, Nova Scotia, on 25 August and straggled unescorted, and miraculously unharmed, across much of the North Atlantic at a leisurely 6 knots. Only a few hours earlier, on the evening of the 6th, the merchantmen had been joined by their escort for the Western Approaches, the destroyers *Scimitar* and *Skeena*, the sloops *Lowestoft* and *Scarborough*, the corvette *Periwinkle* and the armed trawlers *Apollo*, *Westcott* and *Berkshire*. For the convoy's commodore, Rear-Admiral E. Boddam-Whetham, sailing in the steamer *Harpoon*, the sight of these sleek, bustling warships, led by Commander A. M. Knapp in HMS *Lowestoft*, signalled the lifting of a crippling burden of responsibility from his shoulders. The safety of the North Channel lay only two days away, and it now seemed certain to Boddam-Whetham that he would arrive in British waters with his flock intact; no mean feat in those violent days. But, unknown to the Commodore, the convoy was being shadowed.

The U-boat *U65* (Korvettenkapitän Hans-Gerrit von Stockhausen) had been there since dawn, out of sight over the horizon but easily following SC 2's movements by the tall plumes of black smoke reaching skywards from the many old coal burners in its ranks. Von Stockhausen had already contacted U-boat Command at Lorient, and three other boats, *U99* (Korvettenkapitän Otto Kretschmer), *U28* (Kapitänleutnant Günter Kuhnke) and *U47* (Korvettenkapitän Günther Prien), were homing in on his W/T signals.

At this point, with the convoy 100 miles north-west of Malin Head, the Atlantic intervened, lashing itself into the frenzy of an early autumn gale. For the heavily-laden ships of the convoy this was an unkind welcome to home waters, and they rolled and pitched sickeningly as the seas broke over them, but to most minds the deteriorating visibility made up for the discomfort. At least they would be hidden from the prying eyes of the enemy on this last, dangerous stretch of the voyage.

Bad weather knows no favourites, and if the gale came to the aid of the convoy, it also recompensed the U-boats. In the rough seas their low profiles were almost invisible, and they closed in on the surface unseen. Von Stockhausen held on, and was joined in the early hours of the 7th by Prien in *U47*. The weather was perfect for a night attack; dark and overcast, with no moon and visibility about three miles. Prien attacked immediately, torpedoing the 5,155-ton *Neptunian*, loaded with sugar from the West Indies. The Newcastle ship fell astern, and at some time in the dark of that storm-tossed night – no one saw her go – she went down, taking her crew of 36 with her.

In an effort to shake off the attackers, Rear-Admiral Boddam-Whetham took the convoy through a series of emergency turns, but without success. An hour later Prien regained contact and, slipping past the escort screen into the centre of the convoy, struck again. The Liverpool steamer *Jose de Larrinaga*, 5,303 tons, carrying steel and linseed oil from New York to the Bristol Channel, sank in a few minutes. There were no survivors from her crew of 40.

Confusion reigned in the ranks of the merchantmen. The escorts chased their tails, while Prien remained on the surface in the middle of the convoy, hidden by the darkness and the breaking waves. Soon he had the 4,211-ton Norwegian *Gro* in his sights, and she went the way of the others, her bottom laid open by the blast of a torpedo.

Fortunately for SC 2 the dawn comes early in these high latitudes (it was light by the time the change of watch came at 0400), and with the dawn came the throb of Bristol engines as a Short Sunderland flying boat of RAF Coastal Command flew low over the convoy. The U-boats were forced to dive and stay down for the rest of the daylight hours.

It was Günter Kuhnke, in *U28*, who re-established contact with SC 2 after dark on the 8th. He called in the others, and by 2100 the audacious Prien had again crept into the heart of the convoy. At 2124 he sank the 3,840-ton Greek ship *Possidon*. At this point the escorts interfered, and it was 0147 on the morning of the 9th before SC 2 lost another ship. She was the small

British steamer *Mardinian*, nearing the end of her long haul from Trinidad. Kuhnke's torpedo slammed into her engine room, killing six men and sending her spiralling to the bottom. So quickly did she go that her loss went unnoticed, and it was only by chance that 31 survivors were later picked up by the trawler *Apollo*.

As SC 2 lost only five ships out of a total of 53 it cannot be claimed that the attack was a great triumph, but it was the first effective action involving a pack of U-boats working in concert. Even though four of the five ships were sunk by Prien in *U47*, the others were there with him, successfully brought together by Lorient through the use of radio. Moreover, both Rear-Admiral Boddam-Whetham and Commander Knapp were completely confused by the numbers of U-boats, and more so by their new tactic of striking from within the ranks of the convoy, on the surface. If the convoy had been beyond the range of air cover the end result might have been very different.

Prien had now used up all of his torpedoes and, having reported this state of affairs to U-boat Command in Lorient, expected to be ordered back to base. But there was other work to do. The Luftwaffe, continuing its daily bombing of British cities, required advance notice of the weather moving in from the Atlantic, a task usually performed by U-boats not actively engaged with the enemy. The *U47* was well placed for the job, and Dönitz ordered Prien to take her to a point just west of 23° west, and once there to patrol up and down, sending weather reports to Lorient twice a day. This unexpected duty was not welcomed by Prien and his men, who had been looking forward to a spell ashore which they thought they richly deserved. However, their time was to be well spent, for more of the enemy's ships were on the way.

Convoy HX 72, then consisting of 21 ships, sailed from Halifax, Nova Scotia, on the afternoon of 9 September. On the 11th, when it was to the south of Newfoundland, its ranks were swelled by a further eleven ships joining from Sydney, Nova Scotia. Twenty-four hours later, off Cape Race, one ship returned to Halifax but another eleven joined, coming from South American ports via Bermuda. Now 42 ships strong, HX 72 formed into nine columns, led by Commodore H. H. Rogers, RNR, in the 5,201-ton British steamer *Tregarthen*, and set out across the Atlantic for the United Kingdom. This large assembly of merchantmen, most of them British, carrying some 300,000 tons of desperately needed food and war equipment, was escorted by one of its own kind, the armed merchant cruiser HMS *Jervis Bay*. British destroyers were in short supply, and the 22-year-old ex-Aberdeen & Commonwealth liner, armed with seven ancient 5.9in guns and having a top speed of 15 knots, was all that could be spared to protect the convoy on the wide reaches of the North Atlantic. Only when HX 72 reached a point 400 miles west of Ireland would destroyers of Western Approaches Command take over.

From the outset of the voyage Commodore Rogers experienced difficulties with the ships under his command. They were a motley bunch, mostly ageing British tramps, with a handful of Norwegians, two Poles and a Greek, few of them capable of maintaining the convoy's designated speed of 8$^1$/$_2$ knots. Station keeping was bad, and from time to time radio silence was broken by unauthorised transmissions. The loyalty of the British ships was not open to question, but the foreign ships, friendly though they might appear, were an unknown quantity. Concerning one of them, the 6,031-ton Norwegian steamer *Simla*, Rogers had a few days earlier received the following message from the Admiralty:

SS *Simla* has had crew trouble and conflicting reports about reliability of Master have also been received. He is reported as stating that he has run the British blockade and he will do so again. Suggest ship and Master be watched.

The message may just have originated with careless talk in a dockside bar, but it constituted another niggling worry that Commodore Rogers could have done without.

On the morning of the 18th Rogers' troubles increased when a fresh northwesterly gale blew up, causing havoc in the convoy. Being beam-on to wind and sea, the ungainly merchantmen rolled and yawed wildly, the more heavily-laden ships resembling half-tide rocks as the rising seas broke clean over their exposed decks. Station keeping was impossible, and gradually the orderly ranks of the convoy drifted into chaos. Lifeboats, swung out in readiness for a quick evacuation if a torpedo struck, were smashed, cargoes shifted, and a number of ships fell astern. Rogers reduced speed to allow the stragglers to catch up, but the Greek steamer *Mount Kyllene*, listing heavily with her cargo adrift, could do little to help herself. She fell further and further astern, until she was out of sight and on her own. Convoy HX 72 had no destroyer or corvette to stand guard over her. Indeed, it was soon to lose its one and only escort vessel.

At sunset on the 20th, when HX 72 had reached a position just under 500 miles west of Ireland, the *Jervis Bay* was ordered to break away to ride escort on another convoy westbound. As dusk was setting in, the gallant old liner reversed her course, dipped her ensign in salute and steamed off into the gathering gloom at full speed. Six weeks later she went down under the 11in guns of the pocket battleship *Admiral Scheer* while defending Convoy HX 84.

The abandonment of HX 72, leaving 41 merchant ships, mostly unarmed, to conduct their own defence, is indicative of the parlous state of the Royal Navy at that stage of the war. The evacuation of the remnants of the British and French armies from the beaches of Dunkirk had cost 25 destroyers sunk or damaged, and most of those remaining in commission were held in the English Channel to guard against invasion. Churchill was negotiating with President Roosevelt for 50 destroyers in exchange for the use of British bases in the Caribbean and Canada by the US Fleet, but it would be some time before these ships became available.

Meanwhile, HX 72 had to steam unescorted for some 20 hours before making a rendezvous with ships of Western Approaches Command on the afternoon of the 21st. The protective cloak of bad weather, fog or gales would have been most welcome, but, perversely, the North Atlantic had chosen to put on a kindly face. The wind was moderate south-westerly, just sufficient to set the white horses running, while overhead a full moon shone down through broken cloud, bathing the sea in a brilliant light. The visibility was excellent, with isolated rain squalls providing patches of cover. Ideal conditions for skulking U-boats, but bad news for the convoy.

As the night closed in around the serried ranks of slow-moving ships, Commodore Rogers took the only defensive actions open to him, making a bold alteration of course to the southward and, in accordance with Admiralty orders, adopting zig-zag pattern No. 27. The latter considerably slowed down the rate of advance of the convoy, which in any case was making only 7 knots, and the turns involved were so wide that straggling was inevitable. Rogers was not happy.

The routine up-and-down patrol, sending in twice-daily weather reports to Lorient, held no attraction for the U-boat men. It was certainly not a role suited to the man who had audaciously penetrated the defences of Scapa Flow and sunk the British battleship *Royal Oak* less than a year earlier. To Günther Prien, keeping vigil in the spray-lashed conning tower of *U47*, the crushing monotony of the patrol seemed never-ending. Then, on the eleventh day after his successful attack on SC 2, in the last rays of the dying sun, he caught sight of first the smoke, then the masts and funnels, of an inward-bound convoy.

There is no doubt that, throughout the eleven days, *U47*'s regular radio transmissions of weather to Lorient had been listened to by the Admiralty. There then must have been ample opportunity for the source of these signals to be plotted by high-frequency direction-finding stations ashore in the UK. The distance involved was great and substantial errors might be expected to creep in, but nevertheless an approximate position should have been easily obtainable. It is therefore hard to understand why HX 72 was not warned of the danger into which it was steaming. Commodore Rogers had received no inkling of an enemy presence, so he unwittingly took his 41 unescorted merchantmen into the trap.

Soon after sighting HX 72, Prien reported its position, course and speed to Lorient and, being without torpedoes, settled down to shadow the convoy.

Meanwhile, Dönitz was assembling a wolf pack. Two of the other participants in the attack on SC 2, Kretschmer in *U99* and von Stockhausen in *U65*, were still close by, while *U48* (Kapitänleutnant Heinrich Bleichrodt), *U46* (Kapitänleutnant Engelbert Endrass) and *U43* (Kapitänleutnant Wilhelm Ambrosius) were within 380 miles of the convoy. Dönitz ordered these five to form a north-south line on the surface across the expected track of the convoy, with five miles between each boat. Each boat would thus be in visual range of its neighbours, the whole line covering some 30 miles of the horizon. They would have only to wait until the unsuspecting convoy steamed into their sight. Unfortunately, Rogers' large alteration of course after dark foiled this plan, and HX 72 steamed around the southern end of the patrol line unseen. When this became apparent, Dönitz ordered all the U-boats concerned to home in on the convoy at all speed and attack independently.

Kretschmer was the first to arrive at the interception point given by Lorient, but he found no convoy in sight. He submerged to listen with hydrophones, and heard faint propeller noises to the south. Bringing *U99* back to the surface, he motored at full speed on the bearing obtained. He sighted the rear ships of HX 72 at 0030 on the 21st, and set a course to pass astern of the convoy and take up a position to attack from the dark side. With the merchantmen crawling along at 7 knots and *U99* cleaving the water at 17 knots this was not difficult, but the manoeuvre almost ended in disaster. As Kretschmer crossed astern of the convoy the moon went behind the clouds, and he narrowly avoided colliding with Prien's *U47*, then lying almost stopped on the surface, all her crew's attention obviously focused on shadowing HX 72. Kretschmer claims that, shortly after exchanging words with Prien, he sighted a destroyer zig-zagging astern of the convoy, but this must have been a trick of the light or a figment of his imagination, for HX 72 was still unescorted. Such an unlikely possibility did not occur to Kretschmer.

Certainly the presence of an escorting destroyer would have been of great comfort to the master of the 9,154-ton British motor tanker *Invershannon*, rear ship in the port column of HX 72. Carrying a full load of highly inflammable oil, the Glasgow-registered tanker should have been tucked up in the centre of the convoy, out of harm's way, but bad station keeping, exacerbated by the awkward zig-zag pattern, had left her trailing astern. In the bright moonlight the tanker's distinctive silhouette was easily distinguishable, and at 0112 Kretschmer's torpedo caught her squarely in her forward cargo tank. Sixteen of the *Invershannon*'s crew were killed in the explosion; the remainder took to the boats as the smoke and flames roared aft.

By a grim coincidence, a heavy rain squall isolated the *Invershannon* from the rest of the convoy shortly before the torpedo struck, and her plight went unnoticed by the other ships. Commodore Rogers, who was experiencing difficulty in holding the convoy together at the time, did not receive news of the torpedoing for another hour. He then signalled an emergency turn to port, bringing the ships around on to a course of 077°, discontinued the zig-zag and called for a speed of 10 knots, hoping to run away from the danger.

The Commodore's action was in vain, for *U99*, invisible on the dark side, had the speed to outpace the convoy. Kretschmer was soon lining up his sights on another heavily-laden ship, the 3,668-ton *Baron Blythswood*. At 800 yards the Scottish registered cargo ship was a sitting duck, and Kretschmer's torpedo, striking amidships, blew her in half. Loaded with iron ore, she went down in 40 seconds, taking all but one of her crew with her.

It was a bad night for the Scots. Kretschmer's next target, which he brought into his sights half an hour later, was the 5,156-ton Glasgow ship *Elmbank*. She was also hit amidships, but, being laden with timber, did not sink.

Kretschmer still could not accept that the convoy was completely without escorts. Seeing rockets soaring skywards from the fleeing merchantmen, he mistook them for starshell and decided to drop back. He found the *Elmbank* still afloat and fired another torpedo at her, but this struck floating baulks of timber from her cargo and exploded harmlessly. Fire was then opened with *U99*'s 88mm deck gun, but after nearly 90 rounds of ammunition had been expended the fifteen-year-old tramp was still afloat. Attracted by the gunfire, *U47* arrived on the scene, but although Prien then used up all of his 88mm ammunition on the wreck, the *Elmbank* still did not sink. Daylight came, and it was discovered that the *Invershannon* was also still afloat. It took another of Kretschmer's torpedoes – his last – to put her down. He then set the *Elmbank* on fire with phosphorous shells and headed for home, leaving the unarmed *U47* to continue her thankless task of shadowing HX 72.

While Kretschmer and Prien were disposing of the *Elmbank*, the rest of the pack began to arrive. First on the scene, at 0400, was Heinrich Bleichrodt in *U48*, who within fifteen minutes had stalked and sunk yet another Glasgow ship, the 4,409-ton *Blairangus*. Right from the start of the voyage the *Blairangus* had experienced difficulty in keeping up with the other ships, and when Bleichrodt's torpedo found her she was straggling well astern of the convoy. Her loss went unnoticed, except by those involved.

At dawn on the 21st Commodore Rogers, who at the head of the convoy in the *Tregarthen* had been a distant and impotent witness to the night's events, counted ships and found four missing. It was all too clear that the wolves were gathering around his flock and would continue to savage it until help arrived, which would not be for another ten to twelve hours. In desperation Rogers ordered ships in the starboard column to drop smoke floats, under the cover of which the convoy altered course for the rendezvous, now 80 miles to the east. The smokescreen proved only transitory, soon being cleared by the brisk westerly breeze, and as the merchantmen altered to port on to a course of 102°, Prien followed them around. Bleichrodt was also still there, and he would shortly be joined by von Stockhausen in *U65*, Endrass in *U46*, Ambrosius in *U43* and Hans Jenisch in *U32*. Another of Dönitz's leading aces, Joachim Schepke in *U100*, would arrive later.

As the wolves circled, hesitating to attack in full daylight, HX 72 experienced its first stroke of good fortune since setting out to cross the Atlantic. At 1330, more than two hours ahead of schedule, ships of the Royal Navy's Western Approaches Command appeared over the eastern horizon. The convoy was then in position 54° 54'N, 20° 10'W, some 350 miles west of Ireland. The local escort was led by Commander A. M. Knapp in the sloop HMS *Lowestoft*, who twelve days earlier had defended Convoy SC 2 against the first organised pack attack with some success. However, on this occasion Knapp's force was very much depleted. He had with him only the three Flower-class corvettes *Calendula*, *Heartsease* and *La Malauine*, the latter originally built for the French but taken over by the Royal Navy.

The Flower-class corvettes, fast becoming the workhorses of convoy defence in the North Atlantic, were based on the design of a pre-war whalecatcher. Solid, bluff-bowed ships built for heavy weather and displacing a little over 900 tons, they were armed with a 4in anti-submarine gun, one 20mm Oerlikon and a supply of depth charges. Their asdics were primitive, they had no radar, and they were reputed to 'roll on wet grass', a quality which did not improve their fighting capabilities in the turbulent North Atlantic. Undoubtedly the greatest disadvantage suffered by the Flower-class corvettes was their maximum speed of just 16 knots. Dönitz's Type VIICs were able to run rings around them when on the surface.

The arrival of Knapp and his ships caused the U-boats to draw back and put new heart into the 37 ships remaining in Convoy HX 72. They tightened up their ranks and, at Commodore Rogers' urging, worked up speed to a more acceptable 8 knots. HMS *Lowestoft* scouted in the van, *Heartsease* and *Calendula* covered the wings and *La Malauine* zig-zagged astern, keeping a lookout for shadowing U-boats. It was the best that Knapp could do with his meagre escort. The corvettes carried inexperienced crews, and none of the escorts had worked together before.

The wind was westerly, force 2-3, with passing rain squalls, and when darkness came at about 1900 it was complete; the moon was not due to rise for another 2$^1$/$_2$ hours. Rogers took advantage of the cover, discontinuing the zig-zag and ordering an increase in speed to 10$^1$/$_2$ knots. The danger of steering a steady course was obvious, and it was certain that many of the merchantmen would be hard pressed to reach 10 knots, let alone 10$^1$/$_2$, but the Commodore was sure of his decision. He reasoned that a straight course would allow the escorts more freedom of movement, while the extra speed would open up gaps between the ships, reducing the chances of a U-boat firing a spread of torpedoes and finding easy targets. This would not prove to be the case.

While Rogers and Knapp made their preparations for the coming night, the wolf pack, now seven strong, had assembled on the fringes of the convoy, ready to attack as soon as the conditions were right. Schepke, following his usual routine, came in from astern, on the surface, as soon as it was dark, and entered the convoy between the columns. *U100* was trimmed down to her lowest possible silhouette, and no one witnessed her coming.

By about 2130, as the moon lifted above the horizon, bathing the convoy in a weak glow, Schepke was between columns five and six and drawing abreast of the second line of ships. To port was a tempting target, the 8,286-ton Liverpool steamer *Canonesa*, keeping station directly astern of the Commodore's ship, *Tregarthen*. Beyond, and lagging behind the *Canonesa*, so that the two ships overlapped, was the motor tanker *Torinia*, 10,364 tons and loaded down to her marks with precious fuel. Taking careful aim, Schepke fired a spread of three torpedoes.

One torpedo caught the *Canonesa* square in her engine room, blowing a huge hole in her plates through which the sea poured in, quickly flooding the engine spaces. The engineer on watch was killed by the explosion. On deck the damage was equally catastrophic, much of the starboard side of the ship being wrecked; hatchboards and tarpaulins were hurled into the air and one lifeboat was destroyed. When her dazed crew took to the remaining boats, the *Canonesa*'s decks were awash from stem to stern. She sank shortly afterwards.

Schepke's second torpedo sped on past the stern of the crippled *Canonesa* and slammed into the *Torinia*, breaking her back. The tanker's cargo ignited and blew her apart, and she went down, taking all her crew with her. Two minutes later, with only the minimum of manoeuvring required, Schepke fired his stern tube at the ship on his starboard side, the 4,608-ton Newcastle steamer *Dalcairn*. She rolled over and sank.

One of Schepke's torpedoes missed, but in the space of three minutes he had destroyed three merchantmen, totalling 23,258 tons gross and carrying some 35,000 tons of vital cargo, and all this right under the nose of Commodore Rogers.

Looking aft from the bridge of the *Tregarthen*, Rogers was a helpless and astounded witness to the mayhem. To him, and to those on the bridge with him, it seemed impossible that a U-boat could have slipped past the escorts and penetrated deep into the convoy. It was even suggested to Rogers that one of the foreign merchantmen was equipped with concealed torpedo tubes manned by enemy agents; a theory that could well have been plausible on this dark and terrible night. What was real was the flash of the exploding torpedoes, the urgent blaring of ships' sirens, the rockets and flares soaring into the sky. Whatever, whoever, was responsible was laying about the defenceless merchantmen with ruthless abandon. Drastic and immediate action was called for, and the only answer seemed to be to give all ships room for individual action. Rogers ordered the convoy to scatter.

At that time HMS *Lowestoft* was ahead and to port of the convoy, and the first intimation Commander Knapp had of the attack was a red flare fired by the *Canonesa*. Believing the enemy to be outside the convoy, Knapp hauled the *Lowestoft* around under full helm and ran down the port side, firing starshell. She was joined by the corvette *Heartsease*, and the two ships turned the darkness to the north of HX 72 into day with starshell. Their action was futile, for the enemy was not there.

As there was no communication between Commodore Rogers and Commander Knapp, neither knew the other's intentions, and consequently chaos reigned. The torpedoes, the flares, the starshell and Rogers' order to scatter caused panic among the merchantmen, and they fled in all directions. Using signal lamp and loud hailer, Knapp attempted to round them up again, but to no avail. The rout was complete.

The other U-boats moved in for the kill. On the surface they were visible in the light of the moon and the starshell, but they were faster and more manoeuvrable than Knapp's escorts, who could do no more than hurl shells at the fleeting shadows. At 2138 Heinrich Bleichrodt in *U48* torpedoed the *Broompark*. The 5,136-ton British steamer did not sink, and would later reach port unaided. Although the rest of the wolf pack sent torpedoes running in all directions, they found no targets among the twisting and turning ships.

Having reloaded her tubes, *U100* returned to the fray at 2220. Joachim Schepke, master of his trade, then set to work. He first torpedoed and sank the 6,586-ton *Empire Airman*, then crippled the 3,940-ton *Scholar*, which would not sink for another 48 hours. Just before midnight Schepke claimed his second oil tanker. She was the 10,525-ton London ship *Frederick S. Fales*, her loss another hard blow to Britain's struggling war effort. A few minutes after the tanker erupted in a ball of flame, the British ship *Harlingen* (5,415 tons), was attacked and fought back, the only recorded retaliation of the night, apart from a brief depth-charge attack by one of the corvettes. The *Harlingen*'s master reported:

At 2130 GMT convoy attacked by submarines, apparently in large numbers, attack continuing until 0101 GMT 22nd Sept, at which time we were personally attacked by a submarine which emerged right in the path of the moonlight, approx. position 55° 10'N, 17° 53'W.

The wheel was put hard a-port, the submarine being on the starboard beam, and was thus brought right astern. The torpedo fired by him passed close on the starboard bow, quickly followed by another which passed on the port side. We were enabled to get three shots at him with the 4in BL gun. The first shot passed over him, and the second shot, fired with the sights set at 1,400 yards, was followed immediately by a deep thud, the shot striking just beneath the conning tower, which was still awash. The third shot, fired shortly afterwards, we were unable either to see or hear. We resumed our interrupted zig-zag, and saw no further enemy craft.

The *Harlingen's* chief officer later stated that there was a definite explosion after the thud of the shot which struck home, and that he saw the third shot hit in approximately the same position as the second. The submarine then heeled over so far that he was able to see down into the well on top of the conning tower.

The *Harlingen* reported her U-boat by radio and the *Lowestoft* gave chase. After searching for some time without making contact, Knapp decided his services would be better used in rounding up the merchantmen. This also proved to be a hopeless task, for on the orders of Commodore Rogers HX 72 had ceased to exist as a convoy. The ships were scattered far and wide, all fleeing for the safety of the North Channel at speeds of which their well-worn engines had never been thought capable.

The 6,031-ton Norwegian steamer *Simla*, 23 long years in the service of her owners, made a valiant effort to keep up with the others, but she soon found herself alone on an empty sea. She became Joachim Schepke's seventh victim.

At 0446 on the 22nd, in the darkest hour before the dawn, HMS *Lowestoft* was 320 miles west of Malin Head and searching astern of the scattered convoy for stragglers when gun flashes were sighted on the horizon ahead. This was the 7,886-ton Liverpool ship *Collegian*, under attack from Hans Jenisch's *U32*. Commander Knapp increased to full speed, but when he arrived at the scene of the attack, nearly two hours later, the *Collegian* had escaped, although badly damaged by gunfire. Knapp called in two of his corvettes and began and asdic sweep. A possible contact was eventually made and a pattern of depth charges dropped, but with no visible result.

In fact, the U-boats were also speeding for home, having used up all of their torpedoes. Most of the missiles had been wasted, but the victory for Dönitz's wolf pack was beyond all argument. HX 72 had lost eleven ships, totalling 72,727 tons, of which Otto Kretschmer in *U99* had sunk three ships of 17,978 tons, while Joachim Schepke in *U100*, the hero of the action, had single-handedly accounted for no fewer than seven ships of 50,340 tons. It is significant that both Kretschmer and Schepke penetrated inside the convoy before attacking; the commanders of the other U-boats, who had little or no success, were content to launch their torpedoes from afar. The lesson to be learned from this did not escape the attention of Karl Dönitz.

# 3

# The Pack Runs

By mid-October 1940 even Hitler had come to accept that the time for a successful invasion of the British Isles was past. To a visiting Italian Minister he said: 'If I cannot invade them, at least I can destroy the whole of their industry'. He was referring to the continuing raids on British cities by bombers of the Luftwaffe, which on the night of 15 October reached a ferocious crescendo with an attack on London lasting nine hours. In this, the most intense bombing raid of the war thus far, thousands of high-explosive and incendiary bombs rained down, laying waste a vast area of the densely populated city. More than 400 Londoners died in the raid, bringing the total killed in Britain by German bombs, in that one week alone, to 1,567. There was no evident crumbling of morale in the cities, but it was felt that, if the raids continued to exact such a fearful toll, cracks would soon begin to appear. To some extent the RAF was returning the bombs, but always striving to hit only specified military targets. If bad weather or other causes made it impossible to bomb accurately, pilots were ordered to jettison their bombs over the sea. After the October raids on London the RAF was given leave to use its bombs with less discrimination, targeting cities rather than specific installations. The war in the air was moving into a new and more barbaric phase.

At sea it had been that way for some time. Although the threat of invasion had receded, releasing more destroyers for convoy escort duty, there seemed to be no answer to the savage assaults of Dönitz's 'wolf packs'. The German admiral's stated ambition that 'not one day should pass without the sinking somewhere or other of a ship by one of the boats at sea' had been more than realised. On average, 55 Allied merchant ships, totalling nearly 280,000 tons gross, were being sunk by the U-boats every month, the majority of them in the Atlantic. But every achievement has its price. In the case of the U-boat men it was a high one, up to three boats being lost each month out of the 27 or so that were operational. As the Allied convoys became better organised and the expertise of the growing number of escort vessels improved, these losses would inevitably mount.

When Karl Dönitz took command of the U-boat arm, Hitler promised that the German shipyards would turn out about twenty new boats every month, but his promise was not being kept. Demands on Germany's resources by the

Wehrmacht and the Luftwaffe, on which Hitler now based his hopes for victory, were so great that new U-boats were being launched at the rate of only six a month; barely enough to keep pace with the rising losses. While the lost submarines could be replaced, their highly-trained and experienced crews could not. It was rare for any survivors of a sunken boat to return to Germany. This led Dönitz to push his men to their utmost limits, curtailing desperately needed rest periods and slashing the time that boats spent in port after each patrol. Inevitably, this resulted in a discernable lowering of morale in the service.

There is a long-held superstition among seamen, probably associated with the Crucifixion, that to leave port on a Friday is to tempt providence. To sail on Friday the 13th is an open invitation to disaster. So reasoned the crew of *U99* when she was ordered to leave Lorient on her fourth Atlantic patrol on Friday 13 October 1940. Although *U99* was a new boat, less than a year old, she developed a mysterious engine fault that held her in port until after midnight that night. She finally sailed at 0130 on the 14th. In command was Kapitänleutnant Otto Kretschmer, at 28 years old already one of Dönitz's top aces, with 23 ships of almost 100,000 tons to his credit.

The first 48 hours of *U99*'s outward passage across the Western Approaches to the British Isles were uneventful, except for two occasions when patrolling enemy aircraft forced her to dive. Then, on the afternoon of the 16th, when she was 320 miles west of Ireland, a signal was picked up from *U93* (Kapitänleutnant Klaus Korth), reporting the sighting of a large Allied convoy. Anticipating orders, Kretschmer altered course to intercept the convoy and increased to full speed.

In Lorient, Admiral Dönitz acted on the signalled sighting immediately, ordering Korth to continue shadowing and report at regular intervals while a wolf pack was assembled. Within reasonable range of the convoy were *U100* (Kapitänleutnant Joachim Schepke), *U123* (Kapitänleutnant Karl-Heinz Moehle), *U101* (Kapitänleutnant Fritz Frauenheim), *U46* (Kapitänleutnant Engelbert Endrass), *U48* (Kapitänleutnant Heinrich Bleichrodt) and Kretschmer's *U99*. As Kretschmer had foreseen, Dönitz's radioed instructions to these vessels were for them to close on the Allied convoy at all speed. As the day wore on, the reports from *U93* became less frequent and finally ceased altogether, indicating to Dönitz that she had lost contact with the enemy. He then ordered the gathering pack to set up a line of ambush ahead of, and across the track of the convoy, all boats to be in position by 2000 on the 18th. Kretschmer called for more speed, for he feared *U99* might arrive too late to join in the attack.

Convoy SC 7, consisting of 35 ships, fourteen British, six Norwegian, four Greek, three Canadian, three Swedish, two Dutch, one French, one Panamanian and one Danish, left the Canadian port of Sydney, Cape Breton, at noon on 5 October. It was a slow convoy with a designated speed of 8 knots, and would break no records on its Atlantic crossing. In fact, many of the old and sometimes pitifully small ships had never achieved such a speed. Certainly the two Cardiff tramps *Beatus* and *Fiscus*, sister ships staggering under great loads of timber and steel, would be hard pushed to keep up. The same could be said for the two Greek vessels *Niritos* and *Aenos*, built in 1907 and 1910 respectively, whose ancient engines functioned only by faith and a great deal of innovation. As for the tiny Great Lakes steamers *Eaglescliffe Hall*, *Winona* and *Trevisa*, also of a great age, it seemed to be the height of folly that they should challenge this turbulent Western Ocean at all. But perhaps the most revealing indication of the pressing needs of Britain in these dark days was the inclusion in SC 7 of the Norwegian steamer *Snefjeld*. At 1,643 tons gross, this 39-year-old ship, her decks piled so high with timber that only her masts and funnels were visible, presented a ludicrous sight as she struggled valiantly to keep pace with her larger sisters.

Recalled from retirement and charged with the unenviable task of holding this ragged fleet of merchantmen together for the 2,500-mile transatlantic voyage was Vice-Admiral Lachlan Mackinnon, RN. Mackinnon was a man of great experience in the fighting ships, but he had only a limited understanding of the shortcomings and eccentricities of the run-of-the-mill ocean tramp. His talents were to be sorely tested over the coming weeks.

The ship in which Mackinnon flew his flag, as commodore of the convoy, was the 2,962-ton, twin-screw steamer *Assyrian*, owned by the Ellerman & Papayanni Line of Liverpool and commanded by 35-year-old Captain R. S. Kearon. Launched at the beginning of the First World War, the *Assyrian* was a long way from her habitual cruising waters. In the balmy days between the wars she carried general cargoes from Liverpool, Glasgow and south Wales to Spain, Portugal and Mediterranean ports, returning with the produce of these sun-kissed shores. She had accommodation for twelve passengers, and at £1 a day for the 40-day round voyage, the *Assyrian* had been a popular ship with those seeking a long, lazy holiday.

On her current voyage the *Assyrian*'s adequate but not luxurious passenger cabins were occupied by Vice-Admiral Mackinnon, his staff of five signallers and three civilian passengers, making, with her crew of 39, a total complement on board of 48. In her holds were 3,700 tons of food and war supplies loaded in the USA for Liverpool. Her armament consisted of one ancient 4in gun, mounted on her poop deck and manned by a crew drawn from the ship's company, untrained, but nonetheless determined.

The weather was fine and clear, and the sea unusually calm when, ship by ship, Convoy SC 7 cleared Sydney harbour and felt the lift of the long Atlantic swell. An hour of somewhat untidy manoeuvring followed, but finally the ships were formed up in nine columns abreast and set off to cross the ocean, the *Assyrian* leading at the head of column five. Mackinnon had wisely adjusted the convoy speed to 7 knots; even so it was obvious from the amount of black smoke issuing from some funnels that there were those who would be hard pressed to keep up. The *Winona*, in fact, turned back on the first night, when a fault developed in her generator.

The defence of SC 7, apart from the few ill-manned, stern-mounted guns of the merchantmen, was in the hands of the sloop HMS *Scarborough* and the Canadian armed yacht *Elk*. The 1,050-ton *Scarborough* (Commander N. V. Dickinson) was an ex-survey vessel converted for escort duties, armed with two 4in guns and having a top speed of only 14 knots. HMCS *Elk*, as would be expected of a commandeered yacht, was of even lighter calibre. If SC 7 was to reach British waters intact, it would need more than good luck on its side.

Mackinnon was authorised to vary the convoy's course according to prevailing circumstances, but the Admiralty had advised him to steer to the north-east until about 250 miles south of Iceland, before altering down for the North Channel. It was hoped that this northerly route would keep the convoy away from patrolling U-boats until the ocean escort was reinforced by ships of Western Approaches Command. Unknown to Mackinnon and the Admiralty, this was a forlorn hope. Admiral Dönitz, through the *B-Dienst*, the German naval intelligence service, was already aware of the movements of SC 7.

On 28 June 1940 the 7,506-ton British cargo liner *City of Baghdad*, under the command of Captain Armstrong White, sailed from Lourenço Marques, Mozambique, bound for Penang, Malaya. German agents in the Portuguese port notified Berlin of her sailing. Thirteen days later, when *City of Baghdad* was 450 miles off the western coast of Sumatra and nearing the equator, she fell in with the German armed merchant cruiser *Atlantis*, commanded by Kapitän-zur-See Bernhard Rogge. The British ship attempted to escape, but was pounded to a standstill by Rogge's guns. Two of *City of Baghdad*'s crew already lay dead and another was seriously injured, and to avoid further casualties Captain White surrendered. Unfortunately, White omitted to dump his lead-weighted code books overboard before handing over his ship. Within a week or two the entire contents of the Broadcasting for Allied Merchant Ships (BAMS) code was in the hands of the *B-Dienst*. The Admiralty remained ignorant of this catastrophic loss for many months. Meanwhile, *B-Dienst* was busy reading its signals to the convoys and passing them on to Dönitz within a day or so of transmission.

So Dönitz, alerted by radio intelligence, was aware of the sailing of SC 7 from Cape Breton; he also knew the convoy's projected course and speed. This did not bode well for the ships under Vice-Admiral Mackinnon's command, but, ignorant of their betrayal, they sailed on.

Some 48 hours out of Sydney, when clear of Newfoundland, HMCS *Elk* reached the limit of her fuel tanks and, signalling her goodbyes by lamp, turned back for home. With its lone escort, the 1,000-ton sloop *Scarborough*, putting on a brave face as she scouted ahead, SC 7 carried on into the open Atlantic. The weather held fine and clear, which was a mixed blessing, for the billows of black smoke pouring from the tall funnels of the labouring tramps climbed high in the sky, and must have been visible for many miles.

But the ocean would not remain quiescent for much longer. Off Cape Hatteras warm air was rising to form an area of low pressure which would expand and deepen as it tracked north-eastwards around the perimeter of the Azores High. By the morning of the 11th, when SC 7 was 300 miles south of Greenland's Cape Farewell, a full gale was blowing from the north-west. Steaming beam-on to a heavy swell and rough, breaking seas, many of the smaller ships were soon in difficulty. The two remaining Great Lakes steamers, *Trevisa* and *Eaglescliffe Hall*, neither of which had ever experienced such unbridled wrath from the elements, gave up the struggle early on and dropped astern, soon to be lost to sight. Bigger ships began to go as the day wore on and the weather worsened. Two Greeks, the 3,554-ton *Aenos* and the 5,875-ton *Thalia*, their old and poorly maintained engines strained beyond all endurance by the violent rolling and pitching, suffered breakdowns and fell back, wallowing helplessly in the swell. There was no spare escort vessel to stand by these stragglers, and from then on they would have to see to their own defence.

For the next four days the gale blew without let-up, but SC 7, its ranks thinned and ragged, continued to fight its way north-eastwards, the gallant little *Scarborough* zig-zagging ahead in a welter of foam as she rolled her bulwark rails under. Then, on the afternoon of the 15th, the barometer began to rise and the wind eased, allowing the battered ships to re-form and, where possible, repair the damage meted out by the storm. SC 7 was now less than 24 hours, steaming from the rendezvous point at which she would expect to meet her local escort heading out from the North Channel. It was too early to say the race had been won, but an unmistakeable mood of optimism hovered over the convoy.

Then, just before 0100 in the dark of the morning of 16 October, Kapitän-leutnant Wilhelm Schulz, patrolling in U124, sighted the *Trevisa* straggling some 20 miles astern of SC 7. Wireless operators on watch in the convoy listened helplessly to the pitiful distress calls of the little Canadian steamer as she went down. The wolves were at hand.

There followed a harrowing twelve hours, with every ship in the convoy on full alert, with guns manned and extra lookouts posted. A great weight was lifted from Commander Dickinson's shoulders when at last, just before dusk, *Scarborough* was joined by the sloop HMS *Fowey* and the corvette HMS *Bluebell*, the first ships of the local escort to arrive. Between them, the three small warships, however comforting their presence was to the merchantmen, were only a token show of force. None of them had worked together before, ship-to-ship radio communication was poor, and they had no preconceived plan of action in case of attack. However, Dickinson, now Senior Officer Escort (SOE), disposed his forces as best he could, with *Scarborough* on the port bow, *Fowey* on the starboard bow and *Bluebell* astern of the convoy.

As SC 7 braced itself to meet the dangers of the night, the atmosphere on the bridge of the Commodore's ship, *Assyrian*, was electric. Vice-Admiral Mackinnon and Captain Kearon stood side by side, both acutely aware that, if an attack was to be made on the convoy, it must come soon. Many times during the crossing they had roundly cursed the foul Atlantic weather; now, with the wind only a gentle breeze, the sea calm, and a bright moon breaking through the clouds from time to time, they fervently wished they could turn back the clock. For the U-boats conditions could not have been better.

The net Dönitz had strung across the path of SC 7 served its purpose well, and just before midnight on the 16/17th, Heinrich Bleichrodt in *U48* sighted the convoy 250 miles south of Iceland. He reported his find to Lorient, and then, with *U48* trimmed down, took up station astern of the convoy. Admiral Dönitz's orders were not open to interpretation; Bleichrodt's duty was to shadow and report, attacking only when joined by the rest of the pack.

The sight of this great fleet of heavily-laden and highly vulnerable ships crawling eastwards across the moonlit sea would have taxed the resolve of the most resolute U-boat man. For Bleichrodt the temptation to attack was overwhelming. Following his limited success against HX 72, he had then been involved in an attack on HX 77, sinking another three ships and bringing his score for the current patrol to eleven ships, totalling over 58,000 tons. Now just four torpedoes remained and, when they were gone, the probability was that *U48* would be free to go home. Bleichrodt curbed his impatience for almost three hours, then, with dawn less than an hour away with no sign of the other boats, he decided to act alone. Keeping a wary eye on the enemy corvette zig-zagging in the wake of the rear ships of the convoy, he moved in, penetrating the ranks of the merchantmen with ease.

The 9,512-ton French tanker *Languedoc*, sailing under the Red Ensign and her distinctive silhouette clear in the light of the moon, exploded in a sheet of flame when Bleichrodt's torpedo struck. Seconds later the North-East Coast tramp *Scoresby*, SC 7's Vice-Commodore ship, staggered as she was hit amidships, and began to sink. Bleichrodt's third torpedo hit the 4,678-ton *Haspendon*, which developed a heavy list but remained afloat.

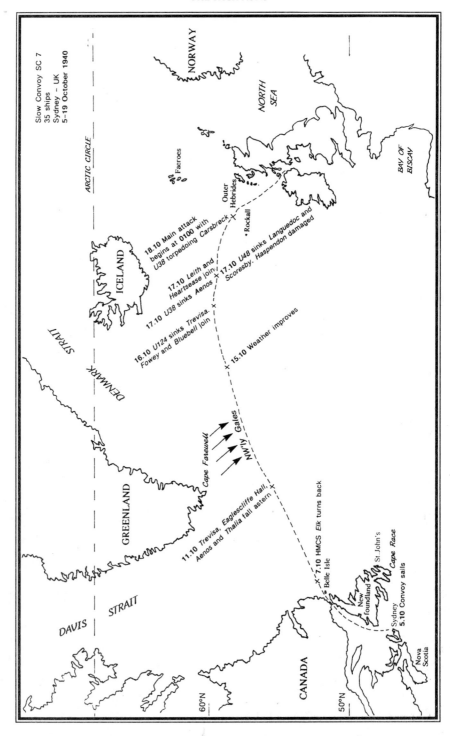

Slow Convoy SC 7
35 ships
Sydney – UK
5–19 October 1940

NORWAY

NORTH SEA

ARCTIC CIRCLE

Faeroes

BAY OF BISCAY

Outer Hebrides

Rockall

18.10 Main attack begins at 0100 with U38 torpedoing Carsbreck ×

17.10 Leith and Heartsease join ×

17.10 U48 sinks Languedoc and Scoresby. Haspendon damaged

17.10 U38 sinks Aenos ×

ICELAND

16.10 U124 sinks Trevisa. Fowey and Bluebell join ×

15.10 Weather improves ×

DENMARK STRAIT

Cape Farewell

NW'ly Gales

GREENLAND

11.10 Trevisa, Eaglescliffe Hall, Aenos and Thalia fall astern ×

× 7.10 HMCS Elk turns back

Belle Isle

St. John's

New Foundland

Cape Race

Sydney

5.10 Convoy sails

Nova Scotia

DAVIS STRAIT

CANADA

60°N

50°N

The simultaneous attack on three ships at once appeared to leave the convoy stunned, and several minutes elapsed before the first rocket soared into the sky. This was followed by a flurry of other rockets and flares fired by the startled merchantmen. The escorts joined in the illuminations with starshell fired at random, and night was turned into day, but no one really knew from which quarter the attack had come, for *U48* had already dived. In the midst of the ensuing panic, Vice-Admiral Mackinnon ordered a 45° emergency turn to starboard, which caused further confusion and allowed Bleichrodt to slip clear of the convoy. But he was not to get clean away. The corvette *Bluebell* was fully occupied, having dropped back to pick up survivors from the torpedoed ships, but *Scarborough* came racing back with her asdics pinging.

Bleichrodt twisted and turned to avoid the probing asdic beam, then came back to the surface and made off into the dark at full speed, and at $17^1/2$ knots she soon shook off the 14 knots British sloop. Now should have been the time for *Scarborough* to return to the convoy, but Commander Dickinson stubbornly persisted in his search for the U-boat, ranging so far afield that the sloop lost all contact with the convoy and would never rejoin. For a while, SC 7 was defended only by HMS *Fowey*, *Bluebell* being still engaged in the search for survivors.

When daylight came, *U48* was out of sight of the convoy, and had altered course to make contact again, when a Sunderland of RAF Coastal Command came roaring out of the sun. Bleichrodt made a record-breaking crash dive, but the Sunderland's depth charges exploded all around the boat as she went down. The lights failed, gauge glasses shattered, and water spurted through strained hatch seals. Bleichrodt went deep and stayed there until the danger from the air was past. Although *U48* was unable to regain contact with SC 7, 24 hours later Bleichrodt put his last remaining torpedo to good use, sinking the 3,612-ton British steamer *Sandsend*, a straggler from a west-bound convoy.

By sunrise on the 17th Mackinnon had succeeded in restoring order within the depleted ranks of SC 7, and was delighted when, at 0700, the sloop HMS *Leith* hove in sight, closely followed by the corvette *Heartsease*. Commander Roland Allen in *Leith* then took over as SOE. The appearance of Sunderlands overhead became more frequent, and the odds on SC 7 surviving appeared to be shortening. Then the unseen enemy struck again. From 60 miles ahead was heard the frantic SOS calls of the *Aenos*, torpedoed by *U38* (Kapitänleutnant Heinrich Liebe). Having fallen out of the convoy on the 11th, the Greek ship had made a lone dash for the UK, only to run into the arms of Liebe, who was patrolling to the north of Rockall.

Throughout the day the weather continued to improve and the convoy made good speed. During the afternoon, being ahead of the schedule advised to the Admiralty, Mackinnon ordered an alteration of course to the northward to lose some time. As no U-boat was then shadowing the convoy, this was a diversion which, but for a cruel twist of fate, might have saved SC 7.

When darkness fell there remained just 220 miles to cover to the shelter of the North Channel, but with only scattered cloud and the moon near full, the slow-moving ships were dangerously exposed. Allen had placed his meagre force, two sloops and two corvettes, to best advantage, ahead, astern and on the wings of the convoy. Asdics pinged monotonously and lookouts scanned the horizon; it promised to be a long night.

On receipt of the report of the sinking of the *Aenos* by *U38*, Dönitz, who by now was concerned at the lack of reports from Bleichrodt, ordered Liebe to search westwards. Basing his calculations on the position and course of *Aenos*, Liebe reversed his own course and proceeded cautiously with extra lookouts posted. His patience was rewarded when he sighted SC 7 late that night. The convoy was on course to pass well to the north of the ambush set up by Lorient.

Shortly after 0100 on the 18th, Liebe slipped easily past the thin defensive screen of SC 7 and torpedoed the 3,670-ton Glasgow ship *Carsbreck*. The attack was not fully successful, for the *Carsbreck* did not sink, but retaliation was swift and Liebe was forced to retire before inflicting more damage. However, his attack succeeded in weakening SC 7's escort even further. The corvette *Bluebell*, already carrying more than 100 survivors from other ships, was ordered by Allen to stand by the *Carsbreck*, and so once again ceased to play a significant part in the protection of SC 7.

When he received Liebe's sighting report, Dönitz at once realised that his boats were too far to the south and radioed them to regroup, forming a line across the convoy's track by 0700 on the 18th. His signal was answered by *U100, U28, U123, U101, U46* and *U99. U99* was then some 100 miles to the south-west of the new patrol line position. Kretschmer put on all speed, but was not in position until 1030. There he established contact with *U46* and *U101*; other boats were nearby.

Half an hour later Liebe reported in again. From the position he gave it was obvious that the convoy had once more altered course, and would pass even further to the north. At 1430 Dönitz abandoned his ambush line and ordered all boats to home in on *U38*, attacking independently when in contact.

With just over an hour to go to sunset, Kretschmer again sighted *U101* and exchanged signals with Fritz Frauenheim by lamp. A few minutes later Frauenheim signalled 'Enemy in sight to port'. Kretschmer swept the horizon with his binoculars and sighted a lone warship on an easterly course. Minutes later the masts and funnels of a large convoy were seen. He altered course to intercept after dark.

Dusk was closing in when SC 7, then 25 miles north-east of the tiny island of Rockall, received orders from the Admiralty to head directly for the North Channel. Mackinnon brought the ships round on to a course of 130°, commencing the final leg of the long ocean passage. The weather remained dangerously fair, with a gentle breeze from the south-east, a slight sea and broken cloud. The moon would soon be up. The sloop *Fowey* (Lieutenant-Commander Robert Aubrey) was ordered to take up station five miles astern of the convoy to search for shadowing U-boats. No doubt Commander Allen's intentions were in the best interests of SC 7, but in detaching *Fowey* he seriously weakened his arm.

Kretschmer was now shadowing a ship which for some reason was romping ahead of the convoy. She was the 5,458-ton British steamer *Shekatika*, loaded with timber. At 1828 Kretschmer submerged to attack, and in doing so allowed the ship to draw ahead. He resurfaced and gave chase, only to find that Moehle's *U123* was already attacking. Her torpedo caught the unsuspecting *Shekatika* squarely amidships but, buoyed up by her timber cargo, she did not sink.

The attack on the *Shekatika* was the signal for the wolves to close in, and a few minutes later Engelbert Endrass, in *U46*, fired a spread of three. The first torpedo missed, but the second and third sank the British ship *Beatus* and the 1,996-ton Swede *Convallaria*, the first and second ships in the port outer column. This sudden onslaught sent *Leith*, *Bluebell* and *Heartsease* racing in all directions, hurling depth charges and illuminating the already moonlit night with starshell, but to no good effect. Not surprisingly, Allen had no clear idea of the whereabouts of the enemy, but he felt obliged to take some action, however ineffectual. The presence of the other sloop would have been of some help, but *Fowey* was still five miles astern. As soon as he saw the starshell bursting, Lieutenant-Commander Aubrey attempted to make radio contact with *Leith*, but failed. He then called for full speed, but at 14 knots *Fowey* would take a full hour to rejoin SC 7. It is said that one man's misfortune is another man's gain, and so it was on this night. As she strained to overtake the convoy, *Fowey* found herself assuming the role of rescue ship, picking up survivors from the *Convallaria* and *Shekatika*. This delayed her even further.

Meanwhile, Frauenheim had torpedoed and sunk the 3,971-ton *Creekirk*, and Kretschmer, while manoeuvring to attack, had been surprised by one of the escorts and obliged to run to the south. It would take *U99* nearly two hours to regain contact. She was back in time to join the rest of the pack in a concerted attack, but whereas the other six boats were content to fire their torpedoes from a distance, Kretschmer slipped through the escort screen and approached the starboard outer column of SC 7. As he did so the moon broke through the clouds, bathing the massed ranks of the merchantmen in a brilliant yellow light. All the ships were zig-zagging independently, but the leading ship of the outer column loomed large in Kretschmer's sights. Using the director to aim off, he fired one bow torpedo, and to his amazement missed. He swung the boat round and fired the stern tube. There was a flash, and the 6,055-ton *Empire Miniver* reared up like a frightened horse. The 22-year-old ship seemed to fall apart before Kretschmer's eyes, and in twenty seconds she was gone. Kretschmer took *U99* deeper into the convoy.

On the bridge of *Assyrian* Captain Kearon witnessed the sudden end of the *Empire Miniver* and immediately put his ship through a series of violent emergency turns before coming back on course and increasing speed. The night had gone quiet again when he sighted a long, low shadow on the water 200 yards on the port bow. As the moon broke through the clouds again, the shadow hardened into the silhouette of a Type VIIC U-boat – Kretschmer's *U99*. Kearon's nerves were bar tight, and without thinking of the consequences he rang for emergency full speed and turned to ram. But Kretschmer took fast evasive action, running ahead of the *Assyrian* and then diving. Kearon gave chase, for he could plainly see the wake of the U-boat's periscope.

The *Assyrian's* engines were 26 years old, but they gave of their best, working up to 10 knots, and she began to gain on the periscope. Then, after about seven minutes, the U-boat resurfaced, now only 400 yards off, and Kearon caught the waft of exhaust fumes as her diesels roared into life. From then on there was no contest, the U-boat drawing rapidly away, altering course to starboard as she went. Kearon followed her round, breaking radio silence to warn the escorts. Pursuer and pursued, now heading to the west, raced down the starboard side of the convoy until Kearon, realising the futility of his action (he had no gun forward) abandoned the chase. He swung the *Assyrian* round under full helm, with her stern to the enemy, and fired one shot from the poop 4in, more as a pointer to the escorts than in the hope of hitting the U-boat. Kretschmer had escaped again.

Over the next hour, with *Fowey* still occupied astern picking up the ever-growing number of survivors, the rest of the wolf pack moved in to savage SC 7. Endrass sank the small Swedish steamer *Gunborg*, Frauenheim and Schepke each put two torpedoes into the Glasgow timber carrier *Blairspey* but she stayed stubbornly afloat, and Schepke again torpedoed the abandoned *Shekatika*.

Kretschmer, who had regained contact with the convoy, joined in the fray. An extract from his war diary best illustrates the heat of the action:

2330 [2130 Convoy Time]: Fire bow torpedo at large freighter. As the ship turns towards us the torpedo passes ahead of her and hits an even larger ship after a run of 1,740m. This ship [*Niritos*, 3,854 tons] of some

7,000 tons, is hit abreast the foremast and the bow quickly sinks below the surface as two holds are apparently flooded.

2355 [2155]: Fire a bow torpedo at a large freighter of some 6,000 tons [*Fiscus*, 4,815 tons], at a range of 750m. Hit abreast foremast. Immediately after the torpedo explosion there is another explosion with a high column of flame from the bow to the bridge. The smoke rises to some 200m. Bow apparently shattered. Ship continues to burn with a green flame.

19 October:

0015 [2215]: Three destroyers approach the ship and search the area in line abreast. I make off at full speed to the south-west and again make contact with the convoy. Torpedoes from the other boats are constantly heard exploding. The destroyers do not know how to help and occupy themselves by constantly firing starshells, which are of little effect in the bright moonlight. I now start to attack the convoy from astern.

0138 [2338]: Fire bow torpedoes at large heavily laden freighter of about 6,000 tons [*Empire Brigade*, 5,154 tons], range 945m. Hit abreast foremast. The explosion sinks the ship. This ship broke in two and both halves sank in a little more than a minute.

0155 [2355]: Fire bow torpedo at the next large vessel of some 7,000 tons [*Thalia*, 5,875 tons]. Range 975m. Hit abreast foremast. Ship sinks within 40 seconds.

0240 [0040]: Miss through aiming error with torpedo fired at one of the largest vessels in the convoy, a ship of the *Glenapp* class 9,500 tons.

0255 [0055]: Again miss the same target from a range of about 800m. No explanation as the fire control data were absolutely correct. Presume it to be a gyro failure, as we hear an explosion on the other side of the convoy some seven minutes later.

0302 [0102]: Third attempt at same target from range of 720m. Hit forward of the bridge [*Snefjeld*, 1,643 tons]. Bow sinks rapidly level with the water.

0356 [0156]: Fire and miss at a rather small unladen ship which had lost contact with the convoy. We had fired just as the ship turned towards us.

0358 [0158]: Turn off and fire a stern torpedo from a range of 690m. Hit aft of amidships. Ship drops astern, somewhat lower in the water. As torpedoes have been expended I wait to see if she will sink further before I settle her by gunfire.

0504 [0304]: Ship is sunk by another vessel by gunfire. I suppose it to be a British destroyer, but it later transpires it was *U123*. Some of her shells land very close, so I have to leave the area quickly. The ship was *Clintonia*, 3,106 tons.

Captain Kearon of the *Assyrian* saw the massacre from the wrong end of the torpedo tube:

There was a period of about an hour when we were free from attack and I had worked up to a position with the *Empire Brigade* on my port side. She had moved up and was ahead of her position. There were some other ships on my starboard quarter. The next thing I saw was a torpedo crossing my bow and I remarked "There goes my next door neighbour", which proved to be correct as the *Empire Brigade* was struck. A few seconds later, at 2323 on 18 October, in position 57° 12'N, 10° 43'W, 170 miles from land, I saw another torpedo coming towards us which hit us in the stokehold on the starboard side, 166ft from the bow. There was only one explosion, which was a dull report, the ship was lifted but no water was thrown up as far as I know; the Chief Engineer said the water came up through his cabin floor, his room being over the after end of the engine room, 40-50ft further aft than where we were hit. There was no flame or smell, but a good deal of smoke. The top sides of the ship on the starboard side were opened up right to the boat deck, there was quite a large hole, and the decks were broken so that we could not use the starboard side of the deck at all. We were actually hit a quarter of a minute before the *Empire Brigade* although I saw the track of the torpedo which struck her before ours.

Up to this time, including the ones I have already mentioned, I had had four torpedoes fired at me, three missed their mark. Altogether I saw the tracks of six torpedoes, ours being the sixth; one hit the *Empire Miniver* and one the *Empire Brigade*. Of the six torpedoes I think four came from the port side and two from starboard. In my opinion there must have been not less than two submarines operating at that time and I think they were definitely picking their marks. After we were struck a

Dutch ship blew up and I believe another ship ahead of us, and later, when I was in the water, another three ships, also ahead of me, were torpedoed. I believe seventeen ships were torpedoed that night, and 21 altogether out of the whole convoy.

When the final reckoning was made, it was found that SC 7 had lost a total of twenty ships of 79,646 tons, while two other ships were damaged but reached port. Of these, Otto Kretschmer sank seven ships of 30,502 tons, and Heinrich Bleichrodt, Karl-Heinz Moehle, Fritz Frauenheim and Engelbert Endrass all added another three ships to their scores. The night of 18/19 October 1940 was aptly named by the U-boat men 'The Night of the Long Knives'.

Kretschmer, Frauenheim and Moehle, their torpedoes expended, returned to the Biscay ports and heroes' welcomes, but Endrass in *U46*, Bleichrodt in *U48*, Schepke in *U100* and Liebe in *U38* remained on station. They were joined by Günter Kuhnke in *U28*, and late on the 19th the fast convoy HX 79, which sailed from Nova Scotia a few days after SC 7, sailed straight into their arms. HX 79 was comparatively well escorted, having with it two destroyers, four corvettes, three trawlers and a minesweeper, but, as was only too common in those early days, the warships lacked experienced crews and had no co-ordinated plan of defence. The result was another massacre to match that of SC7. In the space of nine hours on the night of 19/20 October, HX 79 lost twelve ships totalling another 75,069 tons.

The virtual annihilation by the U-boats of two major convoys in four days, resulting in the loss of 32 merchant ships of 154,715 tons without loss to the attackers, was unprecedented in sea warfare. For Admiral Karl Dönitz it was a complete vindication of his decision to use the U-boats in packs; for Britain and her allies it was another staggering defeat in the long catalogue of defeats that was to become known as the Battle of the Atlantic.

# 4

# Enter the US Cavalry

By the early spring of 1941 Britain had come to accept that she was in for a long and bitter war. Bulgaria and Yugoslavia were under the German heel, Greece was facing invasion, and Rommel had begun to roll back British forces in the Western Desert. Defeat overseas could be lived with, but the savage attacks by German U-boats on the ocean supply lines of the beleaguered islands were another matter. With nearly 50 ships a month going down, cargo space was at a premium, and the implements of war must take precedence. Food imports were slashed, and although the country was a long way from starvation, rationing was strict, and the complaints were loud. Ironically, with less food to eat, the population grew leaner and fitter, and more determined than ever to fight on.

Fortunately for Britain, the tide was at last beginning to turn against the U-boats. In March 1941 Dönitz was dealt a devastating blow by the loss of three of his top commanders in the space of ten days. Günther Prien, darling of the German propaganda machine since his audacious sinking of the battleship *Royal Oak* in Scapa Flow, went first, on 7 March. Still in *U47*, Prien was involved in an attack on the westbound Atlantic convoy OB 293 when the British destroyer *Wolverine* caught him in the act of crash-diving. A well-aimed pattern of depth charges sent *U47*, Prien and all of his crew on their last underwater journey.

Five days later, Otto Kretschmer, in *U99*, and Joachim Schepke in *U100*, met up with the fast Halifax-bound convoy HX 112, escorted by five destroyers and two corvettes under the tenacious Captain Donald Macintyre in HMS *Walker*. Kretschmer lived up to his reputation, penetrating the escort screen on the surface to sink five merchantmen in one fell swoop. Schepke attempted to follow suit, but *U100* was detected by the destroyer HMS *Vanoc*, equipped with the latest Type 271 radar, which was a great deal more efficient than the old radio direction finding (RDF). *Vanoc* gave chase at full speed, ramming the U-boat as she was in the act of diving. Schepke was crushed in his conning tower by the destroyer's bows, and *U100* went down, leaving only seven survivors in the water. It just so happened that when *Vanoc* was hove to, picking up these survivors, with Walker covering her, Kretschmer, who had expended all his torpedoes, chose that moment to submerge nearby, with the object of slinking away. Walker's asdic picked up *U99* as soon as she dropped below the waves, and a swift depth-charge attack so crippled the U-boat that she was forced to resurface. Both British destroyers immediately turned their guns on her, and Kretschmer was obliged to abandon ship, being taken prisoner along with most of his crew. Prien, Schepke and Kretschmer had been the mainstay of the U-boat Arm from the outbreak of war, and between them had been responsible for sinking over three-quarters of a million tons of Allied shipping. Their sudden loss was a great blow to Admiral Dönitz and the German nation.

From then on, things went from bad to worse. On 18 April President Roosevelt announced the extension of the American Security Zone in the North Atlantic to include all waters west of 26° West. Thereafter, the US Navy patrolled this area in force, remaining neutral but at the same time offering a reassuring presence to Allied convoys, and posing a potential threat to the U-boats. In July US troops relieved the British garrison on Iceland, much to the delight of the British, for the Icelanders had been openly hostile to them ever since they had arrived uninvited in May 1940. American supply convoys, escorted by the US Navy, then began to run regularly to Iceland, and it followed naturally that any Allied merchant ship sailing between America and Iceland was offered the protection of these convoys. It was only a small step further for US Navy ships to co-operate actively with the Royal Navy in guarding North Atlantic convoys, and this began in September 1941. This was a clear breach of American neutrality, and howls of anguish arose from Germany, but Hitler, having recently embarked on his ill-fated Russian adventure, was unwilling to provoke the United States, and turned the other cheek. But it was obviously only a matter of time before American co-operation became intervention and shots were exchanged.

On 4 September the US Navy destroyer *Greer*, sailing independently, was nearing Iceland when a British Sunderland flying boat approached her and signalled that a German submarine was submerged 10 miles ahead. The *Greer*'s commanding officer, Lieutenant-Commander L. H. Frost, went to action stations, and when his sonar picked up the submarine he approached warily. Frost's orders were clear and unequivocal; he was to attack only when it was necessary to defend his own ship. The U-boat's commander, Kapitänleutnant Georg-Werner Fraatz (it was *U652*), was acting under a similar restriction from Dönitz, and for some time destroyer and submerged submarine played a cat-and-mouse game, each keeping their distance. Eventually the pilot of the Sunderland, running short of fuel, dumped his depth charges in the vicinity of the U-boat and flew off in disgust. Fraatz, believing he had been attacked by the American destroyer, then loosed off a torpedo in the direction of the *Greer*. The torpedo missed its target, but its track was seen by the Americans. Frost, thereby relieved of the need to continue the ridiculous charade, replied with a pattern of depth charges. The encounter was brief, and *U652* escaped unharmed, but for America the sea war had begun.

Three days later the US merchant ship *Steel Seafarer* was bombed and sunk in the Red Sea by a German aircraft, though whether this was accidental or deliberate is not known. This prompted President Roosevelt to declare: 'From now on, if German or Italian vessels of war enter the waters the protection of which is necessary for American defence, they do so at their own peril'. Soon, US Navy escort vessels were openly providing protection for Allied convoys crossing the North Atlantic. The dangers faced by the U-boats were growing apace, but they still exacted a fearful toll of ships and men.

On 20 October a German radio station in Breslau, broadcasting in English to Britain and North America, made the following announcement:

The DNB has received an eyewitness report on the latest German submarine attack on a British convoy, which led to the sinking of seven freighters and three tankers of together 60,000 tons gross registered tons, as well as two destroyers. By night a German submarine was searching the central Atlantic for enemy shipping. A fresh breeze was blowing from the south-west, conditions of visibility were very poor, there was a driving rain, and the men on lookout had to strain every nerve to penetrate the darkness. Suddenly, the watching men saw some small dark specks on the horizon. "A convoy," reports the officer of the watch. The submarine immediately gets ready for the attack, the dark shadows loom up, larger and larger, and more than twenty ships are counted, apart from the escort vessels.

The submarine fires its first torpedoes, and within an hour three freighters have received vital hits. They fall back in a sinking condition, the jets of flame they send up and the detonations attracting other submarines to the convoy. The wind grows stronger, and a thick mist comes down, so that it becomes difficult for the submarines to maintain contact with the convoy. The destroyers dash frantically hither and dropping depth charges at random, nevertheless, the submarines manage to remain in touch.

In the meantime, Sunderland flying boats arrive on the scene, but still the submarines hang on and in the second night they launch further attacks. The convoy by that time has fallen into disorder and scattered. At dawn one of the destroyers suddenly comes before the torpedo tube of a submarine. The torpedo strikes the destroyer amidships and breaks her in two. The chase goes on. Another day dawns, again one of the escorting destroyers comes within range of a German torpedo, this time probably a ship of the so-called Churchill class. Now a hit is scored on the stern and this destroyer too sinks in a few minutes. The final result of this submarine attack, which was carried out with the utmost tenacity and was spread over several days, was the sinking of seven freighters and three tankers, in all 60,000 gross registered tons of valuable British supply shipping, as well as two destroyers.

Behind this bald account of the savaging of a British convoy broadcast by the German Propaganda Ministry lies the story of an epic battle fought in mid-Atlantic at the turn of the autumn equinox. The ships of Convoy SC 48 faced two powerful enemies, firstly their age-old adversary, the sea, and then the combined might of the wolf packs *Mordbrenner*, *Reisswolf* and *Schlagetod*, mustering between them twenty U-boats. SC 48 won through, but the price paid was enormous.

The slow UK-bound convoy SC 48, a mixed bag of deep-laden and ageing British and Allied tramps, sailed from Sydney, Cape Breton, on the morning of 6 October 1941. Escorted by the Canadian corvettes *Baddeck* and *Shediac*, the convoy entered the Gulf of St Lawrence and headed north for the Belle Isle Strait which separates Newfoundland from the Canadian mainland. The weather in the sheltered gulf was fair, if bitterly cold, and the ships, steaming in good order, maintained a steady 7 knots. The Belle Isle Strait, for once clear of its habitual dense fog, was traversed without incident, and on the night of the 8th SC 48 emerged into the open Atlantic, where its good fortune came to a sudden end in the teeth of a howling gale. For most of those in the ships, being used to the ways of the turbulent Western Ocean, this was no great surprise.

More ships, heavily-laden ore carriers, were on their way to swell the ranks of SC 48, having sailed from the Newfoundland port of Wabana early on the 7th, escorted by the British corvette *Gladiolus*. For the ocean passage the convoy's escort was to be supplemented by the Canadian corvettes *Wetaskiwin*, *Camrose* and *Rosthern*, with the Free French corvette *Mimosa*, all of which had left St John's, Newfoundland, in company at dawn on the 8th. The senior ship of the escort, the destroyer HMCS *Columbia* (Lieutenant-Commander S. W. Davis) had a limited range and would leave St John's on the 9th, to rendezvous with SC 48 at daybreak on the 11th.

Despite the rapidly deteriorating weather, *Gladiolus* and her ore carriers joined the convoy north of St John's on the morning of the 9th, to be followed a few hours later by the balance of the ocean escort. On the orders of the Convoy Commodore, Lieutenant-Commander Harry M. Sanders, DSO, DSC, RD, sailing in the British steamer *Castalia*, the 51 merchantmen then formed into eleven columns, with the seven corvettes taking up station around them.

In the absence of *Columbia*, HMCS *Wetaskiwin*, the senior escort present, took up the lead.

During the night the weather steadily worsened until the wind, then in the north-west, was approaching storm force, and the movement of the sea became heavy and shock-like. The deep-loaded merchant ships, none of them with more than a few feet of freeboard, grimly shouldered aside the threatening ocean, as they had done in countless Atlantic storms in the past. This was their natural element.

Out on the perimeter of the convoy the tiny 900-ton corvettes strove valiantly to provide a credible defensive screen, but much of their effort was spent fighting to save themselves as they were tossed from crest to trough in the angry maelstrom. Driving rain lashed at the convoy, reducing visibility to less than half a mile, and soon the inevitable began to happen, ship after ship falling out, until eleven, including the Commodore's ship, the *Castalia*, were straggling astern. This posed a serious problem for the SOE, who eventually detached *Camrose*, *Rosthern* and *Shediac* to stand by the stragglers. That left the four corvettes *Wetaskiwin*, *Baddeck*, *Gladiolus* and *Mimosa* to cover 40 ships, a near-impossible task in the prevailing conditions.

The bad weather continued without let-up, but by the night of the 14th the main part of the convoy was in mid-Atlantic, having made good a speed of 6 knots since leaving Belle Isle. With the approach of dawn on the 15th came blessed relief for the weary men in their battered ships. The wind backed to the west and fell to a mere moderate breeze, and although the swell was still heavy, the huge, menacing seas began to flatten as the light strengthened in the east. The Master of the *Welsh Trader* had taken over as Acting Commodore, and the ships were steaming in ten columns of four, with *Wetaskiwin* ziz-zagging ahead, *Gladiolus* astern, and *Baddeck* and *Mimosa* covering the flanks. There was no sign of the rest of the convoy, nor of HMCS *Columbia*.

News of the coming of SC 48 had gone ahead of the convoy, and Dönitz gave orders for nine U-boats of the *Mordbrenner*, *Reisswolf* and *Schlagetod* groups, all then in the Eastern Atlantic, to form a separate pack. Once formed, the new pack, codenamed *Raubritter*, took up positions straddling the reported track of SC 48. It was Korvettenkapitän Karl Thurmann, on his fourth war patrol in *U553*, who made the first contact.

At 0400 on the 15th, First Radio Officer N. D. Houston took over the signals watch on the bridge of the 9,552-ton British tanker *W. C. Teagle*, bound from Aruba to Swansea with 15,000 tons of fuel oil. The bridge watch was a new departure for Houston, brought about by the ship's radio receivers having been sealed by the Naval Authorities in Cape Breton because it was thought they might re-radiate if switched on. Accustomed to the warm, twilit world of his wireless room, Houston found the windswept open bridge of the tanker strange, if not a little daunting, but, denied the opportunity to listen in to the ether, he welcomed this opportunity to while away the empty hours.

Since the scattering of the convoy on the night of the 9th/10th, the *W. C. Teagle* had found herself keeping station as third ship in the starboard outer column, not a comfortable position for a loaded tanker. However, on this, the ninth morning out from Cape Breton, all was again quiet; the enemy had either not yet found them, or was not ready to show his hand. The only untoward happening of the previous watch reported to Houston by the Second Radio Officer, whom he had relieved, was the sound of aircraft engines heard overhead at about 0300. As it was most unusual for aircraft, friendly or enemy, to be so far out in the Atlantic at night, Houston assumed a trick of the wind must have been responsible. But as he settled down to wait out the long, dangerous hours of the pre-dawn he was not at ease – and he had good cause not to be.

Karl Thurmann, in *U553*, had been shadowing the convoy on the surface for several hours, radioing directions to the other members of the *Raubritter* pack, who were homing in on him. At about 0500, with the first grey light of dawn showing in the east, Thurmann decided he could wait no longer for reinforcements, and moved in to make a lone attack.

For Radio Officer Houston, keeping watch in the port wing of the *W. C. Teagle's* bridge, the first indication of trouble was a red flash seen to port. This was followed by a muffled explosion, and seconds later, as Houston was running for the alarm bells, came a similar flash and explosion. Thurmann, approaching the convoy from the starboard quarter, had fired a spread of three torpedoes into the massed ranks of slow-steaming merchantmen. The U-boat's first victim was the second ship of column seven, the 4,354-ton, London-registered motor ship *Silvercedar*. Hit squarely amidships, she broke in two, her bow and stern sections floating only briefly before slipping beneath the waves. Twenty-one of her crew went down with her.

Thurmann's second and third torpedoes slammed into the starboard side of the unsuspecting Norwegian steamer *Ila*, a 1,583-ton timber carrier. The *Ila* stayed afloat just long enough for her crew to take to the boats. Meanwhile, in the adjacent column, the *Silverelm*, sister-ship to the unfortunate *Silvercedar*, caught sight of *U553* and attempted to ram. Thurmann was forced to take drastic avoiding action and then crash dived, narrowly avoiding the oncoming bows of the British merchantman. Before diving, *U553* ran close alongside the port side of the *W. C. Teagle*, in full view of Radio Officer Houston and the ship's chief officer. All around them ships' whistles sounded warning blasts and rockets soared into the air, but, despite the commotion, the two officers could not help but notice that the throb of the U-boat's diesels closely resembled the sound of a low-flying aircraft, thus solving the mystery of the earlier report.

The tanker's 4in gun was already manned, but as the U-boat was in line with other ships of the convoy the gun's crew were loath to fire. Houston, on the other hand, was able to take positive action. He raced below to the wireless room, started up the main transmitter, and joined the other ships filling the ether with alarm calls. In the midst of all this frantic activity, the escorting corvettes, one of which was so close to *U553* that she could hardly have failed to see her, took no action at all. This apparent lack of enthusiasm puzzled the men in the merchant ships.

HMCS *Columbia*, having left St John's on the morning of the 9th to rendezvous with SC 48 south of Cape Farewell at dawn on the 11th, had been searching for the convoy for some days. Radio communication was poor in the prevailing bad weather, and with the skies continually overcast the destroyer was unable to fix her position accurately. It is not surprising that the rendezvous was not made. In fact, it was not until 1130 on the 15th, four hours after *U553*'s attack, that Lieutenant-Commander Davis saw the outriders of SC 48 on the horizon. *Columbia*'s arrival was providential, however, for as she approached the convoy her lookouts sighted a U-boat on the surface seven miles to the north-west. Davis warned *Wetaskiwin* of the danger and increased to full speed to attack. *Wetaskiwin* detached *Gladiolus* to join *Columbia*, and as *Mimosa* was still astern, searching for survivors of the two ships sunk earlier, SC 48 was left with only two corvettes to protect the 38 merchantmen remaining. It was fortunate that the *Raubritter* pack had not yet assembled in force.

The U-boat dived as soon as *Columbia* approached, and although the destroyer, assisted by *Gladiolus*, made several depth-charge attacks, no result was obtained. At 1500 the two warships rejoined the convoy, which was then steering a course of 034° at 7 knots. It was only then that a report was received from the Admiralty in Liverpool that one or more U-boats were shadowing the convoy.

One of the 'one or more' shadowers of SC 48 was *U558* (Kapitänleutnant Günther Krech). Coming in from the east, Krech had earlier in the day encountered the 9,472-ton Canadian motor ship *Vancouver Island* sailing independently from Montreal to Cardiff. One well-placed torpedo sent the Canadian ship to the bottom so fast that none of her 73 crew and 32 passengers survived. Thus encouraged, Krech was now eagerly awaiting the coming of darkness and his opportunity to cause mayhem among the ships of SC 48. By then he had in company Kapitänleutnant Joachim Preuss in *U568*. Others were close by.

Lieutenant-Commander Davis now took over as SOE and stationed his escorts where they would be best placed in the event of an attack. With the corvette *Baddeck*, which carried the most up-to-date radar, steaming 4,000 yards ahead, *Columbia* led the convoy, with *Wetaskiwin* on the port wing,

*Mimosa* to starboard and *Gladiolus* bringing up the rear. *Camrose, Rosthern* and *Shediac* were still missing, presumably astern, it was hoped, and escorting the eleven stragglers on a similar course to the main convoy.

Davis thought it unlikely that the enemy would attack in daylight, and in consultation with the Acting Commodore laid plans for a bold diversionary alteration of course after dark. Word was passed to all ships to be ready to alter on the Commodore's signal. When dusk closed in, at about 1800, an uneasy peace settled over SC 48. The threat of the unseen U-boats was very real. The darkness was soon complete, for the moon was not yet up, and the orderly lines of ships, now some 640 miles west of Ireland, steamed on, only the steady beat of their engines and white-frothed wakes betraying their presence. From every bridge eyes peered anxiously into the night, watching not only for the enemy but for the unforeseen actions of one another. With more than 40 ships in close proximity on a dark night, and none carrying lights, the risk of collision was very great.

At 2130 the signal was about to be made for an alteration of course of 45° to starboard when Joachim Preuss struck with his first torpedo. The 6,023-ton British steamer *Empire Heron*, rear ship of the starboard wing column, was hit in her starboard side and went down in a few minutes. *Columbia* was zig-zagging ahead of the convoy when the torpedo struck, and Davis immediately increased to full speed and brought her round under full helm. The destroyer swept down the starboard side of the convoy, firing starshell as she went, but Preuss had already escaped into the darkness. Davis considered giving chase but, deciding the convoy would be too vulnerable without the destroyer, he reversed course and resumed station in the van. *Gladiolus* was ordered to drop back to search for survivors from the *Empire Heron*.

Convoy SC 48 steamed on, alert for further attacks, but none materialised. Midnight came and went, and still all was quiet, but now Lieutenant-Commander Davis grew concerned for the safety of HMS *Gladiolus*. The corvette had been away for three hours, her last signal, sent soon after 2200, reporting she had picked up one survivor and was continuing the search. The *Gladiolus*, commanded by Lieutenant-Commander H. M. C. Sanders, DSO, DSC, RD, RNR, first of the Flower-class corvettes to be built, with two U-boats and almost two years of continuous convoy escort duty behind her, was never seen again. She was later reported sunk in the early hours of the 17th by *U568*, but it seems more likely that she went down before that.

At 0200 the convoy's course was altered to 079°, and at first light on the 16th to 025°. As the hours ticked by it seemed that the diversion must have worked, for the enemy was conspicuously absent. As the day wore on, hopes grew that he had been left far behind. Then, at 1300, a U-boat was reported approaching from the south-west and the spell was broken. Escorts dashed off in pursuit and guns were manned in the merchantmen, but it was a false alarm. The escorts returned, leading what must have been seen by many in the convoy as the fabled US Cavalry. The newcomers 'riding in to the rescue' of SC 48 were the United States Navy Task Unit 4.1.4, consisting of the destroyers *Plunkett*, *Livermore*, *Kearny* and *Decatur*, led by Captain Thebard, USN, in USS *Plunkett*. Word had reached Iceland of the threat to SC 48, and the destroyers had been sent to offer help.

The arrival of the Americans lifted a great weight from Lieutenant-Commander Davis' shoulders, for with the disappearance of *Gladiolus* his already meagre force was stretched far beyond its capability. His instructions were to work in close co-operation with any US ships, and as Thebard was senior he offered overall command of the combined escort to the American. Later in the day a fifth US destroyer, the *Greer*, and the Canadian corvette *Pictou* joined. Thebard then threw a screen around the convoy with his five destroyers, which should have been a formidable barrier for the U-boats. Unfortunately the American captain, probably through inexperience, set the screen too close, at 1,000 to 1,500 yards from the merchantmen. German torpedoes had a range of 2,700 yards.

The Outer Hebrides and the entrance to the North Channel now lay due east at 540 miles, and at 2130 the convoy altered course to 090°. The wind, which was west-north-westerly, had increased to force 5, bringing with it a rough sea and heavy rain squalls, but blowing as it was from astern, the weather, if anything, served to urge the convoy on its way. In pursuit, but unseen, were five members of the *Raubritter* pack, Karl Thurmann in *U553*, Günther Krech in *U558*, Joachim Preuss in *U568*, Heinz-Otto Schultze in *U432* and Ernst Mengersen in *U101*.

Coming off watch at 2000, Radio Officer Houston joined the *W. C. Teagle*'s Master and Chief Officer in the chart room. While the three men were drinking coffee and discussing the day's events, the bridge shook to a loud explosion. They spilled out on deck to find a ship on the port quarter burning furiously and falling rapidly astern. She was the 6,595-ton Panamanian-flag general cargo steamer *Bold Venture*, Karl Thurmann's third victim since he began to shadow SC 48. The Panamanian vessel stayed afloat for ten minutes before sinking in a cloud of steam as the sea quenched her flames.

For the next hour Houston manned the wireless room, listening to the thump of exploding depth charges and the crack of starshell as the convoy's now considerable escort force charged in to the attack. The furore lasted 40 minutes, and then all went quiet. Once again, Thurmann had escaped. Houston returned to the bridge at 2100, knowing full well that there would be no sleep for him that night. He was right. At 2120, as he stood talking to the Chief Officer, there was a muffled explosion and the tanker shook violently. As

Houston ran for the wireless room he saw flames leaping from the after part of the ship. The *W. C. Teagle* had been hit in her after tanks by a torpedo fired by *U558* from beyond the American destroyer screen.

While Houston hammered out the SSSS (submarine attack) signal on his emergency transmitter, other crew members ran out hoses and tackled the blaze, but their efforts were wasted. The *W. C. Teagle* was settling by the stern, and word soon came to abandon ship. Making one last transmission, Houston signed off and hurried aft to the boat deck, where he joined others in clearing away the boats. Minutes later the *Teagle* lifted her bows and began to go down by the stern with a rush. As Houston hurled himself over the side, he saw men on the after part of the ship still fighting the fire, apparently oblivious to the danger threatening.

The shock as he hit the icy water all but paralysed Houston, but when he found himself entangled in a rope (probably one of the lifeboat falls) and being dragged down into the depths, he fought back. His lungs were on the point of bursting when he released himself and shot to the surface to see his ship standing almost vertically as she took her last plunge. He swam away quickly to avoid being dragged down with her. All around him Houston heard cries for help from men in the water. After swimming for a few minutes he found a liferaft and clambered aboard, where, although suffering from shock and numb with cold he felt safe. It was only then that he realised the sea around him had gone quiet. There were no more cries for help. To Houston's great delight he had not been on the raft for more than a few minutes when he saw a ship looming close. He had no means of signalling, but shouted until his voice went hoarse. It was to no avail, for even as he watched there was a bang and the ship erupted in flames. She was the Norwegian tanker *Erviken*, whose master had foolishly reduced speed to pick up survivors when the *W. C. Teagle* was torpedoed. The *Erviken* had made an easy second target for Günther Krech.

Another Norwegian, the 1,369-ton steamer *Rym*, had also dropped back to look for survivors, but when her master saw the *Erviken* go he decided to return to the convoy. It was too late, for *U558* was still there on the surface, and Krech put a torpedo into the little ship's starboard side. The *Rym*, being loaded with timber, stayed afloat for some hours.

Over the next three hours the U-boats made determined attacks from both sides of the convoy, each time being beaten off by the reinforced escort screen. Only Heinz-Otto Schultze, in *U432*, who penetrated the screen and attacked from inside the convoy between columns seven and eight, achieved any success. He torpedoed first the 5,283-ton Greek *Evros*, then the Norwegian tanker *Barfonn*. There were no survivors from the *Evros*, which sank in a few minutes, but the *Barfonn* stayed afloat for some hours, allowing most of her crew to be taken off by *Wetaskiwin*.

Quiet reigned for an hour or so, then, shortly after 0100 on the 17 October came the first American casualties of the Second World War. Joachim Preuss, approaching from the starboard side, fired a salvo of three torpedoes, all intended for the merchantmen. Two missed, and one struck the USS *Kearny*. The *Kearny*, a 1,630-ton destroyer only a few months old and commanded by Lieutenant-Commander A. L. Danis, was hit in her starboard boiler room. Eleven men died and 24 were injured in the scalding hell created by the exploding torpedo. *Kearny* survived and reached Iceland under her own steam, but when news of her dead and injured was released in the USA the country took another step further out of isolation.

The disabling of *Kearny* was compensated for by the arrival of three more British escorts, the destroyers *Veronica* and *Broadwater* accompanied by the corvette *Abelia*. Their arrival brought about a small miracle for the *W. C. Teagle's* First Radio Officer, who, clinging to his raft in the stormy seas, was many miles astern of the convoy and without hope of rescue. It was only by chance that the tiny raft drifted across the path of the *Veronica* and was seen by an alert lookout. Houston was the only man to survive the sinking of the *W. C. Teagle*, and after five hours adrift on the raft was himself near to death.

In what was left of the night, more escorts came pouring in from Iceland and the Western Approaches, and by dawn on the 17th SC 48 was surrounded by a tight ring of eight British destroyers, one Canadian destroyer (*Columbia*), two American destroyers and five corvettes. The USS *Decatur* and USS *Greer* were escorting the *Kearny* to Iceland, and HMCS *Columbia*, now running short of fuel, would leave later that morning. Aircraft of Coastal Command were appearing overhead to complete the cover, but the U-boats of the *Raubritter* pack were still hanging on grimly and making determined attacks from time to time. The defences of SC 48 were now too strong for them, and it was not until the small hours of the 18th that they scored another victory. HMS *Broadwater* (ex-USS *Mason*) was for some reason unknown four miles astern of the convoy when Ernst Mengersen, in *U101*, came across her. Mengersen put a torpedo into the destroyer's starboard side, but was chased off by two other escorts before he could finish the job. *Broadwater* stayed afloat for another twelve hours, but she was so badly damaged that she had to be abandoned and sunk by the guns of her own side.

The remaining 31 ships of the main section of SC 48 reached the safety of the North Channel on the morning of the 20th. Ironically, the eleven stragglers, who for ten days had been crawling behind SC 48 protected by only three corvettes, suffered no attacks, and arrived unscathed except for heavy weather damage.

It cannot be said that the crossing of the North Atlantic by Convoy SC 48 was a complete failure, but the cost, the loss of nine merchant ships totalling

51,093 tons, a destroyer and a corvette, with another destroyer severely damaged, was heavy. Moreover, in the light of the strength of the convoy's escort force, the savaging it received at the hands of the *Raubritter* pack was inexcusable, and must be put down to the inexperience of Captain Thebard, who really should not have taken over as SOE.

After breaking away from SC 48, the *Raubritter* boats were ordered westwards by Dönitz. On 1 November one of their number, Oberleutnant Unno von Fischel in *U374*, sighted Convoy SC 52 135 miles north-east of Newfoundland. This convoy, bound from Nova Scotia to the UK, consisted of 40 merchantmen with a strong Canadian escort of two destroyers and seven corvettes. Von Fischel called in the other boats, and in a running battle lasting some eighteen hours five British merchant ships of 20,413 tons were sunk. So fierce was the engagement that SC 52 finally reversed course and ran for shelter in the Belle Isle Strait, earning itself the distinction of being the only Allied convoy ever turned back by the U-boats. That was not the end of the humiliation of SC 52. Two ships ran ashore in dense fog in the Belle Isle Strait and became total losses, thereby adding another 10,000 tons to *Raubritter*'s score.

# 5

# Along the Great Circle Route

By late November 1941 the Americans were aware that Japanese plans for expansion in the Pacific were about to become reality. The Japanese Combined Fleet, comprising 260 fighting ships including eleven battleships and eleven aircraft carriers, was the most powerful naval force afloat, and had long been straining at its moorings, anxious to open the action. The only credible opposition, the American Pacific Fleet, consisting of about 100 ships, was based on Pearl Harbor in the Hawaiian island of Oahu. Unbelievably, when a message went out from Washington on 27 November, warning all units in the Pacific that war was imminent, the American forces on Hawaii were the only ones not to go on to a full wartime footing. Consequently Pearl Harbor was asleep when the first wave of 180 Japanese carrier-based bombers swooped out of the sky on that fateful Sunday morning of 7 December 1941. One hour and 50 minutes later, when the virtually unopposed attack came to an end, the clear waters of Pearl Harbor ran with blood and a funereal pall of black smoke hid the battered and burning wreckage of eight battleships, three cruisers, three destroyers and five support ships. Ashore, 200 aircraft had been destroyed on their airfields. Altogether, 2,403 men lay dead and 1,178 were wounded. Fortunately the American aircraft carriers were at sea and so escaped destruction, but Pearl Harbor and the big guns of the US Pacific Fleet were no more; at least for the time being.

Germany declared war on America on 12 December, so putting an end to a neutrality that had become a sham. It would now have been expected that the US Navy, already committed to defending British convoys in the North Atlantic, and having been caught so lamentably unprepared in the Pacific, would at least be on full alert in its home waters. This was not so, and the consequences for American merchant shipping were disastrous.

At the outbreak of the Second World War the USA produced 70 per cent of the world's oil, much of which was shipped out of the Gulf of Mexico in tankers. A great deal of this oil was for domestic use, and was carried coastwise to New York and ports in the north. The Gulf ports of Texas also handled 30 per cent of America's cotton crop and vast quantities of timber, potash and sulphur, a proportion of which also went northwards by sea. Consequently a constant stream of shipping plied the eastern seaboard of America, from Florida to

Long Island; deep-draught tankers, fat general cargo ships and lumbering bulk carriers. These ships presented an abundance of soft targets for Dönitz's U-boats, and as soon as hostilities with the US commenced, the Admiral decided to take full advantage of the situation.

Allowing for the two-way Atlantic passage from Biscay, Dönitz calculated that his submarines would be able to spend about three weeks off the American coast. At the end of December he scaled down the attacks on Atlantic convoys, which were becoming more and more hazardous every day, and despatched fifteen boats with orders to make war on the new enemy's coastal traffic.

The first boats of Operation *Paukenschlag* (Drumbeat) arrived on station in the second week of January 1942. They found a situation that never in their wildest dreams had they imagined could exist in time of war. Despite the advice of the British Admiralty, the Americans had not instituted convoys, and all ships were sailing alone and unescorted. Not even the most elementary precautions were being taken. Ships were fully lit at night and used their radios indiscriminately, broadcasting in plain language, giving positions and times of sailing and expected arrival for all to hear. No attempt had been made to black-out the coastal towns at night, so ships sailing close inshore were silhouetted against a backdrop of brilliant illuminations. For any U-boat commander unsure of his own position, it was a simple matter of taking cross-bearings of lighthouses or buoys, all of which were operating on full power. It was as though America could not accept that she was now at war.

On 14 January *U123* (Kapitänleutnant Reinhard Hardegen) opened *Paukenschlag* by sinking the 9,577-ton Panamanian-flag tanker *Norness*. There followed a massacre that would have been beyond belief but for the tragic evidence that floated in the warm waters of the Gulf Stream as it flowed north. During daylight hours the U-boats rested on the bottom in shallow water, coming to the surface at night and using their superior speed to chase the unprepared and unprotected merchantmen, torpedoing and gunning them in plain sight of horrified watchers ashore. The night sky turned red with the glow of burning tankers, bodies littered the beaches and hospitals were filled with injured seamen. Yet the US Navy still refused to organise convoys, and shopkeepers and restaurant owners in the coastal towns, fearing the loss of tourist revenue, refused to dim their lights. The U-boats could hardly believe their luck, and in the first two months of the year 350,000 tons were sunk off the east coast of the United States alone. In Berlin, Knight's Crosses with Oak Leaves were the order of the day.

The Royal Navy offered help, but this was rejected; the official US Navy explanation being that the sinkings were due to mines rather than U-boats. The truth was that, with all destroyers being held with the fleet, the Americans had no anti-submarine defences other than a few small Coastguard cutters. It was only when the destruction of so many tankers threatened a shortage of fuel for domestic central heating and automobiles that America swallowed its pride and asked for help from outside. In February Britain sent ten corvettes and 24 anti-submarine trawlers to organise and escort convoys. Even so, it was not until the middle of May that the first American coastwise convoy sailed. Dönitz then switched his U-boats to the Caribbean, where the climate was warmer and ships still sailed unescorted.

So, in the early months of 1942, Admiral Dönitz faced a situation that most commanders only dream of. Potential targets for his U-boats were so abundant in the Atlantic that there were never enough torpedoes to deal with them. At first he yielded to the temptation to send all available boats to the American coast, thus offering a blessed respite to the long-suffering North Atlantic convoys. This was a major tactical mistake which soon became evident, for it allowed Britain and America to step up the supply of arms by sea to Soviet Russia. When Hitler, whose armies in the East were meeting fierce resistance, became aware of this, he ordered Dönitz to return his U-boats to the convoy routes.

Reluctantly the Admiral again turned his attention to the cold, storm-wracked waters of the north, forming eight boats into wolf pack *Hecht* with the express purpose of attacking eastbound convoys. However, Dönitz was loath to abandon his new-found bonanza in the west completely, and ordered the *Hecht* boats to cross the North Atlantic spread out in line abreast to trawl for convoys as they went. If it so came about that they reached American waters in the process of their foray, so much the better. Ironically, *Hecht* ran into a convoy within a few days of being formed, but the convoy was not one Hitler had had in mind.

On the afternoon of 7 May 1942, watchers on the lonely Scottish island of Islay were treated to a rare sight as a total of 41 merchant ships from Liverpool, the Clyde, Loch Ewe and Belfast made a rendezvous off the island. With a few exceptions, all the grey-painted merchantmen were riding high, in ballast and bound across the Atlantic to load their diverse cargoes of war. For some of the men of Convoy ONS 92 it was their first crossing of this great ocean; for many it would be the last.

As the tired, rust-stained ships idled in the deep water off Islay, warships of the escorting force arrived from Lough Foyle in Northern Ireland and circled them, chivvying and goading like a farmer's dogs marshalling a herd of sheep. The 'farmer' in this case was Captain John B. Heffernan, USN, senior officer of Ocean Escort Group A3. Heffernan, in the destroyer USS *Gleaves,* had also under his command the US Coastguard cutter *Spencer* and a quartet of Canadian corvettes, *Bittersweet, Algoma, Shediac* and *Arvida.* It was not uncommon at this time to have mixed escort groups, although it must be said that none of the participating navies favoured this. In the case of A3, Heffernan and his American ships lacked experience of convoy work, the group had not worked together before, and none of them carried high-frequency direction finding (HF/DF), with which U-boats making radio transmissions could be tracked. Although HMCS *Bittersweet* was equipped with the new 10cm radar, its operators were inexperienced, which rendered the radar virtually useless. Oddly enough, the only ship in the convoy fitted with HF/DF was a merchantman, the rescue ship *Bury*.

In the early days of the war in the North Atlantic, it had been left to the rear ships of the convoy to pick up survivors of torpedoed ships, a practice which all too often led to the rescuing ships themselves being sunk, giving rise to more casualties. In late 1941 the Admiralty requisitioned a number of small, handy merchant ships, and fitted them out for the specific purpose of saving life, one such ship being allocated to sail at the rear of each convoy. It was found that coastal ships with passenger accommodation and cross-Channel ferries were best suited to this work, and the *Bury* was one of the chosen.

In the 1930s the 1,686-ton *Bury*, owned by the London & North-Eastern Railway Company, was a familiar sight on the Harwich to Hook of Holland run, carrying passengers and freight. Built in 1910, she had seen her best days by the outbreak of war in 1939, and her accommodation leaked like a sieve, but she still managed a creditable 11¹/₂kt. When Holland fell, the *Bury's* regular employment ceased, and in 1941 she was taken over for the newly-formed Rescue Service and refitted on the Tyne. She was equipped with powerful motor lifeboats, platforms were built on deck to facilitate the landing of survivors, a complete hospital, staffed by two surgeon-lieutenants and an SBA, was added, and ample medical supplies, blankets and clothing were put on board. As an aid to locating ships in distress, HF/DF equipment was fitted, but the ship was unarmed. Manned by a volunteer merchant service crew and commanded by Captain L. E. Brown, the rescue ship *Bury* entered service in December 1941.

It was late afternoon before Captain Heffernan, having received on board all the relevant paperwork for the ships in his care, turned the bows of USS *Gleaves* westwards and led the way out into the open Atlantic. The merchantmen followed, two abreast, with *Spencer* and the Canadian corvettes on the flanks. Once clear of the land the ships formed up into ten columns of four, with *Bury* bringing up the rear and the escorts positioned on the perimeter.

The weather was clear and sunny, with only a light easterly breeze ruffling the surface of the water, although the surge of the long Atlantic swells could be felt. Captain Lionel Osborne viewed the tranquil scene from the bridge of the Cardiff steamer *Llanover* with a jaundiced eye. A veteran of many Atlantic

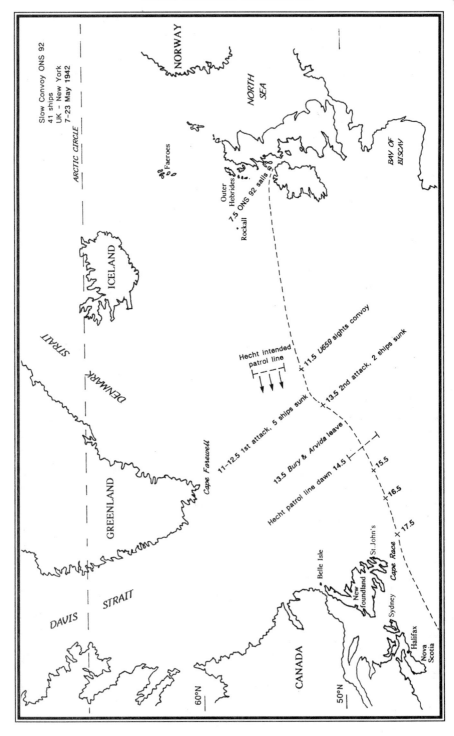

Slow Convoy ONS 92
41 ships
UK – New York
7–23 May 1942

ARCTIC CIRCLE

NORWAY

NORTH SEA

BAY OF BISCAY

Faeroes

Outer Hebrides

Rockall

7.5 ONS 92 sails

ICELAND

DENMARK STRAIT

Hecht intended
patrol line

11.5 U659 sights convoy

13.5 2nd attack, 2 ships sunk

11–12.5 1st attack, 5 ships sunk

Cape Farewell

13.5 Bury & Arvida leave

Hecht patrol line dawn 14.5

15.5

16.5

17.5

GREENLAND

Belle Isle

St. John's

New Foundland

Cape Race

Sydney

Halifax

Nova Scotia

DAVIS STRAIT

60°N

CANADA

50°N

crossings, coal out and grain home, Osborne well knew how fickle the ocean could be. On this occasion the 4,959-ton *Llanover*, lying third in the starboard outer column of ONS 92, was flying light, only her inadequate ballast tanks keeping her propeller immersed, a situation which did not sit comfortably with Osborne. An empty ship earns no money for her owners, and does no credit to her Master, either.

Contrary to Osborne's gloomy expectations, each day dawned fine and clear, and stayed that way. The convoy progressed well, making a good 7kt, with no straggling and very few breakdowns. In the opinion of Captain Heffernan, station keeping was unusually good, and ships were well darkened at night, all of which serves to indicate that, given ideal conditions, a mixed bag of old tramps can be as disciplined as any smart naval squadron. Unfortunately, while this unusually kind face of the North Atlantic made for good convoy work, it was equally on the side of the U-boats.

Allied radio traffic intercepted by German Intelligence had revealed that, since the diversion of the U-boats to American coastal waters, convoys were using the shortest route across the Atlantic, the great circle route. This involved sailing in high latitudes, with all the discomfort that entailed, but the distance saved was in excess of 100 miles. Dönitz therefore first sent the *Hecht* pack northwards into Icelandic waters, with orders to sweep south-westwards in scouting formation. If no contact was made with enemy convoys, then the U-boats, after refuelling from a supply tanker (*U116*) south of the Newfoundland Bank, were to carry on to the American coast, where there was still a rich harvest to be reaped.

The *Hecht* pack was due to begin its sweep south-westwards on 14 May, in about 55°N 30°W, but on the morning of the 11th *U569* (Kapitänleutnant Hans-Peter Hinsch), on her way to the rendezvous, sighted ONS 92. Hinsch immediately broke radio silence and called in the other members of *Hecht*, then settled down to shadow the convoy.

Although *U569*'s conning tower was not visible to the ships of ONS 92, *Bury*'s HF/DF operators were wide awake and quick to fix the bearing of Hinsch's radio signals. Captain Brown immediately advised the SOE of the danger, but Heffernan took no action at that point. Later in the day the Admiralty, also listening in to *Hecht*'s radio traffic, warned of one or more submarines shadowing ONS 92. For reasons unknown, Heffernan still made no move until 1700, when he took *Gleaves* and *Spencer* away from the convoy, sweeping ahead and astern. At 1749 *Gleaves* sighted a submarine on the surface seventeen miles ahead of the convoy, but beyond the range of the destroyer's 5in guns. Heffernan gave chase, but the U-boat dived. Sonar contact was made and *Gleaves* and *Spencer* began a determined but prolonged hunt for the enemy which was to last into the early hours of the

12th. Meanwhile, with the weather fair and visibility excellent, the 41 ships of ONS 92 were left with only four corvettes to defend them. By this time *U569* had been joined by *U124* (Korvettenkapitän Johann Mohr), *U94* (Kapitänleutnant Otto Ites), *U96* (Kapitänleutnant Hans-Jürgen Hellriegel), *U406* (Kapitänleutnant Horst Dieterichs) and *U590* (Kapitänleutnant Müller-Edzards).

The U-boats had a long wait for the darkness they required. It was not until a few minutes before 2100 that the sun finally dipped below the horizon, and, with clear skies, the twilight lasted another hour. Then, as soon as the light failed, ONS 92 went through a series of evasive turns designed to throw any lurking U-boats off the track. The manoeuvre only served to delay the inevitable, and at 2300 Johann Mohr in *U124* made the first attack. Approaching stealthily from the north, he entered the convoy between columns one and two and fired a salvo of three torpedoes. The first hit the 7,065-ton Greenock steamer *Empire Dell*, leading ship of the starboard column. She staggered under the blow and veered out of line, the way falling off her as she did so.

On the bridge of the *Llanover*, two ships astern, the white distress rockets fired by the stricken *Empire Dell* alerted Captain Osborne to the danger. Where there was one torpedo he knew there were likely to be more, and as he punched the alarm bells his eyes scanned the darkness around him. Over the shrill clamour of the bells he heard the cry, 'Torpedo to port!', and he swung round to see an arrow of white foam streaking in from three points abaft the port beam. He ordered the wheel hard to port, in an attempt to swing the ship's stern away from the danger, but it was too late. The torpedo struck the *Llanover* in her after hold, ripped open her hull plates and smashed the propeller shaft, which ran through a tunnel in the hold. The main engine, relieved of its burden, raced out of control, its beat rising to a mad crescendo, then shuddered to a halt as the steam was shut off. The lights dimmed and the *Llanover* settled by the stern as the sea poured into the great empty cavern of her breached hold.

Striving to maintain order in the confusion, Osborne fired distress rockets and then assessed the damage to his ship, which was serious. With the propeller shaft gone, the main engine was useless; the torpedo had also smashed the steering gear, leaving the *Llanover* powerless and rudderless. Then reports came from below that both engine room and boiler room were flooded, and it was painfully obvious that the ship was nearing her end. Having supervised the dumping of the ship's confidential books and papers in their weighted box, Osborne reluctantly ordered his crew to abandon ship, which they did in two lifeboats. All 45 men were picked up by the rescue ship *Bury* within an hour of abandoning. As she returned to the convoy the *Bury* came across 21 survivors from the *Empire Dell*, who she also took on board. The remaining fifteen men of the Scottish ship were picked up by the corvette *Bittersweet*.

After spending almost seven hours chasing a U-boat that had long flown, Heffernan brought *Gleaves* and *Spencer* back to the convoy at about 0100 on the 12th. During their absence the Canadian corvettes had been run ragged by the wolf pack, and three more merchantmen had gone down. Otto Ites, in *U94*, sent the 5,630-ton Panamanian *Cocle* to the bottom, while Johann Mohr increased his score for the night to 21,784 tons by sinking the Greek-flagged *Mount Parnes* and the Liverpool ship *Cristales*. During the attack HMCS *Algoma* sighted a U-boat on the surface and attempted to ram, but without success. None of the other corvettes saw the enemy. *Arvida* and *Shediac* had been fully occupied picking up survivors from the torpedoed ships, which seems nonsensical when there was a well equipped rescue ship with the convoy, but with Captain Heffernan off on a wild goose chase, no one was in charge of the escort force.

The remaining hours of darkness passed without incident, but there could be no relaxing of vigilance. It was a black night, and the wolves were out there somewhere; they could be heard calling to each other over the radio. But they did not attack again.

At 1300 on the 12th Heffernan again took *Gleaves* and *Spencer* away over the horizon to sweep for submarines. Presumably the SOE considered it good practice to go after the U-boats, rather than wait for them to come to the convoy. At 1943 *Spencer* was 27 miles to the north-west of ONS 92 when she sighted two U-boats on the surface and attacked with gunfire. A few minutes later, *Gleaves*, then eighteen miles to the south-east of the convoy, made a sonar contact and dropped depth charges. These sightings partly vindicated Heffernan's policy of seeking out the enemy, but, having achieved his object, he should have taken his ships back to the convoy, for the *Hecht* boats were playing a game with him. When darkness came (it was another calm night, so black that a conning tower would not be seen beyond 500 yards), the wolves pounced again. *Gleaves* and *Spencer* were still absent.

At 2253 Otto Ites slipped past the corvettes and gained his second success of the operation, torpedoing the 4,399-ton British ship *Batna*. *Bittersweet* sighted *U94* on the surface and went after her, but Ites vanished into the darkness. A ship in column two, the tanker *British Power*, sighted more U-boats and fired rockets to warn the escorts. *Bittersweet* responded with starshell, and only then did Heffernan hurry back to join in the defence. He arrived too late to take action.

The dark hours before the dawn brought a lull, but at 0310, as the eastern sky began to pale, Ites struck the last blow, torpedoing the 4,471-ton *Tolken*. The Swedish steamer had only a few hours earlier taken the unfortunate *Llanover*'s place in the starboard column.

While ONS 92 made its painful way eastwards, leaving a trail of sinking ships in its wake, the rescue ship *Bury* followed, searching the troubled waters for survivors. She found the *Cocle's* boats and took on 38 men, one of whom later died from his injuries. At dawn she came across the wreck of the *Llanover*, still afloat but heavily down by the stern. Captain Osborne was prepared to take a volunteer crew back to try to save his ship, but she was too far gone. The corvette *Arvida* helped her on her way with gunfire and depth charges.

Later in the day *Bury* came across two lifeboats and a jolly boat containing 34 men from the *Tolken*, and then two more boats with 40 survivors from the *Batna*. The small ex-North Sea ferry, now with 178 survivors and 62 crew on board, was nearing the limit of her capacity, and was also running short of food and fresh water. Captain Brown requested permission to proceed to St John's, Newfoundland, and this was granted. Fortunately the services of the *Bury* were no longer needed, for during the night of the 13th the U-boats lost touch with ONS 92 and were unable to regain contact.

Ten days later the convoy arrived in New York, seven ships short, and the recriminations began. Given ONS 92's strong escort, it was hard to explain such a grievous loss. Captain Heffernan, however, was of the opinion that the voyage had been successful, and wrote in his report: 'The commanding officers of all the escorts are entitled to credit for a highly satisfactory performance'. Western Approaches Command thought differently, being of the opinion that Heffernan's group failed lamentably in its defence of ONS 92. Captain Brown of the *Bury* commented that, in his opinion, the failure of Heffernan to act on the HF/DF bearings passed to him on the morning of the 11th 'may have contributed greatly to the loss of valuable lives and ships'. The Convoy Commodore wrote: '*Gleaves* was never there when ONS 92 was attacked', which just about sums up the whole sorry episode. The Admiralty complained to Washington, and Heffernan was moved to other duties.

After losing ONS 92 the *Hecht* pack continued on a south-westerly course, and at daybreak on the 14th was 450 miles due east of Newfoundland. Here the U-boats formed a north-west to south-east patrol line across the convoy route, hoping to repeat their previous success. This was not to be, and, having seen nothing by the 18th, they moved on towards the American coast as advised in their orders. They sighted the slow westbound convoy ONS 94 on the 20th, but by this time they were nearing the Grand Banks of Newfoundland and fog swallowed up the enemy ships before an attack could be mounted. All of the U-boats were now running short of fuel, and Dönitz ordered them to rendezvous 600 miles south of Cape Race with the U-tanker *U116*.

Having topped up with fuel and stores from the 'milch cow', the *Hecht* boats then set out for the American coast, but on the 30th Dönitz ordered them to return to the North Atlantic convoy routes. Heading north, they reached a position 600 miles south of Cape Farewell, where it was believed the tracks of both east- and westbound Allied convoys crossed, on the night of the 31st. Almost immediately the westbound convoy ONS 96 was sighted, but the weather took a sudden turn for the worse, and a combination of a strong westerly gale and bright moonlight frustrated the attack. Six days of monotonous patrolling in deteriorating weather passed before the next sighting.

At sunset on 8 June Convoy ONS 100 was five days out from the North Channel, bound for New York. The 37 ships of the convoy were escorted by Escort Group C1, commanded by Lieutenant-Commander J. H. Stubbs in the destroyer HMCS *Assiniboine*, supported by two British corvettes, *Dianthus* and *Nasturtium*, and two Free French corvettes, *Mimosa* and *Aconit*. All of the escorts were equipped with radar, although *Mimosa's* set was temporarily out of action. Stubbs had therefore stationed the French ship astern of the convoy, where he judged the lack of radar would be least felt. The convoy was holding a steady course of 245° and making 7kt in fine weather, with a light southerly breeze and good visibility. The night ahead promised to be as uneventful as the others already past.

That was how *U124*, southernmost of the *Hecht* line, found ONS 100. Mohr made a brief transmission to call in the other boats and began to shadow, remaining on the surface. At 0013 on the 9th he closed in on the unsuspecting *Mimosa* and fired two torpedoes at point-blank range. The French corvette was slipping below the waves with her bottom torn out before those on board realised what was happening.

HMS *Dianthus* (Lieutenant-Commander C. E. Bridgeman, RNR), one of the British corvettes, was some four miles from the *Mimosa* and covering the port side of the convoy when she heard explosions to starboard. A merchant ship in that direction was seen flashing her Aldis lamp, but *Dianthus's* commander decided not to investigate for fear of leaving the port side of the convoy unprotected. Stubbs, in *Assiniboine*, was informed of the happenings astern, and at the same time received a signal from the Admiralty advising that U-boats were shadowing the convoy, but, like Heffernan with ONS 92, he made no move to tighten the defences of the convoy. Under the circumstances, Stubbs' motives for doing nothing were questionable.

Only when dawn broke and *Mimosa* was found to be missing did Stubbs take action. He then discovered that *Aconit*, the nearest escort to *Mimosa*, had picked up a small, unidentified target on her radar at 0015, but had not thought fit to report this. Fearing the worst, Stubbs turned *Assiniboine* about and searched astern of the convoy. He found four men in the water, the sole survivors of the missing French corvette.

Convoy ONS 100 was now 600 miles east-north-east of Newfoundland and ten days' steaming from its destination, New York. Its escort was depleted by 20 per cent, and it was plainly being shadowed by one or more U-boats. Lieutenant-Commander Stubbs realised he might well be facing disaster, and there was very little he could do to avoid it. At noon he sent *Dianthus* to sweep astern for the enemy, warning Bridgeman to stay within visible distance.

At 1600 *Dianthus* was on the convoy's port quarter, distance twelve miles, and shaping her course to cross to starboard. Visibility was good, but the wind had risen to force 4, just strong enough to generate sufficient whitecaps to make a trimmed-down submarine difficult to spot. However, the corvette's lookouts were on their toes, and at 1611 sighted a conning tower fine on the starboard bow at six miles. Bridgeman put the submarine right ahead and rang for full speed, at the same time reporting to *Assiniboine.*

*Dianthus*, her guns and depth charge throwers manned, had begun to surge ahead when her hydrophones picked up a torpedo approaching on the port side. Reacting instinctively, Bridgeman spun the corvette round through 90° to comb the track of the torpedo, which passed harmlessly down the corvette's port side. Seconds later, an asdic contact classified as submarine was reported ahead at 1,400 yards. This left Bridgeman in something of a dilemma, for he now had contact with two U-boats, one visible and the other not. As there was no torpedo track to be seen he opted for the bird in the hand, and resumed his course, calling for more speed. *Dianthus's* engine room responded with almost 2kt more than the corvette had achieved on her trials, but it was not enough, and the surfaced U-boat pulled away, well beyond gun range. Bridgeman gave chase for an hour and a half, but finally had to admit defeat and return to the convoy. He would have been comforted to learn that his tenacity had caused his quarry, *U124*, to lose contact with ONS 100, and that it would be unable to regain it for another two days.

After dark, a cold drizzle set in, making life uncomfortable for those on watch on open bridges. But the severely reduced visibility was a blessing, as it would hide the convoy's movements from the U-boats. At 2100 the Commodore ordered all guns manned throughout the convoy, and then made a bold alteration to the south. Course was resumed at 2230 but, unfortunately, the diversion had not shaken off all of the wolves. Otto Ites in *U94* was still there.

Captain Brinley Thomas, in command of the 4,855-ton London ship *Ramsay*, rear marker of column two, cursed the falling visibility and, when the second alteration of course came, cursed the next ship ahead. She was the 6,147-ton North-East Coast steamer *Empire Clough*, a brand new ship whose engines were giving trouble, causing her to slow down periodically and fall back on the *Ramsay*. She did it again on the alteration of course, and Thomas, forced to reduce speed to avoid a collision, found his ship losing touch with the convoy. In desperation he pulled out of the line and overtook the *Empire Clough*. The *Ramsay* was just three cables ahead of the other ship when Ites, hiding in the darkness to starboard, fired a fan of four torpedoes.

The *U94*'s first torpedo hit the *Ramsay* aft, abreast her mainmast, and the second exploded in her side coal bunkers, sending a column of coal, debris and water high in the air. The British ship went down in five minutes. Captain Brinley Thomas, one of only four who survived the sinking of the *Ramsay*, later reported: 'Before I could get down to the W/T Office vessel was at an angle with bow in the air of 45° and water washing over No. 3 winches. I fell off the lower bridge to deck, scrambled to port side and jumped as the vessel sank . . .' Captain Bastarrechea of the *Empire Clough*, who had watched open-mouthed as the *Ramsay* was destroyed so close on his bow, quickly recovered his composure when his own ship took the second brace of *U94*'s torpedoes in her after hold. Luckily the *Empire Clough* stayed afloat long enough for all of her crew to be rescued by *Dianthus*.

Convoy ONS 100 was now nearing the Grand Banks of Newfoundland, where the cold Labrador Current meets the warm waters of the Gulf Stream. Towards dawn on the 10th the mist turned to fog, and by 0800 visibility was down to 1,000 yards, and one by one the U-boats lost contact. The day and the following night passed without incident, other than the welcome arrival of the Canadian corvettes *Chambly* and *Orillia* to supplement the escort force.

The fog was short-lived, however, and by noon on the 11th the visibility had improved to about 12 miles. By pure chance *U124*, coming up astern of the convoy, regained contact. Mohr just had time to get away a quick signal to the other *Hecht* boats before he found himself under attack by the ever-vigilant *Dianthus*, then sweeping astern. *U124* crash-dived, but the probing beam of *Dianthus*'s asdic reached out, found, and held her. There followed a brutal contest in which Mohr needed all his skill and experience to escape the depth charges raining down on him. The ordeal lasted for over an hour, ending with a ten-charge pattern dropped by *Dianthus* which all but blew *U124* out of the water, but in the end, by dint of his cunning, Mohr was able to slink away.

Contact with ONS 100 was again lost, but *U94* and *U569*, racing in to answer *U124*'s call, came across the 4,458-ton Cardiff tramp *Pontypridd*, which had become lost in the morning mist and was some miles ahead of the convoy. Otto Ites, in *U94*, made the first attack, which came to nothing owing to torpedo failure. Hans-Peter Hinsch in *U569* then took his turn, firing a three-torpedo spread, one of which hit the *Pontypridd* in her forward hold. The other slammed into her stokehold, bringing her to a halt. Both U-boats then stood by on the surface while the sinking ship was abandoned by her crew, the *coup de grâce* being administered by both boats. This was an expensive victory, for the 18-year-old *Pontypridd* died hard, requiring seven torpedoes to sink her.

It was evening before the convoy was again sighted, again by Johann Mohr in *U124*, approaching from the south-east. Unhappily for Mohr, the tenacious little *Dianthus* was still there, keeping watch on the periphery of ONS 100. *U124*'s conning tower was sighted by the corvette at eight miles, and Bridgeman immediately went in to attack, first opening fire with his 4in gun, then following with depth charges when Mohr dived. The chase lasted almost two hours, during which *Dianthus* stalked the U-boat and dropped 28 depth charges. *U124* escaped with only minor damage, but once again, thanks to the skill and dogged persistence of the British corvette, ONS 100 steamed on unharmed.

Despite this second unnerving experience, Johann Mohr did not give up, and at 0223 on the morning of the 12th his persistence was rewarded when he made contact with the back markers of ONS 100 again. On this occasion *Dianthus* was zig-zagging ahead of the convoy, and Mohr approached undetected, torpedoing the 4,093-ton London steamer *Dartford*. The *Dartford* broke up and sank quickly, leaving sixteen survivors struggling in the water. All were rescued, but one died later of exposure.

The *Hecht* pack had struck its last blow at ONS 100 when the convoy was only 400 miles from Newfoundland. To continue to pursue nearer to the land would have been to risk attack from the air. Dönitz ordered the pack to retreat to the north-east, and four days later *U94*, at the southern end of the patrol line, sighted the 48-ship convoy ONS 102 and called in the others. However, ONS 102 proved a hard nut to crack, being stoutly defended by a mixed US/Canadian escort group of two destroyers, two Coastguard cutters and eight corvettes, all under the command of the very able Captain P. Heineman of the US Coastguard. Over three days and nights the *Hecht* boats made repeated attempts to break through the convoy's defences, but each time were thrown back. In one eight-hour depth-charge attack *U94* and *U590* were so badly damaged that they were forced to withdraw. Contact with the convoy was lost, and Dönitz ordered the pack to return home, as some boats were running short of fuel. Early on the morning of the 18th *U124* ran into ONS 102 again, quite by chance, and Johann Mohr claimed another success before he left the area, sinking the American freighter *Seattle Spirit*.

The operation by the *Hecht* pack against the three convoys lasted five weeks, and resulted in only twelve merchant ships and one corvette being sunk. It could not therefore be considered a resounding success, and this was largely due to the effective use of radar by the escorts, a fact which seems to have escaped both Dönitz and the U-boat commanders. On 17 June Dönitz sent the following signal to Johann Mohr, the most experienced commander of the group: 'What are your personal experiences of enemy surface radar?'. Mohr replied:

Altogether seven times yesterday I had to use full speed to dodge destroyers, which, according to the plot, came over the horizon almost straight towards me. Apart from two occasions on which I had to dive, and the destroyers disappeared after dropping deterrent depth charges, I do not think I was sighted. In my opinion all these vessels were merely following normal zig-zag procedure, for when I took evasive action they held to their courses . . .

The conclusion reached by Dönitz was:

'There is still no conclusive evidence of enemy surface radar. That boats were sighted and driven off was due, in many instances, to lack of caution on the part of inexperienced boats, as a result of which the more experienced boats were forced to submerge.'

# 6

# High Summer

Largely as a consequence of the failure of the Americans to protect merchant shipping on their east coast, the first half of 1942 saw the U-boats riding on a wave of success unprecedented in the history of sea warfare. Sinkings worldwide exceeded three million tons, averaging over 500,000 tons a month; in June the figure reached 700,000 tons for the first time. Dönitz reported to Hitler:

> I do not believe that the race between the enemy shipbuilding pro-gramme and the submarine sinkings is in any way hopeless. The total tonnage the enemy can build will be about 8,200,000 tons in 1942 and about 10,400,000 tons in 1943. This means that we would have to sink approximately 700,000 tons per month in order to offset new construc-tion; only what exceeds this amount constitutes a decrease in enemy ton-nage . . . Moreover, the construction figures quoted are the maximum amounts ever mentioned in enemy propaganda as the goal of their ship-building programme. Our experts doubt whether this goal can be reached and consider that the enemy can build only about 5,000,000 tons in 1942. That means that we would only have to sink about 400,000 to 500,000 tons per month to prevent an increase. Anything above that amount cuts into the basic tonnage of the enemy.

German successes at sea, which were far greater than anything being achieved on land, inspired Hitler with a new confidence in the U-boat Arm, and by June 1942 Dönitz was taking delivery of 30 new boats a month. At the end of that month 250 U-boats were either operational or working-up in the Baltic, a vast improvement on the 56 available in 1939. Against this, U-boat losses were run-ning at only just over four a month. Dönitz had good cause to believe he could win this war for Hitler.

As the summer wore on, the Americans, by the use of their considerable air power, finally regained control of their coastal waters, and it became too dan-gerous for the U-boats to ply their trade so far from home. Dönitz now pro-posed to use his gathering strength in full on the North Atlantic convoy routes. His intention was for wolf packs forming up in the western approaches to the

British Isles to lie in wait for westbound convoys, which they would pursue and savage until they reached the waters off Newfoundland. After refuelling from U-tankers, they would then sweep eastwards again to catch the loaded UK-bound convoys. In each case they would have the time and the full breadth of the ocean in which to inflict maximum damage. There were those in Berlin who considered attacking the empty westbound ships a waste of time; to Dönitz a ship sunk was one more ship denied to the enemy, be it loaded or in ballast, and in this the Admiral was right.

Early in the war it had been recognised that the British shipyards, outdated and plagued by restrictive practices, would not be able to keep pace with the losses inflicted by the U-boats. In the mid-1930s a design had been produced in a Sunderland shipyard for a 'standard' merchant ship capable of being turned out quickly and cheaply to meet the needs of an expanding shipping industry, which then ran into recession. The plans were shelved and forgotten, then unearthed again in 1941 and sent across the Atlantic to the great industrial powerhouse that was the United States of America. There the project was put in the hands of Henry J. Kaiser, a construction engineer who had no previous experience of shipbuilding, but who was a go-getting entrepreneur in the best American style. Kaiser modified the plans of the North-East Coast tramp to produce the 7,000-ton, prefabricated, all-welded 'Liberty' ship. Capable of carrying 10,000 tons of cargo at a speed of 11 knots, with minimum fuel consumption, the Liberty promised to be the answer to the crippling losses being suffered at sea by the Allies, soon to include the USA. Using mass production techniques similar to those seen in the automobile industry, shipyards from Maine to California began work around the clock, using semi-skilled and unskilled labour, including many thousands of women. The first Liberty was built in six months, but production increased as the expertise grew. Soon, ships were coming off the stocks at the rate of two a day, the average time from keel to delivery being down to four weeks by the summer of 1942. It remained to be seen whether the U-boats could rise to this new challenge.

In early July 1942 Dönitz formed the *Wolf* group, made up of nine boats, *U552* (Korvettenkapitän Erich Topp), *U607* (Kapitänleutnant Ernst Mengersen), *U553* (Korvettenkapitän Karl Thurmann), *U704* (Kapitänleutnant Horst Kessler), *U90* (Kapitänleutnant Olldoerp), *U71* (Kapitänleutnant von Roithberg), *U558* (Kapitänleutnant Günther Krech), *U43* (Oberleutnant Hans-Joachim Schwantke) and *U132* (Kapitänleutnant Ernst Vogelsang). Of the commanders, Topp, Mengersen, Thurmann and Krech were experienced. The others had only recently joined the ranks of Dönitz's rapidly expanding fleet, and were on their first war patrol.

On the 13th *Wolf* was 600 miles west of Ireland and sweeping westwards when a convoy was sighted to the north of the line. It was at first believed that this was an eastbound convoy, and the U-boats set course to the north-east to make an interception after dark. When it was realised that the convoy was actually westbound it was too late, and contact was lost. The pack then assumed a scouting formation and began their painstaking search for another target. They were in for a long wait.

The British motor vessel *Pacific Pioneer*, 6,734 tons, commanded by Captain H. Campbell, sailed from Belfast on 17 July 1942, bound for New York in ballast. She carried a crew of 66, including eight DEMS gunners who manned her defensive armament, and four passengers, two women and two children. The latter were a rare departure from the norm in these hazardous days, and an added responsibility Captain Campbell could well have done without. The voyage did not begin well. When the *Pacific Pioneer*, in company with several other ships out of Belfast, arrived off the entrance to the Firth of Clyde, where Convoy ON 113 was to assemble, they found only wheeling seagulls and an Admiralty tug trailing a long plume of black smoke. The tug signalled that the Glasgow ships would be six hours late, and advised of a new rendezvous off the north coast of Ireland. It was late afternoon on the 18th before Convoy ON 113, comprising 34 ships, formed itself into nine columns, with the Commodore in the 9,545-ton motor vessel *Empire Rowan* leading column five, and set course for the west. The *Pacific Pioneer* was stationed at the head of column four.

On the far side of the convoy, at the rear of column nine, was the 8,093-ton tanker *British Merit*, commanded by Captain E. G. Dobson. Bound in ballast to Halifax, and thence to an as yet unnamed loading port in the Gulf of Mexico, the *British Merit* was a not over-enthusiastic participant in a new ship defence trial. Before sailing from Glasgow she had been equipped with Admiralty Net Defence (AND), large steel mesh anti-torpedo nets suspended from 50ft-long booms fitted on either side of her masts. The theory was that these nets, when lowered into the water, would protect the vulnerable midships section of the ship against enemy torpedoes. It was also claimed that the nets would reduce a ship's speed by no more than seventeen per cent. Captain Dobson remained to be convinced.

Convoy ON 113's ocean escort was Group C2, made up of the destroyer HMS *Burnham*, commanded by the SOE, Acting-Captain T. Taylor, RN, the Flower-class corvette HMS *Polyanthus*, and the three Canadian corvettes *Drumheller*, *Dauphin* and *Brandon*. Of these, *Drumheller* was detached to escort a merchantman with engine problems back to port, and would not rejoin until five days later. Even before ON 113 began its ocean passage, its escort had been reduced by a fifth. As some small compensation, the North Atlantic was on its best summer behaviour.

Far out to sea, 600 miles west of Ireland, the *Wolf* boats, spread out in a long north-south line, patiently waited for a sighting of the enemy. On the 19th, *B-*

*Dienst* having failed to detect any convoy movements, Dönitz moved the line further to the south. Still the horizon remained stubbornly empty, and on the 22nd, with fuel running low, the boats were on their way to a prearranged rendezvous with a U-tanker when radio traffic emanating from a westbound convoy was picked up. Another patrol line was formed, and late that day Erich Topp, the senior commander of *Wolf*, in *U552*, sighted ON 113 in 53° 45'N, 32° 00'W. The convoy was then making 9 knots to the westward.

The sighting of ON 113 by Topp coincided with the arrival of reinforcements for C2 in the form of the Canadian destroyer *St Croix*, commanded by Lieutenant-Commander A. H. Dobson, RCNR. The *St Croix* was an ex-US Navy four-stacker, one of 50 handed over to the Royal Navy in return for the use of British bases in the Caribbean. Built in 1919 and armed with four 4in and one 3in guns, she had a top speed of 35 knots, and like all of her class was most unsuited to the North Atlantic weather, but she and her crew were well experienced in convoy escort work. Soon after *St Croix* joined, poor visibility set in and Topp lost contact, but not before a great deal of unwise radio chatter between *U552* and the other *Wolf* boats had been intercepted by the Admiralty. This was not picked up by ships in the convoy, who passed an uneventful night in ignorance of the danger threatening.

The 23rd dawned fine and clear, with ON 113 less than three days' steaming from Newfoundland. At noon *Drumheller* rejoined, bringing the escort up to full strength, although the six ships had not one radar or HF/DF set between them. Nevertheless, the SOE, Captain Taylor, zig-zagging ahead in *Burnham*, had confidence in his command, and even dared to hope that the worst might already be over. Then came the warning from the Admiralty of shadowing U-boats, and the war was back in their midst. But the rest of the day passed quietly until, at 1835, *Burnham's* lookouts sighted a speck on the horizon ahead, and the peace was shattered.

Signal lamps flashed, flag hoists snapped in the breeze as they climbed mastwards, and *Burnham* surged forward at 18 knots. Twenty minutes later Taylor established that he had an enemy submarine in his sights, and ordered *St Croix* to join him. The two destroyers raced ahead at 25 knots, their twin bow waves cutting a wide swathe through the water. Left behind, the Convoy Commodore took his ships through a bold emergency turn to port, away from the danger.

With half an hour to go to sunset, *Burnham* had closed the range to 11,000 yards, and Taylor opened fire with his 4in guns. The third round fell close to the U-boat, which immediately dived. For the next five hours the two destroyers patiently combed the area for the submerged enemy, but without success. At midnight, Taylor, concerned for the safety of the convoy, reversed course, *Burnham* and *St Croix* rejoining ON 113 at 0400 on the 24th.

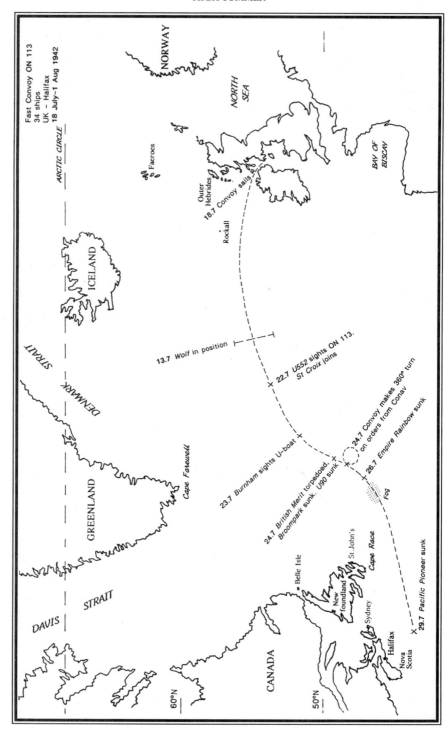

Fast Convoy ON 113
34 ships
UK – Halifax
18 July–1 Aug 1942

ARCTIC CIRCLE

NORWAY

NORTH SEA

BAY OF BISCAY

Facroes

Outer Hebrides

18.7 Convoy sails

Rockall

ICELAND

DENMARK STRAIT

13.7 *Wolf* in position

22.7 *U552* sights ON 113.
*St Croix* joins

24.7 Convoy makes 360° turn
on orders from Conav

23.7 *Burnham* sights U-boat

24.7 *British Merit* torpedoed.
*Broompark* sunk. *U90* sunk.

26.7 *Empire Rainbow* sunk

Fog

GREENLAND

Cape Farewell

Belle Isle

St. John's

New Foundland

Cape Race

Sydney

29.7 *Pacific Pioneer* sunk

Halifax

Nova Scotia

CANADA

DAVIS STRAIT

60°N

50°N

The daylight hours of the 24th again passed without incident, Taylor having stationed *St Croix* ahead of the convoy at maximum visibility distance, with a corvette at the same distance on either side, to keep the shadowing U-boats at arm's length. The convoy remained on a south-westerly course, running at right angles to the direction of the last sighting of the U-boat on the 23rd and, it was hoped, away from the danger.

At 1600 Lieutenant-Commander Dobson signalled the sighting of two U-boats on the surface, one on each bow some 10 miles distant from the *St Croix* and 20 miles ahead of the convoy. Having advised the Commodore to take evasive action, Taylor took *Burnham* to *St Croix*'s aid, cleaving through the water at 27 knots and making smoke to cover the convoy. Dobson had indicated that he was going for the U-boat to port, so Taylor headed to starboard, but after half an hour, with no U-boat visible, he decided to join *St Croix*. The Canadian was then in hot pursuit of a U-boat on the surface and fast closing the gap. At 6,000 yards, well out of range of the destroyer's asdics, the U-boat dived. Dobson, however, was an old hand at this hide-and-seek game, whereas Olldoerp, commanding *U90*, Dobson's quarry, was not. The German twisted and turned, went deep, ran silent, but all to no avail. Dobson guessed his every move and soon had asdic contact. He moved in stealthily and dropped a pattern of three depth charges, which produced oil and wreckage, following it up with another pattern for good measure. The contact was lost.

When *Burnham* arrived on the scene the sea was covered with oil and floating debris, and Taylor was of the opinion that the U-boat had been sunk. He ordered *St Croix* to pick up evidence while *Burnham* stood guard. The result of the search was grisly and conclusive; human remains, lifejackets with flesh still attached, hundreds of pieces of splintered wood, and all the while more oil bubbled to the surface. Olldoerp and his crew in *U90* had made their first and last war patrol.

Returning to the convoy at 2045, *Burnham* sighted a second U-boat on the surface to the north at about five miles, and with *St Croix* in company gave chase. The U-boat dived, and a box sweep of the area by the two destroyers lasting for over an hour proved fruitless. It was now almost dark, and with visibility deteriorating Taylor decided to return to the convoy.

Meanwhile, on orders from CONAV, the US shore control, ON 113 was steering due south, having in effect executed almost a complete circle in mid-Atlantic, a manoeuvre which inspired confidence in no-one, least of all the long-suffering seamen in the merchant ships. On board the tanker *British Merit*, after going through the exhausting process of streaming her heavy anti-torpedo nets for the second time in 24 hours, the consensus was that an undisturbed night's sleep would not come amiss. This seemed unlikely, for U-boats apart, the weather was turning nasty, with heavily overcast skies and the wind increasing from the south.

By 2230 the wind was blowing force 6, accompanied by stinging rain squalls which severely reduced the visibility at times. With the wind and sea ahead, and her nets streamed on either side, the *British Merit* was having difficulty maintaining convoy speed, and steering a straight course was a near impossibility. Captain Dobson fervently hoped that the U-boats were experiencing similar difficulties. Meanwhile he took what precautions he could, posting extra lookouts on the bridge and manning the 4in gun.

At 2253 Dobson, who was in the port wing of the tanker's bridge, heard a dull thud, and assumed that the port-side nets had carried away, which under the circumstances did not surprise him. Then the ship staggered and a huge column of water shot skywards from aft, and Dobson knew she had been torpedoed. So much for the AND. The German torpedo had sliced through the port side net as though it had not been there and exploded in the tanker's engine room.

The lights went out, the main engine ground to a halt, and with no way on her the ship's head fell off, bringing the wind and sea round on to the beam. She began to roll heavily, and Dobson, fearing other torpedoes might be on the way, made preparations for abandoning ship, which with the ship lying in the trough would not be an easy operation.

Conditions in the *British Merit*'s engine room were chaotic. The compartment was rapidly flooding, and the two engineers on watch found themselves in complete darkness, and swimming in a mixture of water and oil. With great difficulty they made their way to the ladder and reached the deck with only a few cuts and bruises. Only then was it discovered that the two greasers of the watch were missing. Chief Engineer Craggs, a man as hard as his name implied, hesitated only for a moment before descending into the darkness of the flooded engine room to look for his missing men. He found one greaser, unable to swim and with a broken leg, clinging to a pipe and in danger of drowning in the rising water. Craggs took the terrified man on his back and carried him to the top of the engine room. The other rating was never found.

After seeing the injured greaser into a lifeboat, Craggs then went below again to assess the damage to the ship. He found that, although the engine spaces were flooded, the water was no longer rising. Most of the ship's tanks were still intact, and although the *British Merit* could no longer move under her own power, she was in no danger of sinking. With St John's, Newfoundland, only 500 miles away, it was possible that she could be towed into port. Captain Dobson ordered the boats away with 32 of his crew while he remained on board with Chief Engineer Craggs and twenty other volunteers, determined to save the ship.

Erich Topp, in *U552*, who had put the Admiralty's net defence to the test and found it wanting, fired his second torpedo at the 5,136-ton Greenock ship *Broompark*, which had already survived one torpedoing earlier in the war. The *Broompark* was hit but also refused to sink, and before Topp could inflict more damage *Burnham* and *St Croix* came racing back. While the two destroyers swept the area with their asdics, Taylor detailed the corvette *Brandon* to pick up survivors from the two torpedoed ships. This *Brandon* did, in Taylor's words, 'in a most seamanlike and efficient manner and deserves praise for the despatch used under difficult conditions'. Conditions certainly were difficult, for it was by now blowing a full gale, with heavy rain, poor visibility and the sea piling up high. Dönitz later commented:

> *U552* succeeded in sinking two ships, but further attacks proved impossible. The situation with regard to the convoy, which was south of Greenland and some 1,500 miles from my command post in Paris, did not seem quite sufficiently clear for me to be able to decide whether any useful purpose could be served by continuing the engagement, or whether I should issue orders to break it off. I therefore exchanged a series of cipher signals with Topp [*U552*], the most experienced of the captains engaged.

> Flag Officer Submarines: What is the weather situation? What speed can you make on course 215°?

> Topp here: West-south-west 8, sea force 7, cyclone. Visibility about 400 yards. Can proceed dead slow on one engine.

> What escort is there? Did anything else make the attack difficult?

> Escort strong. Attack further complicated by sudden advent bad weather which enemy used skilfully to change course through 360°. As a result many boats lost contact.

> Any further action against convoy, for instance against stragglers?

> Convoy's formation perfect in spite bad weather. With weather as it is regard possibility regaining contact extremely unlikely.

> Suppose boats steer south. Do you think this might bring them near the convoy's position? On a south course or a little more?

> Suggest changing course to south-west at dawn as yesterday.

Thanks Topp. Your two ships in the bag anyway, in weather like this.

I therefore ordered the U-boats to break off the action. Our success had been meagre. One boat, *U90* (KL Olldoerp) was lost.

The *Wolf* boats did withdraw, but only because, like the ships of ON 113, their battle had become a defensive one against the might of the sea. While the U-boats fought to stay on the surface and maintain contact with the convoy, the merchantmen simply struggled to stay in line and hold their course. Two of them, the British steamer *Stancleves* and the Norwegian *Harpefjell*, dropped astern, unable to keep up. Even further astern, the two torpedoed ships were still afloat. The *Broompark* had been completely abandoned by her crew, but Captain Dobson and his men were still aboard the *British Merit* and working to save their ship. Dobson wrote in his report:

> All hands now remaining on board worked continuously throughout the night doing what was necessary to tanks lids, hoisting the port after lifeboat and preparing to tow. I slipped the AND nets from the starboard amidships boom to enable boats to lie alongside, but kept the port nets out. As the donkey boiler house was completely wrecked and no steam was available, we fitted connections from the salvage air compressor under the forecastle head to the deck steam pipeline to drive the windlass and winches. The explosion had caused the after guy on the starboard after AND boom to carry away and the boom ran forward bringing up against the davit standard; this buckled it for about ten feet, otherwise, with the exception of the main towing wires slipping a little, the AND gear was intact. After being eighteen hours alongside, the starboard amid-ship boat was hoisted aboard again, her inboard side being slightly dam-aged whilst hoisting, owing to the vessel rolling heavily. At noon the corvette signalled that she had received orders to take us in tow, but at 1600, as we were about to connect the towline, she received fresh orders to return to port with survivors, whilst we received orders to wait for the tugs to arrive. Gun watches and lookouts were maintained throughout.

It must be remembered that all this work was carried on in the most atrocious weather conditions, with the ship lying in the trough of the waves at the mercy of wind and sea, and rolling her scuppers under.

While the volunteer crew aboard the *British Merit* worked to bring order out of chaos, the U-boats closed in again, intent on inflicting more damage on ON 113. Once again they were foiled by the ever-vigilant *St Croix*. At 1800, with the light already failing, the Canadian destroyer sighted a surfaced

U-boat on the starboard bow and went after her. *Burnham* joined in, and the two escorts gave chase at 25 knots, only to see the enemy dive when they were within 3,000 yards. *St Croix* dropped depth charges and Taylor set up a box search, but contact was lost and not regained. At 2000, with the visibility falling and night coming on, Taylor called off the search and the destroyers returned to the convoy.

For much of the night clear skies and bright moonlight obliged the U-boats to keep their distance, but towards dawn on the 26th fog came down, reducing visibility to about 1,300 yards. At 0400 Ernst Mengersen in *U607* and Horst Kessler in *U704* saw an opening, and both fired at the same ship at once. The unfortunate recipient of their torpedoes, the 6,942-ton British motor vessel *Empire Rainbow*, fell out of the convoy with a large hole blown in her side below the waterline.

On hearing the double explosion, Taylor ordered starshell to be fired, but because of the poor visibility this was ineffective. Then the *Dauphin*, stationed on the starboard quarter, reported an asdic contact, and Taylor took *Burnham* to her aid. The Canadian corvette lost contact as quickly as she had gained it, and when the fog cleared at 0430 all that could be seen was the *Empire Rainbow*, abandoned by her crew, drifting astern. Taylor, convinced that the British ship's crew had left her too soon, persuaded them to return. The ship was under way again shortly after she was reboarded, only to be sunk a few hours later by Horst Kessler in *U704*.

Taylor now found that *Burnham* had only 65 tons of oil fuel remaining, just enough for her to reach St John's, which lay 380 miles away. ON 113 was now in range of air cover, and it seemed unlikely that the U-boats would attack in force. Taylor handed over command of the escort to Lieutenant-Commander Dobson in HMCS *St Croix* and then set course for St John's. The *Wolf* group had in fact been dispersed by Dönitz, and were heading south to be refuelled by *U461*. For the next 72 hours the convoy, much of the time in poor visibility, steamed on towards its destination unmolested.

At 0600 on the 29th ON 113 was 250 miles from Halifax when it was again sighted, this time by Ernst Vogelsang in *U132*. This meeting was quite by chance, for, after refuelling from *U461*, Vogelsang had been patrolling Canadian waters alone. He came across a single merchant ship, apparently sailing unescorted, which turned out to be the British ship *Stancleves*, once more straggling astern of ON 113. Vogelsang approached the merchantman on the surface, but she immediately presented her stern to the U-boat and ran away at a surprisingly fast speed for a ship unable to keep up with the convoy. *U132* gave chase, and in doing so she came up with the rest of ON 113.

That evening, having enjoyed an uninterrupted dinner for the first time in the crossing, Captain Campbell was taking his ease on deck outside the

*Pacific Pioneer's* dining saloon. It was a fine, clear evening, with a smooth sea and a light south-easterly breeze. Halifax, Nova Scotia, lay only 140 miles – a mere 15 hours' steaming – away, and with the convoy escort reinforced by the destroyers *Walker* and *Columbia* and the corvettes *Calgary* and *Chicoutimi*, it seemed to Campbell that the worst must be over. True, ON 113 had lost two ships, but the tanker *British Merit* was still afloat and under tow by a tug from St John's.

When Campbell saw a school of whales breaking the surface to port, his first reaction was to call for his passengers to come on deck. They came, the two small girls agog with excitement. It was one of the girls who then pointed out another lone whale surfacing on the quarter minutes later. Campbell turned to look, and froze as he saw a line of bubbles break away from the 'whale' and race towards his ship.

Vogelsang's first torpedo struck the *Pacific Pioneer* immediately under her bridge; five seconds later his second exploded in her No. 5 hold, just abaft the engine-room bulkhead. Campbell's report stated:

> They were both very loud explosions, a column of water was thrown up and the ship took a heavy list to port. I am of the opinion that the submarine fired a salvo of torpedoes blindly into the convoy from about four points off the port bow. Apparently my ship was struck very high up because the tween deck in No. 5, which was an insulated space, had water pouring through the tween deck doors. No oil appeared on the water so apparently the double bottom tanks were not penetrated. A man who was greasing the bearings in the tunnel at the time stated that there was no sign of water there. The Commander of the corvette which picked us up later stated that from No. 91 to No. 93 there was a solid line of ships and it was inevitable that one of them would be torpedoed.

The *Pacific Pioneer* sank 45 minutes after being torpedoed, all her crew and passengers being picked up by the corvette *Calgary* within half an hour of abandoning ship. Convoy ON 113 suffered no more losses and arrived in Halifax at noon next day. Given the circumstances, ON 113 had escaped lightly, losing only three ships. It was the opinion of the Admiralty that even these would not have gone down had it not been for CONAV's decision to put the convoy through a wide 360° turn when the U-boats were to the west of the convoy.

While the *Wolf* boats, weary after their long, frustrating Atlantic pursuit, were refuelling, *U164* (Korvettenkapitän Otto Fechner), was bound for the Caribbean. On 26 July he came upon Convoy ON 115, then 480 miles southeast of Cape Farewell, and sent the usual sighting signal to Dönitz, who ordered all U-boats within 400 miles to close on the convoy. They included the *Wolf* boats.

A fast westbound convoy of 41 ships, ON 115 had left UK waters on 21 July under the protection of the Canadian escort group C3, consisting of the destroyers *Saquenay* and *Skeena* and five corvettes. Acting-Commander D. C. Wallace, RCNR, in the *Saquenay*, was Senior Officer, with Lieutenant-Commander K. L. Dyer, RCN, in command of *Skeena* and Lieutenant-Commander Guy Windeyer, RCN, in the senior corvette *Wetaskiwin*. They were all experienced convoy men. Three of the corvettes, *Wetaskiwin*, *Galt* and *Sackville*, were a well practised team, having worked together for three months. However, once again, none of the escorts was equipped with HF/DF or radar, Wallace being dependent for warning of shadowing U-boats on the much inferior medium-frequency direction finder (MF/DF), this frequency being continuously monitored by the Commodore's ship. It was this set that picked up Fechner's coded transmissions on the 26th, and while ON 115 executed a 90° emergency turn to starboard, *Saquenay* raced astern and began a wide search for the shadower. This came to nothing, for Fechner dived deep at the first hint of trouble and lay low until after dark.

From the U-boats answering Krech's call Dönitz formed a new wolf pack designated *Pirat*, made up of six of the ex-*Wolf* boats, Topp's *U552*, Thurmann's *U553*, von Roithberg's *U71*, Mengersen's *U607*, Krech's *U558* and Schwantke's *U43*, and the newcomer *U164*. With the latter still shadowing, *Pirat* formed a line across the path of ON 115, into which, on the evening of 2 August, the convoy duly steamed. In poor visibility Topp hit two ships with his first spread of torpedoes, the 10,627-ton British tanker *G. S. Walden* and the Belgian steamer *Belgian Soldier* (7,167 tons). Both ships stayed afloat, the tanker reaching port, though the Belgian steamer was later sunk by *U607*. In a second attack Thurmann torpedoed the 9,419-ton British motor ship *Loch Katrine*, which went down with the loss of nine lives.

During this action *U43* was chased and came very near to destruction by the corvette *Sackville*. Hans-Joachim Schwantke described the dramatic incident in his War Diary:

0432: A starshell almost directly astern. Immediately afterwards saw the escort vessel previously sighted about 900 yards ahead and turning at speed, firing as she did so.

0433: Crash dive. Unable to close conning tower hatch. The catch has jammed in the socket. Could find nothing which might be impeding it. Control room hatch made ready for closing. Chief Engineer blew tanks briefly, but I had to get down, and I ordered him to flood. Two men were hanging on to me, and as the water started to pour in, I managed to thrust the catch home (later examination showed that the catch had been turned a little too far, with the result that the straight edges of the catch had come up against the claw lugs on the rim of the conning tower, instead of the bevelled edges). Total delay in diving 20 or 30 seconds. Consequently, we were only 50 or 60ft down, with air vents open and diving at an angle of 15°, when the first depth charge arrived. The whole boat shuddered violently. The lights went out and the electric motors stopped. Papenberg 25m depth gauge and trim indicator out of action. 105m depth gauge rose to 70m and stopped. 25kg pressure gauge at nil. Reports from bow and stern compartments: Depth gauges out of action and registering 0. Starboard electric motor running at full speed, port motor seized up. Boat 5 to 8° down by the bows. Depth gauge remains stationary at 70m. Query – are we on the surface with all our instruments out of order, or are we plunging downwards at full speed? After a test with the piddle cock [a small valve on the outside of the conning hatch used for test purposes] came to the conclusion that the latter surmise was the correct one. Adjusted boat's trim until she was about 7° down by the stern. Within, at the most, half a minute, the boat began to roll. We had broken the surface. Crash dived at maximum angle. Papenberg gauge now working again. At 120m second depth charge came down. Casualties, one man suffering apparently from internal injuries caused by first depth charge.

U43 survived the day, and Schwantke took her home, battered but substantially intact, and she was quickly back in service. HMCS *Sackville* also flushed out two more *Pirat* boats, scoring a direct hit on *U558*'s conning tower with a 4in shell as she crash-dived. Günther Krech and his men reached base safely.

The action of the *Wolf*/*Pirat* pack against Convoys ON 113 and 115 resulted in the sinking of six ships of 35,398 tons, with two tankers damaged. This, against the loss of one U-boat and damage to two others, did little to further Dönitz's efforts to make inroads into the enemy's ability to carry cargoes.

# 7

# The Day of the Amateur

On 14 September 1939, just eleven days after the outbreak of war, *U39* was cruising to the west of the Hebrides when she sighted a high-sided warship approaching. To the delight of Kapitänleutnant Glattes, commanding the new Type VII U-boat, this turned out to be the 22,000-ton British aircraft carrier *Ark Royal*, pride of the Royal Navy's air arm. A destroyer escort was close by the carrier, but Glattes dived and succeeded in approaching to within 900 yards before firing a spread of two torpedoes. The torpedoes were of the magnetic-pistol type, and both exploded prematurely, *Ark Royal* not suffering so much as a blister on her paintwork. On the other hand, *U39* came in for the full fury of the depth charges of the destroyers *Faulkner*, *Foxhound* and *Firedrake*, and was blown to the surface. Glattes and his crew abandoned their boat before she went to the bottom, the first German U-boat to be sunk in the Second World War.

By the summer of 1942 Dönitz had lost 98 U-boats, and with them had gone many of his best men, trained before the war and hardened in battle. Experienced submarine commanders and petty officers, the backbone of the service, were irreplaceable, and yet, ironically, the trickle of new U-boats coming out of the yards had grown to a flood. By August 330 boats were in commission, and the day of the hand-picked, highly-trained U-boat crew was past. In order to keep sending his boats out into the Atlantic, Dönitz was reduced to conscripting officers and men from the surface fleet; from destroyers and cruisers, and even from merchant ships. Good seafarers though they might be, the submarine was an alien concept to these men, and although they were put through a very thorough, if truncated, training course, they lacked experience in underwater warfare. In many cases Dönitz's much-vaunted U-boats now went to sea manned by young ratings on their first voyage, supervised by petty officers unused to handling submarines, and commanded by men more at home on the bridge of a surface ship than in the conning tower of a U-boat.

Late on the night of 15 June, as the wolves were returning to the Atlantic, the 8,402-ton London steamer *Port Nicholson*, commanded by Captain Jeffery, was en route from Halifax to Boston in Convoy XB 25. It was a voyage that should have proved uneventful; unfortunately, Dönitz had left behind a rearguard on the American coast. Off Cape Cod, XB 25 was sighted by *U87*

(Kapitänleutnant Joachim Berger), and she at once moved in to attack. The *Port Nicholson* was a big ship, highly conspicuous among the collection of slow-moving coastal traffic, and Berger, one of the dwindling band of experienced U-boat commanders, was quick to single her out.

Two torpedoes hit the British ship in her engine room, stopping her in her tracks and killing two of her crew. She quickly settled by the stern, and seemed in imminent danger of sinking, so Captain Jeffery gave the order to abandon ship. The survivors were taken on board a Canadian corvette which then stood by the *Port Nicholson*, which remained afloat all night. Next morning, Jeffery, his chief officer and the lieutenant commanding the corvette boarded the crippled ship with a view to salvage. A few minutes after the party boarded, to the horror of those watching, the bow of the *Port Nicholson* reared up and she slid beneath the waves stern first. Captain Jeffery, his chief officer and the Canadian lieutenant were not seen again.

The demands of war were great, and within a month twelve of the survivors of the *Port Nicholson* found themselves mounting the gangway of another ship bound for the UK. She was the 3,807-ton *Cape Race*, out of Glasgow and under the command of Captain J. Barnetson. The *Cape Race* carried a crew of 51, including five DEMS gunners who manned her armament of one 4in, one 12-pounder, one 20mm Oerlikon and six 0.303in Marlin machine-guns. Under Barnetson's command the *Cape Race* had twice fought her way through to Russia on the northern convoy route, so she was no stranger to the hazards of war. On this occasion she was to cross the Atlantic in the slow convoy SC 94, her cargo consisting of 1,040 tons of steel and 1,230 standards of timber for Manchester. In one way, the arrival on board of the *Port Nicholson* survivors was fortuitous. Only a few days earlier, Barnetson's chief engineer had been landed ashore sick, and the ship was in danger of being held in port for want of a First Class Certificate in the engine room. As luck would have it, Second Engineer J. Eltringham, one of the *Port Nicholson's* survivors, possessed such a certificate, and was able to step into the sick man's shoes.

Convoy SC 94 sailed from Sydney, Cape Breton, on 31 July, escorted by the British destroyers *Lincoln* and *Wanderer* and the Canadian corvettes *Chambly*, *Barrie* and *Matapedia*. The convoy consisted of 30 merchant ships, mainly British, with the Commodore sailing in the 4,817-ton London steamer *Trehata*, commanded by Captain Lawrie. The weather was characteristically foggy, and it was late on the afternoon of 2 August before the Belle Isle Strait was cleared. The local escort was then relieved by Escort Group C1, a joint British/Canadian force led by the corvette HMS *Primrose* (Lieutenant-Commander A. Ayer, RNR). *Primrose* had with her the destroyer HMCS *Assiniboine* and four other corvettes, HMS *Dianthus*, HMS *Nasturtium*, HMCS *Orillia* and HMCS *Chilliwack*, all old hands on the Atlantic battlefield. The

Canadian ships were, as usual, without HF/DF or 271M radar, although *Assiniboine* did have RDF. The British ships were better equipped, *Nasturtium* having 271M radar and the others RDF. The latter, which had a fixed aerial, was of great assistance in station keeping and coastal navigation, but was of very limited use for detecting U-boats. Its discrimination was poor, and it was necessary to weave the ship continually from side to side in order to search.

It had been intended that three more merchantmen, escorted by the corvette *Battleford*, would join from St John's, Newfoundland, before dark that night, but in the poor visibility prevailing the rendezvous was not made. *Battleford* and her charges did not meet up with SC 94 until the morning of the 3rd, and then only after a great deal of highly dangerous use of the radio telephone.

Throughout the rest of the day the fog persisted, and the convoy, 33 ships steaming in nine columns abreast, crawled north-eastwards at a speed that was little more than steerage way. *Assiniboine* zig-zagged ahead, *Dianthus* covered the rear, and the other corvettes kept station on the flanks, all hidden in the silent fog. On the bridge of the *Trehata*, leading at the head of column five, the Commodore's signallers worked valiantly to hold the convoy together.

The inevitable happened in mid-afternoon, when the Commodore initiated a 30° alteration of course to starboard by sound signal. This consisted of a pre-arranged number of blasts on the *Trehata's* steam whistle, to be repeated by all ships as they altered course. Fog is a notorious distorter of sound, and six merchantmen on the port side of the convoy, along with the escorting corvettes *Nasturtium* and *Orillia*, failed to hear the alteration signal and continued on the original course. The loss of a large section of the convoy did not become apparent until the fog lifted at daylight on the 4th. *Dianthus* was sent to search for the missing ships but returned after three hours, having made no contact. That evening, *Dianthus* and *Chilliwack* made a further, more extensive search, but again without success. The sea was calm and the visibility excellent, but it was as though the eight ships had disappeared from the face of the ocean. At 0930 on the 5th the SOE, in HMS *Primrose*, became concerned for the safety of the ships and broke radio silence. *Orillia* at once answered, reporting the breakaway section to be 33 miles on SC 94's port beam. *Assiniboine* was despatched to collect the lost sheep, and the convoy altered course to converge.

Dönitz received early word of the sailing of SC 94 and had nominated an attacking force, codenamed *Steinbrink*. This was to be made up of nine boats, all except one on their first patrol and manned by largely inexperienced crews. The exception, *U593*, commanded by Kapitänleutnant Gerd Kelbling, was on her third patrol, but her first and only action had been two months earlier in US coastal waters, when she damaged one ship and sank another, both sailing independently and without escort. Kelbling and his men had no experience of convoy action. *U704* (Kapitänleutnant Horst Kessler) had been

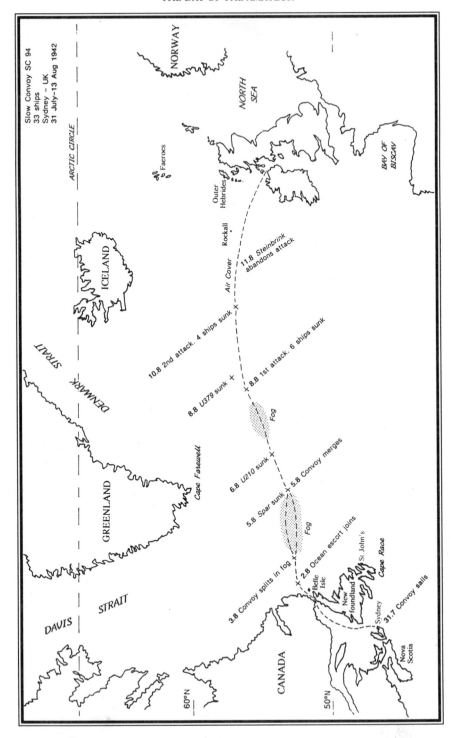

Slow Convoy SC 94
33 ships
Sydney – UK
31 July–13 Aug 1942

NORWAY

NORTH SEA

BAY OF BISCAY

Faeroes

Outer Hebrides

ARCTIC CIRCLE

Rockall

11.8 *Steinbrink* abandons attack

ICELAND

Air Cover

10.8 2nd attack. 4 ships sunk

8.8 *U379* sunk

8.8 1st attack. 6 ships sunk

Fog

DENMARK STRAIT

Cape Farewell

6.8 *U210* sunk

5.8 *Spar* sunk

5.8 Convoy merges

GREENLAND

Fog

3.8 Convoy splits in fog

2.8 Ocean escort joins

Belle Isle

New foundland

St. John's

Cape Race

Sydney

31.7 Convoy sails

DAVIS STRAIT

CANADA

Nova Scotia

60°N

50°N

briefly involved with the attack on ON 113, but without tangible success. The others, *U176* (Korvettenkapitän Reiner Dierksen), *U379* (Kapitänleutnant Paul-Hugo Kettner), *U210* (Kapitänleutnant Lemcke), *U595* (Kapitänleutnant Jürgen Quaet-Faslem), *U597* (Kapitänleutnant Eberhard Bopst), *U660* (Kapitänleutnant Götz Baur) and *U438* (Kapitänleutnant Rudolf Franzius), were all newcomers to the deadly game of 'kill or be killed' that was the Battle of the Atlantic. One potential member of the group, *U335*, failed to join, being sunk by the British submarine *Saracen* off Norway as she set out for the rendezvous.

The assembly point for *Steinbrink* was 400 miles north-east of Newfoundland, where Dönitz intended to set up a patrol line across the track expected to be followed by SC 94. Having left Brest on 22 July, *U593* was still in the Bay of Biscay when the order came, and Kelbling, anxious to add to his meagre score, headed out into the Atlantic at full speed. His progress was delayed by rain squalls, and later by fog, but he arrived at the rendezvous 24 hours ahead of the others. The ocean was empty of enemy ships, and eight days of frustration and monotony were to pass before *U593*, stationed at the northern end of the patrol line, heard the brief radio telephone exchange between *Primrose* and *Orillia*. Kelbling homed-in on the bearing.

Having established the position of the main convoy, the 'lost' ships formed up in two columns of three and, with *Nasturtium* to port and *Orillia* to starboard, altered course to close with SC 94. Speed was now of the essence, and black smoke poured from the funnels of the gaggle of old tramps as they strove to put the miles behind them. In the flat calm the ships surged forward, but with the visibility estimated at 30 miles, the efforts of their sweating firemen served only to advertise their presence. Gerd Kelbling saw their smoke long before the ships lifted over the horizon.

At 1350 *U593* was in position on the starboard bow of the six-ship convoy, and taking careful aim at the leading ship, the 3,616-ton Dutch steamer *Spar*, Kelbling fired a single torpedo. One minute later he fired a second. Kelbling's first torpedo ran true and blasted open the *Spar*'s hull in way of her engine room. The sea poured in and she began to sink; 20 minutes later she was gone, leaving the sea covered in wreckage through which two heavily-laden lifeboats threaded their way.

Kelbling's *U593* was well placed to do untold further damage, but his second torpedo, which missed its target, gave her away, and the wrath of the gods descended on her. Lookouts on the *Nasturtium* spotted the torpedo track, and the corvette heeled under full helm as she ran down the track at full speed, hurling depth charges as she went. *Orillia* had by this time obtained a weak asdic contact on her starboard bow, and she weighed in with a pattern of ten charges. The destroyer *Assiniboine* was then only six miles off, and she raced in at 20 knots to join the fray. *U593* was fortunate in being able to slip away with only minor damage.

While *Nasturtium*, covered by *Orillia*, stopped to pick up the 36 men and a dog who survived the sinking of the *Spar*, *Assiniboine* made a careful sweep of the area up to a depth of eight miles in all directions. At 1620 it seemed her patience might have been rewarded, when a large splash, followed by bubbles, was seen about one mile ahead. The Canadian destroyer increased to maximum speed to investigate, but no asdic contact was made. Kelbling, having used his periscope briefly, was gone, sinking down into the depths on silent routine.

The five remaining stragglers rejoined SC 94 during that night, and on the morning of the 6th the convoy was once more in nine orderly columns, steering a course of 068° at 7 knots. The senior escort, HMS *Primrose*, was in the van, with *Assiniboine*, *Chilliwack* and *Battleford* covering the starboard side while *Dianthus*, *Orillia* and *Nasturtium* kept station to port. Morning star sights established the convoy's position as 290 miles south-south-east of Cape Farewell. The weather remained fair, but the sky was overcast and the visibility, although still good, was down to eight miles. All was quiet, but no one in the ships doubted that the enemy was all around them, watching and waiting. They were correct, for wolf pack *Steinbrink*, called in by Kelbling, had arrived.

The first confirmation of the imminent danger came while the breakfast fires of the galleys were still smoking. At 0845 *Assiniboine* reported sighting an unidentified object on the horizon fine on the port bow of the convoy. *Primrose* ordered her to investigate, and the destroyer surged forward as her powerful engines were opened up. SC 94's shadow, *U593*, had been caught unawares on the surface, and was faced with the alternatives of diving or running. Wrongly believing that he was being pursued by a corvette, Gerd Kelbling chose to run. It was a race that could have only one end. *Assiniboine's* top speed was in excess of 26 knots; the U-boat, at best, would make no more than 17$^1$/$_2$. Steering a course slightly to starboard of the surfaced submarine, *Assiniboine* gave chase, and within ten minutes was in easy gun range. She opened up with her forward 4.7s, firing three quick salvoes, all of which fell close to *U593*. Kelbling dived and turned to port to run away underwater.

*Dianthus* had been sent to assist the destroyer, and was coming up on her port quarter. *Assiniboine* reached the last known position of the U-boat at 0857 and began an asdic search, the first leg being on a north-westerly course. When the destroyer had run some three miles on this course, *Dianthus*, still some way astern, reported a contact. *Assiniboine* turned towards the corvette and immediately obtained a firm contact at 600 yards. She moved in on this, laying a pattern of ten depth charges set to 100 and 225ft, then followed this with another full pattern set to 150 and 385ft. The shock waves of the underwater explosions were felt in the ships of the convoy, many miles astern; in *U593* the effect was devastating.

By this time *Dianthus* had arrived on the spot and was reporting a firm asdic contact. *Assiniboine* stood by, acting as directing ship, while the corvette attacked using charges with shallow settings, for it was thought that the U-boat was not far below the surface. The assumption appeared to be correct, for when contact was lost with the target it was at a range of less than 100 yards. So, in spite of the expenditure of a great deal of fuel and numerous depth charges, *U593* escaped again, but not for long. *Assiniboine* and *Dianthus*, steaming in line-abreast five miles apart, were still patiently quartering the ocean when Kelbling surfaced again at 1412 and began retiring to the south-east at full speed. The U-boat was immediately sighted by *Assiniboine*, but fog patches were now forming, and although the destroyer increased speed to 22 knots *U593* found refuge in the fog. She had, however, been damaged by the fierce depth-charging, and Kelbling judged it was time to retire from the fray and return home for repairs.

*U593* was in-between fog patches, and hidden from her pursuers, when she met up with *U210* (Kapitänleutnant Lemcke). Throughout the day Lemcke had been steering on a parallel course to SC 94, but had not sighted the convoy. Before he went on his way, Kelbling gave Lemcke the position, course and speed of the convoy, cautioning him to look out for the enemy warships chasing *U593*. Lemcke thanked him, and assuming the escorts had returned to the convoy, set course to intercept SC 94 after dark.

*Assiniboine* and *Dianthus* had not given up the search, and, as luck would have it, altered on to a northerly course which took then directly into the path of *U210*. At 1536 the U-boat suddenly appeared out of the fog only a mile ahead of *Assiniboine*, and the destroyer at once went into the attack. It was too late for Lemcke to dive, and he ran at full speed for the nearest fog patch. Once concealed in the fog Lemcke assumed he would be able to make good his escape, but he was not aware that *Assiniboine* was equipped with radar, albeit in its earliest form.

Having lost sight of the U-boat in the fog, *Assiniboine* increased speed and, after steaming for about a mile, altered course to the south. Almost at once an RDF contact was obtained on her starboard bow at 1,200 yards. Visibility was by now down to 600 yards, but a minute later *U210* was sighted by eye at very close range, and *Assiniboine* opened fire.

Had Lemcke then crash-dived, he might possibly have got away, but it is more likely that his boat would have received a similar hammering from the escorts as that dealt out to *U593*. However, the German commander chose to fight it out on the surface, and there followed a gun battle at point-blank range, with the U-boat taking violent evading action, all the time attempting to get inside the destroyer's turning circle and underneath her big guns. In this Lemcke was partly successful, but by going astern on one engine *Assiniboine* was finally able to manoeuvre into a position to ram. Her commanding officer's report stated:

> It was impossible to depress the 4.7in guns sufficiently at this range, but I ordered them to continue firing, more to keep the guns' crews busy while under fire than in any hope of hitting. One hit was gained on the conning tower, however.
>
> During most of the action we were so close that I could make out the Commanding Officer on the conning tower bending down occasionally to pass wheel orders. A gun's crew appeared on the deck and attempted to reach the forward gun but our multiple 0.5in machine-guns successfully prevented this.
>
> Three or four times we just missed him. The officers left the conning tower in order to dive and in the few seconds during which he was on a steady course we rammed him just abaft the conning tower. He was actually in the process of diving at the time.
>
> I turned as quickly as possible to find him surfacing again but slightly down by the stern, still firing and making about 10 knots. After a little manoeuvring we rammed him again well abaft the conning tower and fired a shallow pattern of depth charges as we passed. Also one 4.7in shell from "Y" gun scored a direct hit on his bows. He sank by the head in about two minutes.
>
> *Dianthus* appeared out of the fog just in time to see him go. The yell that went up from both ships must have frightened U-boats for about ten miles in the vicinity.

The deadly duel between destroyer and submarine, fought in complete isolation in the swirling mists of the grey Atlantic, lasted no more than fifteen minutes, and its conclusion was inevitable. But before she went *U210* exacted a price from *Assiniboine* for her victory. Her machine-guns and 40mm cannon raked the destroyer from end to end, setting fire to drums of petrol stowed on her deck, which in turn set fire to her bridge. One rating was killed and one officer and twelve other ratings wounded. The ramming of the U-boat had also severely damaged *Assiniboine*'s bows, and she was obliged to return to port. Thirty-eight of *U210*'s crew were picked up by *Assiniboine* and *Dianthus*, but Lemcke was not among them. He died when a shell hit the U-boat's conning tower, without the satisfaction of knowing that his courageous fight had robbed SC 94 of the protection of her only destroyer.

For the next 36 hours SC 94, with its thin defensive ring of corvettes around it, pushed steadily eastwards, while the wolves of *Steinbrink* circled warily, seeking an opportunity to pounce. Operating at night on the surface, they made four successive attempts to break through the ring, but each time they were beaten back. Early in the afternoon of the 8th, when the convoy had reached the mid-point of the passage, the U-boats changed tactics and approached at periscope depth. Captain Barnetson had a grandstand view of the attack from the bridge of the *Cape Race*.

At 1230 on the 8th August the Commodore's ship, SS *Trehata*, No. 51, was torpedoed on the port side, then the SS *Kelso*, No. 52, also on the port side, followed by the American ship on my starboard quarter, the SS *Kaimoku*, No. 73. I saw a great column of smoke and flames burst out of the port side of this vessel, the whole ship seemed to explode, then she sank quickly. A fourth ship, SS *Anneberg*, No. 63, was also torpedoed but she was astern of me and I did not see on which side she was struck. All four ships were torpedoed within a period of about five minutes.

I was very close to the *Kelso*, which was immediately on my port beam, and I saw her sink in about five minutes; ten minutes after she had disappeared, at about 1300, there were two violent underwater explosions, within about half a second of each other, which appeared to come from the *Kelso*, one taking place forward and one aft. Actually, I thought my ship had been torpedoed and rang "stop" on the engine-room telegraph, but finding I had been mistaken I rang down for the engines to be restarted. We also sent out a W/T message stating we had been torpedoed, but cancelled it later by radio telephone.

Yet Barnetson did not see the whole dramatic picture. In all, five ships were torpedoed, the fifth being the 7,914-ton Greek steamer *Mount Kassion*. Only two U-boats were involved, *U176* (Korvettenkapitän Reiner Dierksen) and *U379* (Kapitänleutnant Paul-Hugo Kettner), but the suddenness of their vicious attack on that calm and sunny afternoon sent panic sweeping through the convoy. The crews of three British ships, the *Empire Moonbeam*, *Empire Antelope* and *Radchurch*, also thought they had been torpedoed, and abandoned ship in a hurry. This uncharacteristic display of pure funk by British merchant seamen was partly redressed when the men of the two *Empire* ships reboarded. The master of the *Radchurch* had stood by his ship, but nothing would induce his crew to rejoin him, and the 32-year-old Cardiff tramp drifted forlornly astern of the convoy until Reiner Dierksen ended her humiliation with a torpedo.

Another British ship, the *Empire Scout*, took over as Convoy Commodore, and the rest of the afternoon passed uneasily but without incident, *Battleford* and *Orillia* being engaged in picking up survivors from the sunken ships. In all, 201 survivors were taken on board the corvettes out of a total of 242 known to be in the merchantmen. Convoy SC 94, meanwhile, was left weakly defended, with only four corvettes to cover the remaining merchantmen, one of which, the *Cape Race*, was straggling astern. When Captain Barnetson came to restart his engines following the savaging of the convoy by *U176* and *U379*, he found that the devastating explosions aboard the sinking *Kelso* had damaged the *Cape Race*'s propeller shaft bearings and fractured the main injection inlet. For the next hour the *Cape Race* drifted engineless in the rear of the convoy while Chief Engineer Eltringham earned his unexpected promotion. Anxiously pacing the silent bridge of his ship, Barnetson felt helpless and desperately vulnerable.

The fragile peace came to an abrupt end when, at 1710, the corvette *Dianthus* (Lieutenant-Commander C. E. Bridgeman), keeping guard on the port bow of the convoy, sighted a surfaced U-boat on her port beam. The corvette's radar was out of action at the time, and contact was lost when the U-boat disappeared into a rain squall. Bridgeman steered for the squall, and after half an hour the enemy was again seen. *Dianthus* gave chase, and again lost her quarry, but at 1845 her perseverance was rewarded by the sight of two U-boats some six miles ahead and lying close to each other, apparently stopped. They were *U176* and *U379*, exchanging information following their successful hit-and-run attack on SC 94.

When *Dianthus* came in sight Dierksen quickly made off in an easterly direction, but Kettner was slow to move, and soon found himself under fire. The range was 12,000 yards and, aiming and firing with admirable precision, the British corvette's gunners got off twelve rounds of high explosive (HE) before Kettner made a hurried and undignified departure below the waves. None of *Dianthus*' shells found their target, and it seemed that *U379* had made good her escape. *Chilliwack* joined *Dianthus*, and the two corvettes carried out a thorough asdic sweep of the area, but no contact was made. Sunset came, and *Chilliwack* rejoined the convoy, leaving *Dianthus* to continue the search alone. By 2054, with darkness setting in, Bridgeman decided he would make one last sweep, concentrating on the spot where *U379* had been seen to dive. It was a lucky decision; a quarter of an hour later a signalman on the bridge of the corvette sighted the U-boat on the surface, attempting to slink away into the darkness. Bridgeman lit up the area with eight rounds of starshell, panicking Kettner into diving again.

This time the corvette's asdic operators obtained a good, hard echo at 2,500 yards, and *Dianthus* went in like a terrier after a rat, attacking with a five-depth-charge pattern set shallow. Two minutes later *U379* came to the surface and was immediately caught in the beam of the corvette's powerful searchlight.

Bridgeman opened up with all guns and turned to ram. *Dianthus* struck the U-boat a glancing blow forward of her conning tower and rode up over her, dropping six depth charges set to explode at 50ft as she drew clear. Lieutenant-Commander Bridgeman described what followed in his report:

> U-boat sank after ramming four times and firing seven rounds of 4in, 100 rounds of pom-pom and several belts of Hotchkiss. Target was well illuminated by searchlight and snowflakes. Pom-pom was highly effective. At the fourth ramming U-boat's bow lifted and struck *Dianthus* on the starboard side of the forecastle.
>
> These nineteen minutes between the surfacing and sinking of the U-boat can be described as very lively and gave our crew the opportunity for which during the whole commission they had striven so hard.
>
> Immediately the U-boat sank, the First Lieutenant and Chief ERA made a survey of the damage and commenced shoring up, whilst every attempt was made to pick up survivors. In spite of bringing one of our prisoners to the bridge to urge his countrymen in the water to swim alongside, it proved a slow process, they only appeared capable of shouting.

The *U379* sank at 2206 on 8 August in 57° 11'N, 30° 57'W, thus bringing to an end her first and only war patrol. Only five survivors were picked up by *Dianthus*, whose bows were stove in by the ramming, resulting in 4ft of water in her lower messdeck. Bridgeman, aware that another U-boat was somewhere close by, and anxious to quit the area as soon as possible, dropped a Carley float for the other Germans in the water and set course to rejoin the convoy. With her forward bulkhead shored up she steamed at 6½ knots throughout the night, rejoining SC 94 again at 1300 on the 9th.

While *Dianthus* had been away the convoy's escort had been reinforced by the destroyer HMS *Broke*, which took over as Senior Escort from *Primrose*. *Broke*'s introduction to SC 94 was sudden and brutal. Soon after she had taken up her station on the starboard beam, the convoy made two large alterations of course, during which the destroyer got badly out of position. While she was crossing ahead of the convoy to regain her station she was bracketed by torpedoes passing both ahead and astern of her. A white swirl of water, indicating a diving submarine, was sighted, and *Broke* charged in, firing depth charges. No results were observed, but the destroyer's swift action probably forestalled an attack on the convoy. There were no more alarms that night.

On the afternoon of the 9th, with SC 94 some 700 miles to the west of Ireland and an equal distance south of Iceland, US Navy Catalina amphibians and RAF Liberator bombers arrived overhead. With these long-range aircraft circling on the fringes of the convoy, the shadowing U-boats were forced to take refuge below the surface. The Polish destroyer *Błyskawica* also joined that afternoon, but her stay with SC 94 was brief. On being sent by *Broke* to investigate a reported U-boat sighting, her gyro compass became unserviceable and she wandered away, losing touch with the convoy.

The morning of the 10th dawned fine and clear, with a force 4 north-westerly wind blowing, accompanied by a moderate sea and swell. There was still no sign of the missing Polish destroyer, and *Primrose* was detailed to search astern for her. The British corvette, then stationed on SC 94's port quarter, reversed course, and within fifteen minutes had sighted a shadowing U-boat five miles astern of the convoy. Altering course towards the enemy, *Primrose* closed at full speed, opening fire with her 4in gun at 1,300 yards. The U-boat dived as soon as the shells began to fall around her, and the usual hide-and-seek game followed. *Primrose* was joined by *Battleford*, and the two corvettes began a systematic asdic search, dropping depth charges whenever a likely contact was made.

While *Primrose* and *Battleford* were away, the defence of SC 94 was left to HMS *Broke* and four corvettes, one of which, *Dianthus*, was severely damaged and in no condition for a fight. Bad weather over Iceland and Ireland prevented the arrival of air cover that morning, leaving the convoy open to attack. The uneasiness was felt throughout the 26 merchantmen remaining afloat. The *Cape Race*, her main engine again functioning sweetly, was back in position as second ship in column six. Captain Barnetson reported:

Everything went well until the morning of 10th August. Weather that day was overcast, but visibility was good, moderate sea and north-westerly wind force 4. We were steaming at 7 knots, steering 086°, when at 0930 GMT, on the 10th August, in position 56° 45'N, 22° 50'W, we were struck by a torpedo on the starboard side abreast of the mainmast. Just before we were hit the ship ahead of us, SS *Empire Reindeer*, No. 61, was torpedoed, being struck on the starboard side, the SS *Oregon*, No. 52, also on the starboard side. I saw the track of a torpedo cross our bows, which struck the *Oregon*, then we were hit, all three vessels being torpedoed within a few minutes of each other, as in the first attack on the 8th.

This attack on SC 94 had been mounted by *U660* (Kapitänleutnant Götz Baur) and *U438* (Kapitänleutnant Rudolf Franzius). Baur fired a single shot followed by a two-torpedo spread, and then another single shot. He hit first the 4,439-ton Greek steamer *Condylis*, No. 33 (this was not seen by Barnetson), then the 6,008-ton British ship *Oregon*, then the 6,259-ton *Empire Reindeer* and, finally, the *Cape Race*. The *Oregon* did not sink until later, the *coup de grâce* being administered by Franzius in *U438*.

The *Cape Race* was hard hit, the torpedo blasting a huge hole in her hull in way of her No. 4 hold, into which the sea was pouring. But there appeared to be a chance of saving her. As a precautionary measure Barnetson ordered most of his crew to abandon ship; this they did in three lifeboats. Four men remained on board; Captain Barnetson, Third Officer A. McCallum, and the ship's boatswain and carpenter. Barnetson later reported to the Admiralty:

> The vessel did not appear to be sinking very rapidly, but at 0950 the *Oregon*, which had been abandoned, sheered to starboard and rammed us practically amidships on the port side, smashing the port lifeboat which had been lowered to the water's edge, and making a large hole in the port side of the ship. Fortunately, there was nobody in the lifeboat at the time. The ship was settling slowly by the stern with the forecastle head rising out of the water, but after being rammed she started to sink very rapidly and I thought it was time to get away. After a good deal of difficulty the four of us still on board managed to clear away the remaining lifeboat, the vessel finally sank by the stern, and disappeared at 1000, the timber stacked on the after deck floating off as the stern went under.

Captain Barnetson, all of his crew, and the twice-torpedoed survivors of the *Port Nicholson* were later picked up by the corvettes *Nasturtium* and *Dianthus*. In all, the two escorts saved 117 men from the four torpedoed ships. Only eleven lives were lost.

Following this latest attack, there was again some confusion in the ranks of SC 94. The Commodore ordered an emergency turn to port, but on the signal to turn, for some unknown reason, the ships in columns seven, eight and nine sheered off to starboard, and for the second time during the passage the convoy was split in two. At the same time, *Broke* and *Orillia* both obtained asdic contacts and went racing off in different directions. A full hour passed before order was restored to SC 94.

Later that morning the convoy came under almost continuous air escort by RAF Liberators from Aldergrove and US Navy Catalinas from Iceland. At 1017 Catalina K-73 sighted a surfaced U-boat five miles south of the convoy and swept in to attack, dropping five depth charges. The U-boat's stern was still visible when the charges exploded all around her, and five minutes later oil was seen bubbling to the surface. Two more U-boats were spotted by aircraft during the day, but both dived before an attack could be launched. At 2008, with the last of the light fading, Liberator F-120 sighted a conning tower 20 miles on the port quarter of the convoy and attacked at once, dropping six depth charges set to 25ft only four seconds after the U-boat had disappeared in a swirl of foam. After 40 seconds an underwater eruption was seen, believed by the Liberator's crew to be the result of the U-boat blowing main ballast tanks. An hour or so later Catalina G-73 sighted another U-boat ten miles astern of SC 94, steering north. A depth-charge attack was carried out, but no results were observed.

The intense activity of the patrolling aircraft kept the wolves of *Steinbrink* at bay until destroyers of Western Approaches Command arrived in force early on the 12th. It was then too dangerous for the U-boats to ply their deadly trade, and Dönitz called them home.

Considering the inexperience of most of the U-boat commanders, the *Steinbrink* operation, with eleven Allied merchant ships of 53,241 tons and some 70,000 tons of vital cargo destroyed, can be judged a success. On the other hand, the cost to *Steinbrink* was high; three U-boats (including *U335*, sunk off Norway) lost and four damaged. As to C1, its defence of SC 94 had been vigorous and, under the circumstances, effective. However, it was of some concern to the Admiralty that two ships, *Assiniboine* and *Dianthus*, had, in their enthusiasm to destroy U-boats by ramming, put themselves out of action as effectively as if they had been torpedoed.

# 8

# The Threat from the Air

August 1942 ended with the U-boats still in the ascendancy, having sunk over half a million tons of Allied shipping in the Atlantic during the month. However, the cost of maintaining this level of sinking was rising at a frightening rate, ten U-boats a month failing to return to base. Although these losses were more than compensated for by the increased output of the German shipyards, it was the constant drain on his pool of trained men that worried Admiral Dönitz. It was an inescapable fact that when a U-boat went down for the last time, all too often it took all its crew with it. Those few who did survive invariably ended up in Allied prisoner-of-war camps. No matter how hard Dönitz's training schools worked to intensify and shorten their courses (and there was a limit beyond which they could not safely go), they were finding it increasingly difficult to turn out enough replacement crews to meet the growing demand.

The pattern of U-boat losses was also changing, around 50 per cent now being the result of growing Allied air activity over the convoys. Very-long-range (VLR) Liberators of 120 Squadron, now based in Iceland, were able to stay aloft for up to eighteen hours, and so had reduced the air gap south of Greenland to about 600 miles; some three days' steaming for the average convoy. Rapidly advancing technology would further increase the range of these aircraft, and meanwhile they had new ways of searching out their prey. Submarine spotting had once been largely a matter of keeping a sharp lookout with noses glued to the perspex, but the fitting of air-to-surface vessel (ASV) radar and the Leigh Light brought about a dramatic change.

The Leigh Light, a high-power searchlight fitted to the underside of an aircraft and used in conjunction with ASV, enabled the aircraft to come in low over the water at night and bomb with considerable accuracy. A surfaced U-boat suddenly caught in the beam of a Leigh Light was like a frightened rabbit trapped by the headlights of an oncoming car. Often, before the decision could be made whether to dive or fight it out on the surface, the depth bombs were whistling down. To the U-boat men the Leigh light, or *das verdammte Licht*, as they called it, was one of the most demoralising weapons they had ever had to face. And unless they were in the Greenland gap, its threat was with them all the time. Even the passage across the Bay of Biscay, once made quickly and safely on the surface, had turned into a dangerous ordeal. The coming of

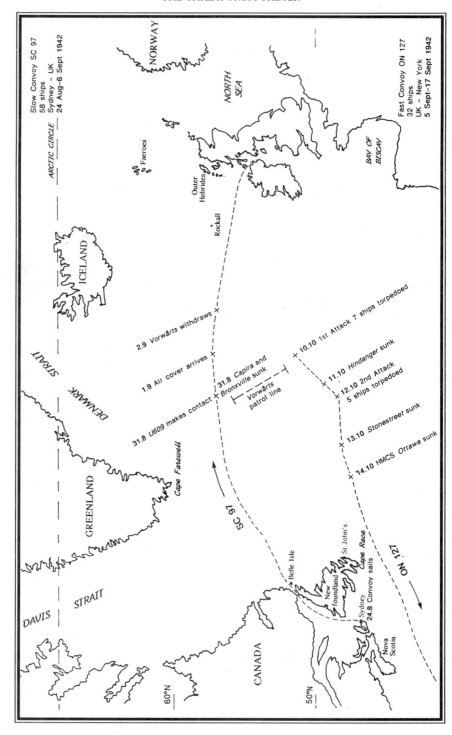

Slow Convoy SC 97
58 ships
Sydney – UK
24 Aug–6 Sept 1942

Fast Convoy ON 127
32 ships
UK – New York
5 Sept–17 Sept 1942

NORWAY

NORTH SEA

ARCTIC CIRCLE

BAY OF BISCAY

Faeroes

Outer Hebrides

Rockall

ICELAND

DENMARK STRAIT

2.9 Vorwärts withdraws

1.9 Air cover arrives

31.8 U609 makes contact

31.8 Capira and Bronxville sunk

Vorwärts patrol line

10.10 1st Attack 7 ships torpedoed

11.10 Hindanger sunk

12.10 2nd Attack 5 ships torpedoed

13.10 Stonestreet sunk

14.10 HMCS Ottawa sunk

Cape Farewell

GREENLAND

SC 97

Belle Isle

St. John's

New Foundland

Cape Race

Sydney

24.8 Convoy sails

ON 127

DAVIS STRAIT

CANADA

Nova Scotia

60°N

50°N

the Leigh Light forced them to travel submerged day and night, with all the extra time and discomfort that entailed.

The abortive attack on Convoy SC 97 at the end of August 1942 was ample proof of the growing ascendancy of Allied aircraft over the Atlantic. A convoy of 58 ships, SC 97 sailed from Sydney, Nova Scotia, on the morning of 24 August, escorted by Escort Group C2. This was a multinational force consisting of the British destroyers *Burnham* and *Broadway*, the US Coastguard cutters *Bibb* and *Ingham*, the Canadian corvettes *Drumheller*, *Brandon*, *Dauphin* and *Morden*, and the British corvette *Polyanthus*. Although such a mixed bag of warships brought inevitable problems in co-ordination, C2 was a force to be reckoned with, as the U-boats would discover.

At this time Dönitz had two packs operating simultaneously on the North Atlantic convoy routes. The *Lohs* group of nine boats was then 500 miles west of the Azores and refuelling from the U-tanker *U462*, while *Vorwärts*, with thirteen boats, was making a sweep to the south-west. It was *Vorwärts'* that finally located SC 97 but, unfortunately for the U-boats, they did not meet up with the convoy until it was 600 miles south-west of Iceland, within range of Allied land-based aircraft.

Soon after first light on the 31st, Klaus Rudloff in *U609*, stationed at the northern end of *Vorwärts* patrol line, made contact. The weather was perfect; calm, with a slight swell and maximum visibility. Rudloff came through the escort screen from ahead, and dived under the convoy to make a submerged attack from the port side. At 0705 he sank two ships with one salvo, the 5,625-ton Panamanian steamer *Capira* and the 4,663-ton Norwegian motor vessel *Bronxville*. Not surprisingly, this caused some confusion in the convoy, with merchant ships opening fire indiscriminately in all directions. On the other hand, SC 97's escort, led by Commander T. Taylor, RN, in HMS *Burnham*, reacted swiftly and vigorously, and *U609* only narrowly escaped destruction.

For the torpedoed seamen the calm weather was an unusual blessing, and the entire crew of the *Bronxville* was picked up. Those in the *Capira* were not so fortunate. The torpedo had struck in her empty forward hold, which immediately filled with water. The Panamanian went down bow-first in a few minutes, only sixteen of her crew of 54 surviving.

Other *Vorwärts* boats came racing in during the night, but pulled back when they were given an equally hot reception by Taylor's ships. On the following morning six U-boats were gathered around the convoy, but before they could mount an attack a US Navy Catalina arrived from Iceland and the opportunity was lost. From then on SC 97 had continuous air protection from the US Navy, and the *Vorwärts* boats were forced to remain submerged. Consequently the convoy left them behind. One boat, *U756* (Kapitänleutnant Klaus Harney), made the mistake of staying on the surface too long and was sunk by a Catalina, bringing her first and only war patrol to a sudden end.

The nights were moonless, and with SC 97 making large alterations of course under the cover of darkness, *Vorwärts* lost contact with the convoy. On the morning of 2 September the pack was called off. Dönitz commented:

> By systematically forcing the boats under water, [air cover] made them lose contact at evening twilight, thus spoiling the best prospects for attack of all boats in the first four moonless hours of the night . . . The convoy operation had to be broken off in the morning of 2.9 as it no longer seemed possible for boats to haul ahead in the face of the expected heavy enemy air activity . . . by increasing the range of their aircraft the English have succeeded in gaining air control over a great part of the North Atlantic with land based planes and narrowing the area in which U-boats can operate without threat from the air.

When *Vorwärts* next went into action it took care to attack in the Greenland Gap, where the skies were empty.

Convoy ON 127, westbound from the UK to New York, assembled at the entrance to the North Channel during the daylight hours of 5 September. Originating from the Clyde, Loch Ewe, Liverpool and the Bristol Channel, the convoy consisted of 32 ships, many of them oil tankers in ballast. The ocean escort, C4, which joined when the convoy was abreast of Lough Foyle, was largely Canadian, led by Lieutenant-Commander A. H. Dobson, RCNR, in the destroyer HMCS *St Croix*. He had with him a second destroyer, HMCS *Ottawa*, the Canadian corvettes *Sherbrooke*, *Arvida* and *Amherst*, and the British corvette *Celandine*. *Ottawa*, an ex-Royal Navy destroyer armed with four 4.7in guns, was commanded by Lieutenant-Commander C. A. Rutherford, RCN.

Soon after sunset that day, ON 127, steaming in eight columns of four, set course to the westward. In the ranks, and returning to sea again only three weeks after her harrowing crossing with SC 94, was the Honduras-registered steamer *Empire Moonbeam*. Keeping company close by was the 8,029-ton British tanker *Empire Oil*.

As ON 127 put the Irish coast astern, 600 miles out in the Atlantic the *Vorwärts* boats, alerted by *B-Dienst*, were setting up the usual ambush in the path of the convoy. There were thirteen boats in the pack, but apart from Korvettenkapitän Otto von Bülow, in *U404*, few of the commanders could lay claim to be well experienced in submarine warfare. Rudloff in *U609* had opened his score with SC 97, Horst Höltring in *U604* had sunk a Soviet submarine in the Baltic in June 1941, and on 25 August, while on his way to join *Vorwärts*, met and sank the Dutch ship *Abbekerk*. Hans-Jürgen Hellriegel in *U96* and Joachim Deecke in *U584* each also had a Soviet submarine to their credit, but had claimed no further victims. The others, Klaus Harney in *U756*, Hans Stock in *U659*, Struckmeier in *U608*, Richard Becker in *U218*, Joseph Röther in *U380*, Karl Hause in *U211*, Adolf Oelrich in *U92*, Friedrich Mumm in *U594* and Heinz Walkerling in *U91*, were all complete novices. *Vorwärts* was strong in numbers but short on experience.

Convoy ON 127 was four days out from the North Channel when, on the evening of 9 September, it was sighted by the southernmost U-boat in the *Vorwärts* line, which had by then been reinforced by boats from the *Stier* group. The weather was fine, with a light south-south-westerly wind, slight sea and good visibility, but the U-boats lost contact with the convoy after dark and did not find it again until daylight on the 10th. By this time the Admiralty had detected the presence of the U-boat packs, and a stream of urgent signals warned ON 127 of the imminent danger.

The morning passed without incident, noon sights putting the convoy 750 miles south-west of Cape Farewell, beyond the reach of Allied aircraft from either side of the Atlantic. The ships were steering a course of 260° at a speed of $7^3/4$ knots. The destroyers *St Croix* and *Ottawa* zig-zagged ahead and the corvette *Sherbrooke* was astern, while *Arvida*, *Amherst* and *Celandine* covered the flanks.

On board the *Empire Oil*, the third ship of column four, there was an air of subdued expectancy. The 8,029-ton British tanker was in ballast and gas-free, and therefore no more vulnerable than any other ship of the convoy, but Captain Marshall was too experienced to drop his guard. As far as possible, normal sea-going routine was kept, but the tanker's gun crews were stood-to at their guns, and on the bridge, and at various other vantage points, seven lookouts kept watch for the enemy.

At 1220 Hans-Jürgen Hellriegel in *U96* had succeeded in penetrating the escort screen and was at periscope depth between columns one and two of the convoy. He turned first to port and fired a single torpedo, which hit the 4,241-ton Belgian steamer *Elisabeth van Belgie*, the second ship in column one. Swinging round to starboard, Hellriegel then fired a spread of three, two of which found targets in the 12,190-ton British tanker *F. J. Wolfe*, the second ship in column two, and the 6,313-ton Norwegian tanker *Sveve*, occupying a similar position in column three.

This not unexpected but nonetheless devastating interruption of a tranquil late summer afternoon brought about an immediate reaction in the convoy. The Commodore ordered an emergency turn to starboard, and the ranks of merchantmen swung sharply with a commendable precision prompted by the urgency of the situation. The corvette *Sherbrooke* dropped back to stand by the torpedoed ships, while the other escorts closed in around the convoy, their asdics probing for the enemy. Hellriegel was long gone, and they swept in vain. At 1325 *St Croix* obtained what was thought to be a firm contact, and dropped a pattern of depth charges, but with negative results.

Of the torpedoed ships, the *F. J. Woolfe*, as might be expected of a large tanker in ballast, remained afloat and held her position in the convoy; the *Elisabeth van Belgie* and the *Sveve* were clearly beyond help. Lieutenant-Commander Dobson ordered *Sherbrooke* to sink these ships by gunfire when she had picked up survivors. Meanwhile, ON 127 closed ranks and steamed on.

The remaining hours of the afternoon passed with agonising slowness, for now that the wolves were running there was no relaxing. Asdics pinged monotonously, nervous gun barrels covered every wavelet and scores of glinting binoculars quartered the horizon with ceaseless vigilance. The *Empire Oil*, like all the other ships, was closed up to action stations with every eye straining, but no one saw the periscope break the surface between columns four and five. *U659* had slipped through the escort screen and was deep in the heart of the convoy. Hans Stock was about to fire his first shot in anger, and the *Empire Oil* was in his sights. Captain Marshall's report describes what happened next:

We were struck by a torpedo aft on the starboard side in the engine room . . . There was a dull thud, debris, smoke and steam rose high into the air, but there was no flash and no water was thrown up. The vessel immediately stopped and settled by the stern, falling away 2 points to starboard. As Gunlayer Jones was badly injured by the explosion, we carried him along to one of the boats, all of which were ready swung out, and I gave orders for them to be prepared for lowering. I then went aft to ascertain the extent of the damage and it appeared that the bunker bulkhead and stokehold bulkhead were both holding.

A minute or two later the track of a torpedo was seen to pass across our bows about 150ft ahead, the small feather of water was plainly visible travelling through the water, but it passed us harmlessly without exploding. Four minutes after the first explosion we were struck by a second torpedo, this time well forward on the port side in way of Nos. 7, 8 and 9 wing tanks. No one on board saw the track of this torpedo but it was seen from two other ships. Apparently the track was seen to cross our stern, travelling from port to starboard, along our starboard side, across our bows, then it described a circle between the two columns of ships (then five cables apart) and struck the ship as stated. Both the Captain and the AA Lieutenant on board the *Empire Moonbeam* saw this, and the Lieutenant fired at it with a machine-gun. There was no flash with this explosion and no water was thrown up. The deck in the way of No. 8 tank was torn a little, one of the midships tanks was damaged, as well as the three wing tanks, and No. 3 lifeboat, the motor boat, was badly damaged. Fuel oil from the fore-deep bunker was pouring out, the main pipeline was smashed, water was leaking through the valves, and there was a huge hole in the port side of the ship extending from deck level to well below the waterline and 25ft in length. The plastic protection around the bridge was undamaged.

The *Empire Oil* was listing heavily to starboard, her engine room, rapidly filling with water, was a shambles of broken machinery, and the damage to her hull was extensive. Clearly she was beyond saving, and Marshall now gave the order to abandon ship. This was done in good order, 51 men getting away in two boats; the two men on watch in the engine room when the first torpedo struck were missing, believed killed by the explosion.

When Marshall's ship was torpedoed, HMCS *St Croix* was astern of the convoy investigating an asdic contact. Dobson immediately reversed course and raced back up between columns four and five, obtaining an echo at 800 yards ahead. This was *U659* making good her escape, and for a while it seemed that Hans Stock had lingered too long after claiming his first victim. *St Croix* was joined first by the corvette *Celandine* and then by *Ottawa*, the three ships saturating the area with depth charges. Stock was forced to go deep, and darkness had fallen before he deemed it safe to creep away.

Having given up the search for the enemy, *St Croix* and *Ottawa* screened each other while they picked up survivors from the torpedoed *Empire Oil*, *St Croix* taking on board Captain Marshall and 26 of his crew, and *Ottawa* taking the remaining 24. The tanker was then still afloat, and it was hoped she could be taken in tow, but that night she provided a first target for Joachim Deecke in *U584*, who delivered the *coup de grâce* with two torpedoes.

By the time they had snatched the last exhausted survivor from the water, *St Croix* and *Ottawa* were 30 miles astern of ON 127, and with the light now fading they hastened to rejoin the convoy. They were ten miles from the rear ships when the wolves of *Vorwärts* struck again. Taking advantage of the darkness and the absence of the front row of ON 127's escort, Otto von Bülow in *U404*, Struckmeier in *U608* and Richard Becker in *U218* made a concerted attack, *U404* and *U608* coming in from the port side and *U218* from starboard. Struckmeier's torpedoes missed, but von Bülow hit the 7,417-ton Norwegian tanker *Marit II*, while Becker put one of the two torpedoes he fired into another Norwegian tanker, the 7,361-ton *Fjordaas*. Neither ship sank, and both would eventually reach port.

*St Croix* and *Ottawa* were alerted to the attack by starshell and snowflake rockets fired by the corvettes. They were too late to join in the counter-attack, but as they neared the convoy *St Croix*'s radar picked up a small echo passing to port at fourteen miles. Dobson hauled the destroyer round and raced in to cross the wake of a submarine which had just dived. A shallow pattern of depth charges was dropped, but no further contact was made.

With the two Canadian destroyers back on station, the U-boats found it difficult to close in on the convoy, even though all of the group's radar sets were now out of action. Just before midnight the corvette *Arvida* reported sighting a submarine on the surface at 1,000 yards, and attacked with a ten-charge pattern when the boat dived. At the same time *Amherst* also attacked a contact on the port bow of the convoy. Twenty minutes later, *Ottawa* flushed out another U-boat on the port quarter and attacked, but with no visible result. At 0121 *Celandine* sighted and attacked a U-boat on the surface with what were reported as 'very promising results'. In the face of such vigilance, the U-boats then retired to a safe distance for the rest of the night, during which *U96* came across and sank the 415-ton Portuguese trawler *Belaes*, which had inadvertently strayed into the battle zone.

Next afternoon the *Vorwärts* boats again began to probe the defences of ON 127. *St Croix*, scouting some 15 miles ahead of the convoy, chased a surfaced U-boat, while *Ottawa* depth-charged a contact close ahead of columns three and four. It was not until a little before 1600 that *U584* broke through the screen and torpedoed the leading ship of the port column, the 4,884-ton Norwegian motor vessel *Hindanger*. She remained afloat, and was sunk before dark by the guns of the corvette *Amherst*. As she disappeared beneath the waves, a lone Liberator of 120 Squadron from Iceland flew overhead. The aircraft was operating at the extreme range of its endurance, and its presence in the vicinity of the convoy, however comforting, was brief.

*St Croix*, *Amherst* and *Sherbrooke* were all away from the convoy on various missions when, at 2121, Joseph Röther in *U380* succeeded for the first time in approaching close enough to use his torpedoes to good effect. He fired a spread of four and, after hearing three detonations after four minutes and 40 seconds, claimed three hits, but his torpedoes all went wide. *U211* was hard on the heels of *U380*, and Karl Hause had more luck than Röther. His three torpedoes were well aimed, two of them slamming into the biggest ship of ON 127, the 13,797-ton whale factory ship *Hektoria*, and the other finding the *Empire Moonbeam*. The *Hektoria* took on a very heavy list and the *Empire Moonbeam*'s engine room was flooded, but again, both ships being without cargo, they did not sink at once. *Arvida* took off their crews and then stood by to see if there was a possibility of saving one or the other, or even both. It was a forlorn hope, and the corvette abandoned her vigil after two hours. No sooner had she gone to rejoin the convoy than *U608* moved in to finish the job begun by *U211*. The *Hektoria* was reported as sinking at 0051, and the *Empire Moonbeam* just over an hour later, at 0159 on the 12th.

With yet another of ON 127's escorts away, Adolf Oelrich in *U92* entered the fray, firing a four-torpedo spread aimed at HMCS *Ottawa*. Oelrich claimed a hit, but the destroyer was unscathed. In the midst of the confusion caused by this attack, the British steamer *Emperor Thackeray* hit a submerged object, which may well have been a U-boat, but was more likely a torpedoed hulk floating just below the surface. The *Empire Thackeray* suffered no apparent damage to her hull.

*St Croix, Amherst* and *Sherbrooke* rejoined the convoy, but the attacks continued throughout the night, all escorts being heavily engaged in beating off marauding U-boats. There was a period of quiet before dawn, and it was assumed the enemy had withdrawn, then as the first grey light of the coming day appeared on the horizon astern, Otto von Bülow in *U404* crept up unseen on the starboard quarter and fired three single torpedoes. Two missed, but the third found a target in the rear ship of column six, the 9,272-ton Norwegian motor tanker *Daghild*. Von Bülow claimed he heard sinking noises, but the *Daghild* stayed afloat, once again demonstrating the extraordinary capacity of an unloaded tanker to absorb punishment.

When the distress rockets soared up from the torpedoed Norwegian, Dobson ordered his ships to carry out Operation *Raspberry*, which entailed all escorts turning outwards to illuminate their sectors with starshell. Nothing was seen of the enemy in the immediate vicinity of the convoy, but HMS *Celandine*, standing by torpedoed ships some miles astern, caught sight of the low silhouette of a U-boat in the light of the starshell. The U-boat, apparently unaware of the presence of the corvette, was 1,000 yards ahead of *Celandine* and evidently shadowing ON 127. *Celandine* gave chase at full speed, but when she was within 500 yards the U-boat crash-dived. The corvette ran on and dropped a shallow pattern of depth charges which appeared to blow the U-boat to the surface. The submarine soon dived again, and after a second depth-charge attack all contact was lost. Ten minutes later *Celandine* surprised another shadowing U-boat, which she also forced to dive, following up with a well-aimed depth-charge pattern. She was then ordered to rejoin the convoy.

At sunrise, Dobson, believing that all daylight attacks had come from ahead, disposed his force in the van of the convoy, with *St Croix* and *Ottawa* on the wings and *Amherst* and *Sherbrooke* in the centre. *Celandine* and *Arvida* were still astern. To some extent Dobson's tactics were vindicated, for during that day no fewer than three U-boats were sighted ahead of the convoy and attacked. On the other hand, sightings were also made astern and on each beam. The U-boats, although keeping their distance, still had a tight ring around ON 127. At 1649 an underwater attack was tried, with one boat dropping back into the convoy from ahead, but she was picked up by *St Croix*'s asdics. Dobson attacked with a pattern set to 50ft, and then turned under full helm to run down between columns five and six, following his prey. *Celandine*, stationed astern of column six, reported hydrophone effect, but neither ship made asdic contact. Once more the intruder had slipped away.

The night passed quietly, and on the morning of the 13th the first air cover arrived from Newfoundland and the shadowing U-boats kept a discreet distance from the convoy. Only one unfortunate straggler, the Panama-flagged, American-owned steamer *Stone Street*, limping along some miles astern with boiler trouble, fell to a torpedo from *U594* (Kapitänleutnant Friedrich Mumm). Thirteen of the *Stone Street*'s crew went down with her.

The unexpected sinking of the American ship cast a shadow over the convoy, and the remainder of the day passed with the ships in a state of alert. Then, just on dusk, the R/T burst into life with a brief message from HMS *Witch*, reporting that she and HMCS *Annapolis* were six miles ahead, coming from St John's with orders to join C4. Convoy ON 127 was now less than 400 miles east of Newfoundland, and with the prospect of the escort being reinforced by two more destroyers, albeit both of First World War vintage, it seemed possible that the long nightmare might be over at last. But it was not to be, for lurking somewhere between the approaching destroyers and the convoy was Heinz Walkerling in *U91*. The U-boat was a newcomer to the Battle of the Atlantic, but Walkerling, in the recommended manner, was attempting to drop back on ONS 127 to be in a position to attack after dark.

The convoy was now approaching the notorious Grand Banks of Newfoundland, and the damp smell of fog was in the air, prompting Lieutenant-Commander Dobson to order *Witch* and *Annapolis* to remain ahead until daylight. The first contact with the newcomers – or so it was thought at the time – was made by *Ottawa*, then on the port bow of the convoy. At 2152 the Canadian destroyer reported two unidentified radar echoes five miles ahead, which she was about to investigate. Dobson advised Rutherford that his radar contacts were probably *Witch* and *Annapolis*, and in doing so may have signed *Ottawa*'s death warrant, for it is possible that Rutherford went in with his guard down.

Thirteen minutes later the transient peace of the night was shattered when *Witch*'s R/T burst into life, reporting, 'Believe *Ottawa* torpedoed'. Shortly after this, two white rockets soared into the sky ahead, and Dobson hauled *St Croix* over and increased speed. In less than five minutes *Ottawa* was sighted on *St Croix*'s port bow, apparently stopped but on an even keel. She had been hit by a torpedo fired by *U91* and, although badly damaged, was at that moment in no danger of sinking. But as *St Croix* swept up on *Ottawa*'s starboard side, Walkerling turned his sights on her and fired again.

The torpedo missed Dobson's ship and crashed into the already crippled *Ottawa*. The second explosion broke the destroyer's back and she sank immediately. Increasing to full speed, Dobson pulled clear of the sinking ship, ordering the corvette *Celandine* to close in to pick up survivors while *St Croix* went after the U-boat.

Almost at once *St Croix's* asdics picked up an echo on the port bow, which she proceeded to follow, Dobson having first warned ON 127's Commodore to make an emergency turn. The underwater bearing moved to port, then to starboard, as Walkerling twisted and turned to shake off the probing beam of *St Croix's* asdic, but in vain. At 2255 the destroyer was running over the U-boat and Dobson, reducing to 10 knots, fired a medium pattern of depth charges.

At 2305 the corvette *Arvida*, which Dobson had ordered to screen *Celandine* while she picked up survivors from *Ottawa*, reported 'Tanker torpedoed on starboard side, survivors in water and in boats, proceeding to *Ottawa*'. It is not known what prompted this signal, for no other ship was torpedoed, although Adolf Oelrich in *U92* had fired a spread of three torpedoes and claimed three hits at about that time. The consternation caused in the convoy, which was then in the process of making an emergency turn, was alone worth the expenditure of three torpedoes.

Meanwhile, *St Croix* continued to pursue *U91*, and at 2310, hearing fast hydrophone effect, increased to full speed. Within five minutes the wake and conning tower of a submarine was sighted close under the port bow. Starshell was fired, then Dobson opened up with his 3in gun, but the gun's crew were unable to see the target and their fire was ineffective. *U91* crash-dived when the bows of the destroyer were within 20 yards of her. Dobson dropped a pattern of charges set to 100ft, following which there was no further contact. Walkerling had escaped.

Returning to the convoy, Dobson stopped engines when he observed flares on the water, which he presumed were being burned by survivors of the torpedoed tanker, and ordered *Arvida* to screen *St Croix* while she picked up the men. A few minutes later the SOE had second thoughts, deciding it was too dangerous for the destroyer to remain stopped with U-boats in the vicinity. The grisly task of pulling out the survivors, who turned out to be from *Ottawa*, was left to *Arvida* and *Celandine*. Of the destroyer's complement of 188 only 76 men survived, many of whom were badly injured. Lieutenant-Commander Rutherford, who had been seen to pass his lifejacket to a rating unable to swim, was not among the survivors.

The U-boats made one more effort to smash their way through the defences of ON 127 that night, but they were beaten back by the escorts, some of whom were now running short of fuel and depth charges. Next day continuous air cover was provided from Newfoundland and the opportunity for further attacks was past. The convoy reached New York on 17 September without further loss.

Without doubt, the battle honours for ON 127 went to the boats of the *Vorwärts* pack, and the convoy gained the distinction of being the only one during 1942–43 at which all of the U-boats sent against it fired their torpedoes. The final reckoning was six merchantmen of 44,113 tons sunk, four others damaged, and Canada's finest destroyer, HMCS *Ottawa*, lost. Only one U-boat was damaged in the action. Later, when all the relevant inquiries had been made, Lieutenant-Commander Dobson was criticised for his conduct of the defence of the convoy. In particular, his use of escorts to sink damaged merchantmen was questioned. An internal minute drawn up by the Admiralty in Liverpool commented:

> There is an unnecessary waste of escorts' efforts to sink damaged freighters. At 0200Z *Sherbrooke* has managed to get 25 miles astern of the convoy in order to sink torpedoed ships. At 1928 on the same day *Amherst* is detached to sink torpedoed ships. What is *St Croix's* idea, what is his meaning? He is helping to reduce our tonnage by weakening the escort and completing the enemy's work.

It does seem in retrospect that the defence of ON 127 by C4 was at times noticeably unco-ordinated, with escorts acting independently when they should have been working as a tight-knit team. At one time, it was said, the reaction to a U-boat attack was so confused that two of the corvettes opened fire on each other.

While the *Vorwärts* pack was occupied with ON 127, other packs in the North Atlantic were not enjoying a similar success. On her way to join the *Lohs* pack east of Newfoundland, *U216* sighted the slow eastbound convoy SC 99, but lost contact when pounced upon by the escorts. Next day, *U440* came up with the same convoy, but was again chased off, and was so damaged by depth charges that she had difficulty in submerging. The planned attack on SC 99 was called off on the 14th, but on the following day fresh boats arriving were formed into a new pack, *Pfeil*, and sent against the westbound ON 129. Contact was made, but fog and bold action by the escort screen thwarted any attack. Next day, in improving visibility, two boats sighted the escort screen, but were lured away while the convoy took bold avoiding action. All contact was lost, and on the 18 September Dönitz called off the action.

By the end of September very-long-range Liberators of 120 Squadron, RAF, were reaching out 800 miles into the Atlantic from Iceland, but this was still not enough to bridge the Greenland air gap completely. The Admiralty now proposed to do this by converting merchant ships to carry aircraft. Six bulk grain carriers and six oil tankers were being fitted out as Merchant Aircraft Carriers (MAC), with offset bridges, 400ft-long flight decks, arrester wires, crash barriers and all the usual equipment of an escort carrier. Only older-type Fairey Swordfish single-engined biplanes were suitable to operate from such a short flight deck, and it was proposed that the MAC ships would carry four of these, flown and maintained by the Fleet Air Arm (FAA). The ships would sail under the Red Ensign, carry up to 80 per cent of their usual cargo, and be manned by merchant seamen. It was a bold concept, a typical British compromise, and, as time would tell, it worked.

Also in September 1942 the first 'Support Group' was formed for the North Atlantic. This consisted of four destroyers, four frigates and two sloops. The destroyers were ageing, but with highly-trained crews, modern radars and new weapons the support group was a formidable force, designed to operate independently of the convoys, hunting the U-boat wolf packs with the aid of aircraft. It was most unfortunate that the first group met with very severe weather on its first operational cruise and recorded no successes. Soon afterwards, with every possible escort ship required for the Allied landings in North Africa, the support group idea was dropped, but it would prove its worth later in the war.

# 9

# The Decoy

In the autumn of 1942, faced by insistent and often hysterical demands from Soviet Russia for the opening of a Second Front, Britain and America at last agreed to attempt a landing on German-held territory. The disastrous raid on Dieppe in August, which had cost the British and Canadian force 3,000 casualties and all of its equipment, ruled out another Channel crossing, but there remained North Africa, a goal long discussed by Churchill and Roosevelt.

In the Western Desert, Rommel's Afrika Korps was encamped within 100 miles of Alexandria with its supply lines stretched to far beyond the limits of prudence. To the west, Morocco and Algeria lay exposed, guarded only by French troops of suspect allegiance, and whose defences were known to be somewhat antiquated. The plan drawn up was for the British Eighth Army to begin a rolling advance westwards from El Alamein, while Anglo-American forces landed simultaneously at Casablanca, Oran and Algiers. Caught in the middle, Rommel would be forced to fight his final African battle on two fronts.

Operation *Torch*, as the North African seaborne landings were codenamed, was to involve 350 troop transports escorted by 500 warships, sailing in seven convoys from American and British ports. This led to a huge increase in shipping activity and concentrations of men and supplies in ports on both sides of the Atlantic. Inevitably, the German High Command soon became aware that a large-scale invasion was imminent. Numerous reports from agents pointed to North Africa, but it was well known that the Allies were masters of the art of rumour spreading, and this location was treated with the utmost suspicion. German intelligence favoured Dakar, and their preference was accepted, although what possible reason the Allies could have for invading Vichy French-held territory 1,500 miles south of Gibraltar does not seem to have been seriously considered. In the Atlantic Dönitz mustered his U-boats, and by the end of October 40 German and Italian submarines were stationed in a long line stretching south-eastwards from the Azores, lying in wait for the Dakar-bound Allied invasion force.

The landings at Casablanca, Oran and Algiers were set for dawn on 8 November, the first troop convoy sailing from a US port on 19 October and the second from the Clyde on the 22nd of that month. Within a few days the whole 800-strong armada was on the high seas. The defence of such a huge force, spread over several million square miles of ocean, was a major operation involving all available Allied warships and aircraft. Heavy surface ships patrolled the Denmark Strait and the Faroes Gap to meet any threat from German capital ships lying in Norwegian ports, fast anti-submarine attack groups swept the Bay of Biscay, and long-range aircraft covered every accessible part of the North Atlantic. For good measure, bombers of the US 8th Air Force attacked Brest and other U-boat bases. Yet all this would have come to naught if the U-boats then at sea had been alerted. Dönitz's wolves, concentrated 40-strong off the Azores, had the capability of creating such havoc among the packed troopships that the whole enterprise might have foundered in mid-ocean.

The skies were kept clear of inquisitive Focke-Wulf Kondors by Allied air activity, but the one great stroke of good fortune to attend Operation *Torch* was the coincidence that no U-boats were at the time en route to operational areas south of Gibraltar. Had only one such boat sighted the smoke marking the passage of one of the convoys, the game would have been up. As it was, every convoy, every ship involved in the invasion, arrived off the beaches unharmed, largely due, some would say, to a deliberate sacrifice offered up for the safe conduct of Operation *Torch*.

The West African state of Sierra Leone, founded in 1787 as a colony for freed slaves, is hot, humid, and home to most of the nastier diseases known to man. At the beginning of the 19th century the colony's only deep-water port, aptly named Freetown, played host to ships of the Royal Navy engaged in the suppression of the slave trade. In the inner harbour, watched over by the guns of Fort Thornton, captured slavers, sometimes a dozen at a time, lay at anchor, while boats loaded down with the poor wretches they had illegally shipped rowed for the shore and freedom. In 1942, after more than a century of leisurely commerce, Freetown's harbour once more bustled with activity. The port had become a major assembly point for convoys, a repair and refuelling point for the Royal Navy and a refuge for torpedoed ships. The boats still rowed ashore, but in place of freed slaves they carried the haggard survivors of ships lost in the surrounding shark-infested waters. The approaches to Freetown were a fertile hunting ground for the U-boats.

On the morning of 16 October 1942 the hot sun rose on a crowded harbour as the rain clouds of the night cleared away. From Cape Sierra Leone to King Tom Point, the 37 merchantmen that were to comprise Convoy SL 125 were anchored in close proximity to one another. All fully fuelled and watered, and with steam up, the ships were awaiting the order to weigh anchor and begin the long and hazardous passage north. Largely British, they had come from the far reaches of the Empire, carrying oil from the Persian

Gulf, sugar from Mauritius, tea and manganese ore from India, timber from the Gulf of Guinea and copra from the Far East. All but one were loaded to their gunwales. The exception, which stood out among this collection of cargo liners and long-haul tramps, was the 11,989-ton *Président Doumer*, an ex-French passenger liner managed by Bibby Line, with several hundred servicemen on board. Anchored nearby was British India's 5,283-ton *Nagpore*, a long way from her usual trading waters and carrying the convoy Commodore, Rear-Admiral C. N. Reyne.

At 1000, under a clear blue sky marred only by distant thunder clouds, the clank of windlasses echoed across the shimmering waters of the harbour as anchors were hove home. Half-an-hour later the *Nagpore*, her yardarms festooned with flags, led the way out of the harbour. The others followed in single file, Aldis lamps clattering as they passed name and destination to the signal station on Aberdeen Hill. Keeping close in to Cape Sierra Leone, one by one they altered to starboard and steamed out to sea, leaving Carpenter Rock with its skeletal remains of a wrecked Elder Dempster ship well to port. Outside, patrolling up and down and rolling uncomfortably in the long swell, were the ships of SL 125's escort, comprising a sloop, four Flower-class corvettes and an armed trawler. They were concerned to see the convoy under way and clear of the land, for there were times when it seemed that the U-boats prowling off Freetown outnumbered the great hammerhead sharks that frequented these waters. The SOE was not aware that, on Dönitz's orders, the U-boats had moved north some time ago.

The sun was at its zenith when the last ship cleared Carpenter Rock, and the next hour was passed in forming the convoy into nine columns abreast, a not inconsiderable feat for 37 heavily-laden, slow-manoeuvring merchantmen. But at long last it was done, and course was set to the north-west. The Admiralty track laid down for SL 125 passed close to the Cape Verde Islands, well to seaward of the Canaries and then midway between Madeira and the Azores, before running due north to the approaches to the North Channel. It was a wide diversion, likely to prolong the passage by more than a day, but was considered necessary to avoid waters closer to the African mainland, where U-boats were known to patrol regularly – or so it was said.

Twenty-four hours out of Freetown, with the convoy well clear of the coast, the escorting sloop and armed trawler turned back, leaving the delicately named corvettes *Cowslip*, *Crocus*, *Petunia* and *Woodruff* to stand guard over SL 125 until the Western Approaches. The task facing these four rust-stained little ships, each armed with only a single 4in gun and a few racks of depth charges, was daunting indeed.

The total inadequacy of SL 125's escort was clear to Captain W. B. Blair, Staff Captain of the 6,148-ton cargo liner *Stentor*, as he made his rounds on deck and watched the four corvettes position themselves to best advantage around the convoy. In the event of a concerted attack by a pack of U-boats they would be, at best, like yapping terriers defending a flock of sheep. Steaming in the lead of column nine, the *Stentor* was particularly exposed. Homeward bound from the Far East, she was loaded with 6,000 tons of general cargo and carried the convoy's Vice-Commodore, Captain R. H. Garstin, RNR, and his staff of six. She also had on board 125 passengers, mostly Army personnel, which with her crew of 114 gave her a total complement of 246. If the worst happened, her lifeboats would be grossly overloaded – assuming they all got away,

Similar thoughts passed through the mind of Captain G. L. Evans, who viewed the departure of the two escorts from the bridge of the *Pacific Star* with equal misgivings. His 7,951-ton twin-screw refrigerated ship, carrying 5,000 tons of meat from Argentina to Liverpool, was on the *Stentor*'s port beam, leading column eight. It occurred to Evans that it might have been much less dangerous to have made the long run home from the Plate unescorted at the *Pacific Star*'s full speed of 15 knots, rather than dawdle at 7 knots in this thinly defended convoy, but the Admiralty would have their way, and having steamed over 3,000 miles alone and unharmed, Evans had been ushered into Freetown and into the arms of SL 125. On sailing, his ship had been appointed DF Guard for the convoy, which involved his radio officers keeping constant watch on the U-boat frequencies. This meant that the *Pacific Star* would have the doubtful privilege of being one of the first to be warned of the approach of danger.

The progress of the convoy northwards was slow, for some in its ranks, hoary old tramps like the Swedish *San Francisco* and the Danish tanker *Anglo Maersk*, were hard pressed to maintain even 7 knots. So at times SL 125 proceeded at the rate of its slowest member, which was a mere snail's pace. However, the weather was fine and warm and the enemy conspicuous by his absence, so the passage of time was pleasant enough. Ships took advantage of the time and weather to catch up on neglected maintenance. Dakar was passed without incident on the 21st, and by the morning of the 23rd Cape Blanco was abeam 320 miles over the horizon to starboard. Course was altered to due north, to pass midway between Madeira and the Azores.

It so happened that, on this day, Admiral Dönitz, unhappy that so many of his operational U-boats were idling off the Azores with no sign of the long-awaited Allied invasion convoys, decided to send some of them south to the Freetown area. He formed the *Streitaxt* pack comprising eight boats; *U509* (Kapitänleutnant Werner Witte), *U604* (Kapitänleutnant Horst Höltring), *U203* (Kapitänleutnant Hermann Kottmann), *U409* (Kapitänleutnant Hanns-Ferdinand Massmann), *U659* (Kapitänleutnant Hans Stock), *U510*

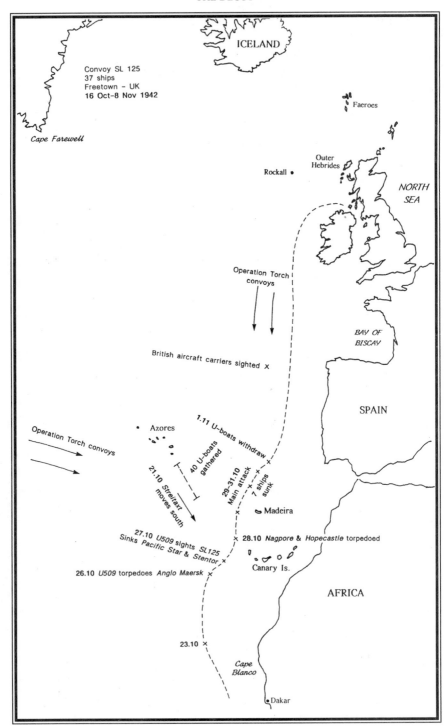

Convoy SL 125
37 ships
Freetown – UK
**16 Oct–8 Nov 1942**

ICELAND

Faeroes

Cape Farewell

Outer
Hebrides

Rockall •

NORTH
SEA

Operation Torch
convoys

BAY OF
BISCAY

British aircraft carriers sighted ✕

SPAIN

Azores

*1.11 U-boats withdraw*

Operation Torch convoys

*40 U-boats gathered*

*21.10 Streitaxt moves south*

*29–31.10 Main attack*

*7 ships sunk*

✕ Madeira

**28.10** *Nagpore & Hopecastle* torpedoed

**27.10** *U509 sights SL125
Sinks Pacific Star & Stentor*

Canary Is.

**26.10** *U509 torpedoes Anglo Maersk* ✕

AFRICA

23.10 ✕

Cape
Blanco

• Dakar

(Fregattenkapitän Karl Neitzel), *U103* (Kapitänleutnant Gustav-Adolf Janssen) and *U440* (Kapitänleutnant Hans-Heinrich Geissler). Karl Neitzel had sunk three ships off the West Indies in the 'happy days' of August 1942, Horst Höltring was briefly, but unsuccessfully, engaged in the attack Convoy SC 97 later that month, and Hans Stock had torpedoed and damaged the tanker *Empire Oil* in ON 127 in September. The other boats and their commanders were without combat experience, all being on their first war patrol.

Two days after setting off on their run south from the Azores, the *Streitaxt* boats were to the west of the Canary Islands when they sighted a deep-laden tanker escorted by two destroyers, heading in for the African coast. The U-boats gave chase, but the destroyers were vigilant and no boat was able to get close enough to torpedo either the tanker or her escort. The chase did, however, generate a great deal of radio activity between the U-boats, all of which was duly listened-in to by Allied ears. At that time SL 125 was some 240 miles south-west of the Canaries, but although it must now have been apparent that the convoy was steering into the midst of a U-boat pack, no warning was issued by the Admiralty.

The Atlantic Ocean is wide, and SL 125 might still have slipped unseen past the *Streitaxt* boats had it not been for an unfortunate turn of the cards. For some time the Danish tanker *Anglo Maersk*, commanded by Captain Valsberg and managed for the Ministry of War Transport by Houlder Brothers of London, had been experiencing engine problems, much to the chagrin of Rear-Admiral Reyne and the escorts. At noon on the 25th the *Anglo Maersk*'s engines failed completely and she dropped out of the convoy to lie stopped for 27 hours while her engineers worked frantically to rectify the fault. She was under way again on the afternoon of the 26th, and making full speed to rejoin the convoy, when she had the great misfortune to cross paths with *U509*. Werner Witte, who had become separated from the other *Streitaxt* boats, put a torpedo into the tanker, but although it was damaged the *Anglo Maersk* did not catch fire. Captain Valsberg and his crew stayed with her, and she limped along at 7 knots, only to be torpedoed again by *U604* on the evening of the 27th. This time the tanker went down, but her crew of 37 abandoned in good order and eventually reached the Canaries.

Witte needed no crystal ball to tell him that the *Anglo Maersk* was a straggler from a convoy likely to be nearby and, having left her lying crippled, he pressed on, using the Danish tanker's initial heading as a pointer to greater things. Four hours later *U509* was in sight of the rear ships of SL 125. Witte called in the other boats.

In the late afternoon of 27 October, when *U509* began shadowing SL 125, the convoy was 170 miles west of the island of Palma and steaming on a northerly course at 7 knots. The last of the North-East Trades were blowing;

warm, gentle winds. The sea was quiet, and the sky azure blue and dotted with clumps of fine-weather cumulus. It was a day that, in times past, would have warranted steamer chairs and gin and tonics on deck to watch the sun go down. Now, with the horrors of war never far removed, the atmosphere in the ships was relaxed but cautious.

The very brief transmission by *U509* was missed by the radio officer on DF guard in the *Pacific Star*. The first that Captain Evans, or anyone else in the convoy, knew about the impending danger was at 1750, when the *Nagpore* hoisted the two-flag signal 'WF', meaning 'enemy submarine in the vicinity'. An emergency turn signal followed soon afterwards, and the convoy wheeled away from the danger, its four-corvette escort hovering nervously around the perimeter. A tense hour passed, during which the sun went down and darkness drew a protective cloak around SL 125. At 1930 Rear-Admiral Reyne deemed that the shadowing U-boat reported to him by the Admiralty had been shaken off, and course was resumed to the north. In fact, *U509* had by then found her way through the thin escort screen under the cover of darkness, and was to starboard and ahead of the convoy. Witte waited for the leading ships to enter his sights, then fired two torpedoes.

Captain Evans had seen the *Pacific Star* settled down on to her course and was about to leave the bridge when the first of Witte's torpedoes slammed into the starboard side of the Blue Star ship, exploding in her No. 1 hold. Evans saw a bright yellow flash from forward, followed by a muffled explosion. A column of water, carrying splintered hatchboards and carcasses of frozen meat, was thrown high in the air, some of the debris raining down on the bridge. There was a stink of burnt cordite. The escorting ships were momentarily stunned by the sudden attack, then HMS *Woodruff*, stationed on the starboard beam of the convoy, recovered and lunged forward, dropping a single depth charge. The corvette's asdic had not yet picked up an echo, and her action was purely reflex; more a gesture of aggression than anything else.

Aboard the *Stentor*, Staff Captain Blair was at dinner in the officers' saloon when the double explosion rattled the plates. Believing the explosions to be depth charges, Blair resisted the temptation to rush out of the saloon and, assuming an air of nonchalance to reassure the passengers, slowly made his way out on deck. Once out of sight he sprinted for the bridge. He was on his way up the ladder when the ship staggered under the force of the explosion below decks and leaned heavily to port. Witte's second torpedo had hit the *Stentor* just forward of the bridge, ripping open her deep tanks containing 250 tons of highly inflammable palm oil. When Blair reached the open deck the oil was ablaze and flames were leaping 200ft in the air, engulfing the fore part of the bridge. Burning oil, cascading back on to the deck, was flowing aft along the alleyways and into the passenger accommodation. The *Stentor* was rapidly becoming a funeral pyre for all on board.

Immediately following the torpedoing of the *Pacific Star*, *Cowslip*, *Crocus* and *Petunia* raced to the starboard side of the convoy to join *Woodruff*, and all four escorts fired starshell and dropped depth charges. They did not sight *U509*, but so aggressive was the response of the corvettes that Witte was forced to retire into the darkness at full speed before diving. Fortunately *U509* was then the only boat in contact; the others, hurrying in to answer Witte's signal, were still some hours away.

When the furore had died down, Captain Evans took the opportunity to assess the damage to the *Pacific Star*. Accompanied by his chief officer and carpenter he went forward, where he found No. 1 hold in a shambles. Closer examination showed that the torpedo had penetrated the starboard side on the waterline and, although the 45ft-wide hold was fully loaded with meat, had passed through the cargo and blown another hole in the port side. The *Pacific Star*'s hull was open to the sea on both sides. Evans later reported:

> I ordered the men to stand by the boats, and carried on. I increased speed as much as possible, but during the night we dropped astern of the convoy. Although the engines were doing revolutions for 10 knots, we could only make five. During the night the weather deteriorated, many of the torn plates on the starboard side being broken off by the seas. We carried on at the rear of No. 8 column until 0245 on the 28th, when the last ship of the convoy was no longer in sight, so rather than become a straggler I decided to fall out and endeavour to make Gibraltar. Weather continued to deteriorate, the wind reaching gale force with a high sea, so at 0330 I altered course for the Canaries which were only 350 miles away, Gibraltar being 900 miles.

The situation aboard the *Stentor* became hopeless within a few minutes of the torpedo striking, and the order was given to abandon ship. Staff Captain Blair reached the boat deck to find the evacuation already in progress:

> I saw Captain Williams by No. 3 boat whilst I was on my way to my own boat, which was No. 7. I also saw the Vice-Commodore being led along the deck by a Major Turner. As I passed the Vice-Commodore I heard him say "I am blind" and I also noticed that Major Turner had both his hands badly burned.
>
> I went to the boat deck and saw No. 5 and 7 boats safely away. I then turned round with the intention of going to the after well deck in order

to release the rafts, but before I had time to do so the ship sank bow first, and I found myself in the water. The ship sank in eight minutes at 1943.

Blair reached a raft and was later rescued by HMS *Woodruff*; others were not so fortunate. One of *Stentor's* eight lifeboats had been destroyed by the explosion, and another by the ensuing fire. Number 4 boat could not be reached because of the flames, and No. 3, Captain Williams' boat, capsized as the ship sank, throwing all its occupants into the sea. Only four boats got away safely, along with several rafts. In all, *Woodruff* picked up 202 survivors, ten of whom were injured. Captain Williams and twenty of his crew, the Vice-Commodore, Captain Garstin, and 23 passengers were unaccounted for and believed drowned.

Before dawn on the 28th, SL 125 had closed ranks and was proceeding on a course of 012° as fast as the slowest ship would allow, a laboured 6¹/₂ knots against a north-westerly gale-force wind and rough sea. There was no doubt in anyone's mind that the U-boats had not finished with them, and when the sun rose behind a heavy overcast many feared what this forbidding looking day might bring. Aboard the *Président Doumer*, riding high out of the water and rolling crazily, her passengers, wracked by the horrors of seasickness, were past caring about the future.

The *Pacific Star*, meanwhile, was running south-east before the gale for the Canaries. When, in mid-morning, the ship's motor launch was smashed by a following sea, Captain Evans began to fear for the safety of his men. He later wrote in his report:

All this time the vessel was slowly going down by the head, as No. 2 hold was flooding through the bulkhead and torn deck plating, until on soundings being taken we found No. 2 hold was completely full and No. 3 hold had 23ft of water in it. By the evening of the 28th the weather was becoming so bad that I considered it unwise to remain on board. We had five boats left. I ordered the three starboard boats away, as this was the lee side, then turned the ship to make a lee for the port boats. One port boat was launched without much trouble, but whilst we were waiting for the Chief and Second Engineers to come up from below the ship slewed round and by the time the last port boat was lowered it was on the weather side of the ship, which made it very difficult to get clear of the ship. We finally abandoned ship by 1800 on the 28th, having shut off the engines, but leaving the pumps going as the vessel was going down steadily by the head all the time. I did not attempt to abandon ship in a hurry as it was a very dark night, the weather was bad and I had 97 men to get safely away.

While Captain Evans was making his last preparations to leave his doomed ship, SL 125 was 120 miles west-south-west of Madeira and sailing into the gathering gloom in worsening weather. *U509* was still the lone shadower, and as soon as darkness fell Werner Witte moved up on the leading ships and fired a two-torpedo spread. The Commodore's ship, the 5,283-ton *Nagpore*, was the first victim. As she rolled heavily in the rising swell, a torpedo caught her amidships and she broke in two, sinking within ten minutes. Rear-Admiral Reyne and eighteen men escaped in one lifeboat, but the *Nagpore's* master, Captain Tomkin, and eighteen others perished.

Witte's second torpedo found its mark in the hull of the 5,178-ton British motor vessel *Hopecastle*, which, although severely damaged, did not sink. She dropped astern and was soon alone. In the early hours of the 29th she was found by *U203*, and Hermann Kottmann used his deck gun and a torpedo to finish the job begun by Witte.

Although SL 125's escort was weak, Witte was at a dangerous disadvantage in being the lone attacker, and he held off for the rest of the night and during daylight the next day. When he made another foray, after dark on the 29th, he was again unlucky. His torpedo hit the Donaldson Line's 7,131-ton *Corinaldo* squarely, but she also remained afloat. Her destruction was left to the other wolves now closing in, but she did not die easily, absorbing three more torpedoes from *U659* and *U203* before being sunk by gunfire from the latter.

Despite being sorely harassed by the corvettes, Witte continued to probe the defences of SL 125, and at 2015 broke through to put two torpedoes into the 4,772-ton motor vessel *Brittany*. The heavily-laden ship sank in a few minutes, taking with her 13 of her crew and one passenger. By this time Witte had at last been joined by other members of the *Streitaxt* pack, Hanns-Ferdinand Massmann in *U409* and Hans Stock in *U659*. Massmann, although a complete novice, soon opened his score with a well-aimed torpedo at the small British tanker *Bullmouth*, which stubbornly refused to sink. Another hour elapsed before Hans Stock manoeuvred into position to administer the *coup de grâce* with two more torpedoes. The *Bullmouth* erupted in a sheet of yellow flame; her master, Captain Brougham, and his crew of 47 perished as she went down.

When the flames of the burning tanker had been quenched by the sea, calm once again returned to SL 125, but over the horizon to the south-east another drama was being acted out. Having successfully evacuated all of his men from the crippled *Pacific Star*, Captain Evans had stayed close to the ship, hoping to reboard. His report states:

We lay to all night in the hope of reboarding in daylight, but by next morning, 29th, it was too rough to return, seas were breaking right over the ship forward and aft, and the fore deck was awash. We had sent out an SOS message before leaving, but nothing came along, so three of the boats set sail for the land, leaving two boats, in charge of the Second Officer and myself, to stand by. The two boats remained alongside all the 29th, in the hope of help arriving, as I intended to reboard if a ship came along to stand by us, but nothing came, the weather continued bad, and the men began to get a little restive. However, we stayed in the vicinity all that night until daylight on the 30th, by which time the ship was becoming waterlogged. The starboard propeller was completely out of the water, as she had now taken a list to port, and the ship was so low in the water that she was not drifting, whereas the boats were, so I decided to give up all hope of reboarding and set sail for the Canary Islands.

While Evans said his last farewell to his doomed ship, the *Streitaxt* boats were gathering around SL 125. Just before dusk that evening, Horst Höltring brought *U604* in at periscope depth and torpedoed the 11,998-ton troopship *Président Doumer*. The explosion ripped open the liner's thin plates in way of her engine room, the lights went out and she took a heavy list. Not unexpectedly, panic broke out among the troops on board, many of whom jumped overboard. Others mobbed the lifeboats, with the result that boats were upended in their davits and fell 50ft on to those struggling in the water below. A total of 260 men were lost, either in the water or with the ship went she went down.

It was now the turn of Hans Stock again, who brought *U659* in on the surface under cover of darkness to put two torpedoes into the 6,405-ton *Tasmania* on the other side of the convoy. Höltring in *U604* had also surfaced, and turned his sights on the 3,642-ton *Baron Vernon*. Two torpedoes streaked towards the elderly Scottish tramp and struck her amidships. One failed to explode on impact, but the other was sufficient to blast the bottom out of the ship.

There was then a pause, during which the four escorting corvettes, who had run their bearings hot chasing the shadowy U-boats, cleared their decks of empty shellcases and waited, wondering from which side the next attack would come. Their wait was not prolonged; *U409* slipped unseen into the ranks of nervous merchantmen and added the 6,373-ton *Silverwillow* to her score. The senior man of *Streitaxt* pack, Fregattenkapitän Karl Neitzel in *U510*, had now arrived on the scene, and he quickly found a target in the 5,681-ton Norwegian steamer *Alaska*, seriously damaging her. In just over two hours the convoy had been ripped apart, and five ships were sinking or crippled. Only one of these, the *Alaska*, would stay afloat.

In the midst of the mayhem, Captain Cameron, commanding the *Baron Elgin*, turned his ship about and began to pick up survivors, weaving his way carefully through the boats, rafts and men littering the sea astern of the convoy. As he was going about his errand of mercy, Cameron became aware that a surfaced U-boat was slowly circling his ship. Other men might have abandoned those in the water, but Cameron was made of sterner stuff. Ordering his gunners to hold their fire, he carried on with the rescue, keeping a wary eye on the U-boat and fearing the torpedo that might come at any minute. But the German submarine commander also had the quality of mercy, and after a while he withdrew silently into the night, leaving the *Baron Elgin* to carry on her work.

The last U-boat to be involved with SL 125 was *U103*, commanded by Gustav-Adolf Janssen. At some time before midnight on the 30th, Janssen found the abandoned *Tasmania* and sank her with two torpedoes. Soon after that, Admiral Dönitz ordered *Streitaxt* to break off from the convoy and go in pursuit of two British aircraft carriers reported 280 miles west of Cape Finisterre. This order was later rescinded, but by the time the U-boats relocated SL 125, aircraft and destroyers had come to its aid and a resumption of the attack was impossible.

The savaging of Convoy SL 125 by the *Streitaxt* boats was a major disaster, resulting in the loss of twelve ships of 80,000 tons and the lives of 426 men, to say nothing of the cargoes. However, the sacrifice of the Freetown–UK convoy – and there is to this day a strong suspicion that it was a deliberate sacrifice – kept the U-boats occupied while the huge Allied convoys for Operation *Torch* slipped by on their way to the North African beaches. When, on 8 November, Dönitz received news of the landings, he at once ordered all U-boats between Cape Verde and Gibraltar, and all those in the North Atlantic with sufficient fuel, to make for the beaches and there cause maximum disruption. They were too late, for when they arrived there was an impenetrable screen of Allied destroyers and aircraft around the landings.

On the afternoon of 31 October Captain G. L. Evans led the *Pacific Star's* lifeboats into Santa Cruz, Las Palmas. Despite the ordeal they had been through, not one man of the British ship's crew of 97 had been lost. Their reception in this supposedly neutral port was not as might be expected. Captain Evans reported:

> The Authorities were definitely not on our side, the majority of the officials, particularly the Military, are strongly Spanish in feeling, certainly not pro-British, whereas the ordinary man in the street is very much on our side . . .
>
> I was interrogated by both the Captain of the Port and the Military Commissar. The former asked me to complete a questionnaire containing such questions as: what our Naval escort consisted of; the distance

apart of the ships in columns; ports of departure and destination; the position of the ship when torpedoed; nature and amount of cargo; what was my opinion of the Naval aspect of the war, and if I had seen any bomb damage during the war to ports and installations . . .

Needless to say, Evans gave the Spanish no information that might have been of use to the enemy, and it was with great relief that he and his men boarded a ship for home a few days later.

# 10

# A Good Note on Which to
# End the Year

Captain J. B. Hodge, master of the British tanker *Empire Spenser*, was no stranger to the hazards of war. However, it did occur to him that there were safer ways of crossing the North Atlantic than on top of 10,000 tons of high-octane aviation spirit. Any winter passage of this angry ocean is a challenge, but as 1942 drew to a close, with some of the worst storms of the year raging, the *Empire Spenser*'s homeward run promised to be one to remember. And then, of course, there were the U-boats.

Although 87 German submarines had been sunk during the year, Dönitz's fleet had increased to 393, 212 of these being operational. By the end of November 1942 their total score for the year stood at 1,094 Allied ships of nearly six million tons sunk, most of these going down in the Atlantic, including a disproportionate number of British oil tankers. As a result, oil reserves in Britain had reached an all-time low of 300,000 tons, with imports down to only two-thirds the level of 1939. Now, with the battle for the Allied supply beaches in North Africa a lost cause, Dönitz had returned most of his U-boats to the Atlantic, and the stage was set for a grand finale that would mark 1942 as a year of catastrophe for Allied merchant shipping.

On 27 November, as the climax of the Battle of the Atlantic drew near, the 8,194-ton *Empire Spenser* set sail from New York. As a loaded oil tanker she presented a prime target for the U-boats, and steps had been taken to disguise her distinctive silhouette. Her original funnel, right aft as in all tankers, had been removed, and a dummy funnel erected close abaft the bridge, while canvas screens rigged on deck gave the appearance of extra accommodation amidships, as in a general cargo carrier. It was a crude disguise, but seen through a periscope on a dark night it might make the ship seem a less inviting target. Captain Hodge reserved his judgement on this, but he did have some confidence in the *Empire Spenser*'s AND nets. With these heavy steel mesh curtains streamed on either side of the ship, she might lose a knot or two of speed, but her chances of survival would be greatly increased.

The *Empire Spenser* sailed from New York on 27 November and, having cleared the Ambrose Light, joined the ranks of Convoy HX 217, bound for the United Kingdom. The convoy comprised 33 ships escorted by Escort Group B6, with Commander S. Heathcote as Senior Officer in the destroyer HMS

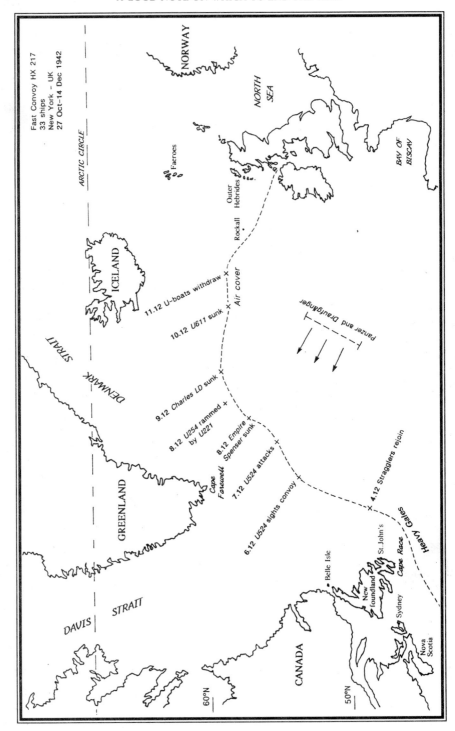

**Above:** A Convoy makes drastic changes of course to avoid U-boats. (Imperial War Museum)

**Below:** A salvo of depth charges explodes around a U-boat caught on the surface by a Coastal Command aircraft; the tail gunner is also machine-gunning the U-boat. (Imperial War Museum)

**Above:** HMS *Starling* carrying out a depth charge attack in February 1944. (Imperial War Museum)

**Opposite page, top:** Two U-boats meeting in the mid Atlantic. (Imperial War Museum)

**Opposite page, bottom:** One of the largest convoys of the Second World War carries British and American forces to land on the North African coast in Operation 'Torch'. (Imperial War Museum)

**Opposite page, top:** Commander Weir of the Royal Navy giving landing instructions to a captured U-boat commander (in the white cap). (Imperial War Museum)

**Opposite page, bottom:** The end of a U-boat. Damaged by a depth charge, the Atlantic 'reptile' was forced to the surface, where it was sunk by British guns. Two of the U-boat's crew can be seen swimming towards the destroyer, and another is on the conning tower about to leave the doomed submarine. (Imperial War Museum)

**Above:** Biscay base under attack. Allied bombs explode on the U-boat harbour at Lorient. (Imperial War Museum)

**Above:** Torpedoed. British merchant seamen survivors on one of the emergency life rafts that all merchant ships carried. (Imperial War Museum)

**Opposite page, top:** U-boat commander (Kapitänleutnant Hans Ey) takes the con. (Horst Bredow)

**Right:** *U82* returns from patrol.

A British bren-gunner guards Dönitz, with Albert Speer (Minister of Armaments and Munitions) and General Jodl, as they go into captivity. (IWM BU6708)

*Fame*, the Polish destroyer *Burza*, the British corvette *Vervain*, and three Norwegian corvettes, *Potentilla*, *Rose* and *Eglantine*. *Fame*, damaged a month earlier when she rammed and sank *U353* in a spectacular defence of Convoy SC 104, was only recently returned to service. In the rear of the convoy was the 2,259-ton rescue ship *Perth*, owned by the Dundee, Perth & London Shipping Company. Although built in 1915, the *Perth* still showed the fine lines of the crack coastal passenger steamer she had once been, still managed a respectable 14 knots and was equipped with HF/DF. She was a valuable asset to the escort force, and a reassuring presence to the those who manned the deep-laden merchant ships, who might at some time have need of her services.

Much against Captain Hodge's wishes, the *Empire Spenser* had been allocated position No. 101 in the convoy, as lead ship of the starboard wing column; the last place one might expect to find a ship loaded with a lethal cargo of high-octane fuel. The Belfast-registered tanker was a sound ship, built only that year, heavily armed with a 4.7in, a 12-pounder and four 20mm Oerlikons, and she had her anti-torpedo nets. Nevertheless, to station her first in the line of the enemy's fire was indeed tempting providence.

While HX 217 was forming up to begin its perilous Atlantic crossing, two of Dönitz's wolf packs, the *Panzer* and *Draufgänger* groups, were gathering in mid-ocean near the convoy routes. On the 29th one of the *Draufgänger* boats, forced to submerge when a patrolling Catalina swooped out of the skies, heard propeller noises when underwater. These were presumed to come from the eastbound convoy ON 151, known to be somewhere in the vicinity, and on receiving word of the contact Dönitz ordered the 22 boats comprising the two groups to form a patrol line across the expected track of the convoy. Some hours later *U603* (Kapitänleutnant Hans-Joachim Bertelsmann) reported sighting masts and funnels on the horizon, but then lost contact in poor visibility. Later, two of the *Panzer* group heard hydrophone effect when submerged, but, despite a careful search, nothing was seen. Convoy ON 151 had slipped through the net.

Meanwhile, HX 217 had run into bad weather which rapidly deteriorated into a howling gale. Before long a number of ships were forced to heave-to, drop out from the ranks and fight their lonely battles against wind and sea astern of the convoy. The *Empire Spenser*, her AND nets streamed, was one of the first to run into trouble. Heavy seas carried away the hoisting gear for the starboard nets, and these became so entangled that they could not be hauled inboard. All the weight of the nets was on the forward boom, and, as the weather worsened, Hodge feared the boom might collapse, allowing the heavy steel mesh to drift aft and foul his propeller, possibly with fatal results. He decided to heave-to and slip the starboard nets before this catastrophe happened. Despite the seas breaking over the tanker's weather deck, the slip was accomplished with comparative ease. There then seemed little point in attempting to rejoin the convoy, perhaps sustaining more heavy-weather damage in the process, so Hodge elected to remain hove-to until the seas moderated. It was the morning of 4 December before the *Empire Spenser*, along with several other stragglers, caught up with HX 217 and eased back into the ranks, the tanker being ordered once more to take up the lead of column ten. With the starboard AND nets irretrievably lost, her exposed outboard side was without protection.

For some time the Allies had been using very high frequency (VHF) radio to communicate between ships in a convoy. This was thought to be secure, for transmissions on these high frequencies were rarely audible above 30 miles and, in any case, the U-boats, it was thought, were not equipped with VHF. However, word of this policy had reached Dönitz, and experiments were being conducted using specially trained radio operators in selected U-boats equipped with VHF receivers. One of these boats was *U524*, commanded by Kapitänleutnant Freiherr (Baron) Walter von Steinäcker and sailing with the *Panzer* group. On the evening of 4 December Steinäcker's operators picked up transmissions in English on 124.5m, estimated to be emanating from at least ten ships. As the range of the German VHF receiver was not known, it could not be established how far off the enemy ships were, but there seemed little doubt that there was a substantial convoy in the offing. Dönitz ordered all boats to move north-east at full speed to intercept.

Fittingly, Baron von Steinäcker's *U524* was first to make contact, sighting HX 217 at midday on the 6th. The convoy was then on the eastern edge of the Greenland Gap without air cover, and the time was opportune for an all-out attack. Von Steinäcker signalled the other boats to join him and settled down to shadow the convoy, reporting his progress to Dönitz every four hours.

That evening four other boats joined *U524*, but poor visibility precluded any attack. The night passed with the ships of HX 217 unaware that the wolves were gathering around them. At 0645 on the 7th, in the darkest hour before the dawn, von Steinäcker approached the convoy on the surface and fired a four-torpedo spread. Two detonations were heard, but no hit was seen. All of the torpedoes went wide, and the Baron suffered the indignity of being chased and depth-charged by HX 217's escort. The element of surprise was now lost to the U-boats, and their chances of success worsened with the coming of daylight, which brought with it air cover for the convoy.

The first aircraft to arrive from Iceland was Liberator 'H' of 120 Squadron, RAF Coastal Command, piloted by Squadron Leader Terry Bulloch, DSO, DSC. Bulloch, a long-range pilot of exceptional ability, had flown 800 miles through high winds, heavy icing and thick cloud to reach HX 217. Once overhead he spent seven hours covering the convoy, sighting eight U-boats on the surface, all of which he attacked vigorously with depth charges and cannon fire. Bulloch bracketed one U-boat with six depth charges and claimed to have inflicted serious damage. The result of this attack was never confirmed, but the avenging presence of the Liberator over the convoy kept the U-boats down and denied them the opportunity to get to grips with HX 217.

At about 1300, having reached the limit of his aircraft's endurance, Bulloch turned for home, reaching his base in Reykjavik safely after being airborne for 16 hours and 25 minutes. But 'H' did not leave until she was relieved by another Liberator, piloted by Squadron Leader Desmond Isted, who kept up the pressure on the U-boats. During the afternoon Isted made five sightings and four attacks. When darkness fell on the 7th, HX 217 was still intact and pushing steadily eastwards despite the numerous U-boats probing at its defences. Air cover continued throughout that night, causing Dönitz to write in his diary:

> When the first night of the attack began we awaited reports in a state of intense expectation. As the night progressed, however, I began to feel anxious. Within a short space of time my command post picked up 11 messages in English, emanating from the convoy's air escort and reporting that U-boats had been sighted and attacked. The air escort of this particular convoy seemed to be exceptionally strong, even during the hours of darkness.

As if to offset the huge advantage afforded HX 217 by the continuous air cover, there was a marked improvement in the weather. The clouds moved away, visibility increased, the wind dropped to a gentle breeze from the south and the sea subsided, although a heavy swell persisted. Conditions were now ideal for the wolves to move in.

Best estimates say that seventeen U-boats were in contact with HX 217, and it was inevitable that, sooner or later, one would break through its defences. Again it was Baron von Steinäcker in *U524* who succeeded first, having reached a position to starboard of and abreast the leading ships as midnight approached. At 2355 he fired two two-torpedo spreads in quick succession. The first narrowly missed the destroyer HMS *Fame*; the second streaked towards the unprotected starboard side of the *Empire Spenser*.

No one on board the tanker saw the line of bubbles to starboard as one of von Steinäcker's torpedoes homed in on her from out of the darkness. When the torpedo ploughed into No. 1 cargo tank, some 100ft from the stern, the explosion was subdued, but the ship shook violently, and a tall column of gasoline shot into the air, erupting into flame as it fell back on the after deck. Diesel oil poured out of the nearby bunker tank, and this too caught fire. Within minutes the whole of the starboard side of the after part of the ship was ablaze, the wind blowing the flames right across the deck from starboard to port. Behind the flames 35 men were trapped in the after part of the ship, including Captain Hodge. One of the two available lifeboats aft was filled with gasoline and on fire, and the flames were spreading to the other one.

It was fortunate for Hodge and his men, then sheltering on the port side and being driven nearer and nearer to the ship's rail, that the two engineers on watch below kept the engine running. This enabled Chief Officer C. Siemsen, who had the watch on the bridge, to swing the ship round to bring the wind on the port quarter, so that the flames were blown to starboard. Siemsen's initiative allowed Second Officer A. N. Chapman to launch the port, after lifeboat and take off 21 of the men trapped aft, many of whom were without shoes or outer clothing. Chapman took the crowded boat across to the rescue ship *Perth*, which was now standing by the *Empire Spenser*.

It had been intended that Captain Hodge and the thirteen men still remaining in the after part of the tanker would wait for Chapman to return with the boat, but when, at 0130, No. 2 cargo tank caught fire, their position became untenable. The sea around the *Empire Spenser*'s stern was a blazing inferno, with flames leaping 10ft in the air and trailing two miles astern. There was, however, a clear patch to windward, and as the tanker had by then stopped, Hodge and his men succeeded in abandoning ship using liferafts. As they paddled away it could be seen that the *Empire Spenser*'s back had been broken by von Steinäcker's torpedo. Chief Officer Siemsen, whose prompt action had saved Hodge and his men, remained on board, and with twenty men still in the fore part of the ship attempted to fight the blaze with chemical extinguishers. It was a gallant action, but doomed to failure. Siemsen was soon forced to put his men into the only lifeboat left intact and row away, leaving the *Empire Spenser* to her fate.

With the burning tanker dropping astern, HX 217, then 300 miles southwest of Cape Farewell and with just over 1,000 miles to go to the North Channel, continued on a north-easterly course at 10 knots. Continuous air cover, and the unstinting efforts of Heathcote's escorting force, kept the U-boats at bay throughout the remaining hours of that night and all next day, and it was the wolves who suffered the next casualty in deteriorating weather on the night of the 8th. Kapitänleutnant Hans Trojer, in command of *U221*, described the incident in his war diary:

Proceeded in pursuit of convoy at high speed. 2134 night dark, sea strength 5, squalls of rain. German U-boat sighted through rain squall on starboard bow. Turned away with full rudder, but could not avoid sharp blow on after pressure hull. Collision hardly seemed noticeable to us.

The other boat remained afloat, but started to settle in the water. Observed a few pocket torches and about 30 men in lifejackets and escape gear. Switched on searchlights and warned men to keep calm. Constant shouts for help. Used Sander [line throwing] pistol and heaving lines in attempts to help, but all attempts frustrated by heavy seas. Some of my own men attached to lifelines went overboard, but could do nothing. Only one petty officer and three men succeeded in grabbing lines and were hauled aboard, in spite of heavy sea, which was breaking over bridge. It was *U254*. After we persisted in our efforts for two hours, during which the searchlight was in constant use, two star shells were fired to the east of us and a vessel switched on two lights.

Dönitz had always been aware of the risk of collision when operating a pack of U-boats against a convoy at night, but the loss of *U254* (Kapitänleutnant Hans Gilardone), the first of its kind, came as a severe shock. As a result of this accident Dönitz resolved that, in future, no more than thirteen to fifteen U-boats should be in the immediate vicinity of a convoy at any one time.

Unaware of the fatal collision between two of their number, the other U-boats involved with HX 217 continued to press home the attack against the convoy, but it was not until the morning of the 9th that they again tasted victory. At 0521, *U758* (Kapitänleutnant Helmut Manseck) crept in under the cover of darkness and fired a single torpedo before being pounced upon and put to flight by the Norwegian corvettes *Potentilla* and *Eglantine*. The torpedo went wide and exploded harmlessly at the end of its run. Then, shortly before dawn, Korvettenkapitän Karl Thurmann in *U553* found the 5,273-ton Liverpool-registered motor vessel *Charles L. D.* straggling astern and sank her with one torpedo.

The North Atlantic was back in its angry winter mood, and the bad weather prevented air cover on the 9th, but a superhuman effort by Heathcote's destroyers and corvettes, whose asdics and radar were severely affected by the weather, frustrated attack after attack. During the long night that followed, *U758* twice succeeded in breaking through the ring of guns and depth charges surrounding the convoy, but once again Helmut Manseck's torpedoes were wasted. At dawn on the 10th HX 217 was 300 miles south of Reykjavik, and heavy air support arrived in the form of the Lockheed Hudsons of 269 Squadron, Coastal Command, and the Catalinas of US Navy Patrol Squadron VP-84. One of the latter surprised *U611* on the surface and depth-charged her to destruction. That was enough for Dönitz, who aborted the failed operation, which had cost him the loss of two U-boats against two merchantmen of 13,467 tons sunk.

Throughout the rest of December the weather in the North Atlantic was so atrocious as to cause even the U-boats to suspend their activities. Their combined sinkings during that period amounted to only four merchantmen and one British destroyer. As the end of the year approached, with no improvement either in the weather or the fortunes of war, Dönitz gathered his scattered U-boats together and formed the *Spitz* and *Ungestüm* packs. These two packs, twenty boats strong, were ordered to scour the southern part of the North Atlantic, where it was believed Allied convoys were being routed to avoid the worst of the weather. A few days earlier, on the morning of 18 December, Convoy ONS 154 had cleared the North Channel, bound for Halifax, Nova Scotia. With the best of intentions the Admiralty had instructed the convoy commodore, Admiral Egerton, to steer a south-westerly course towards the Azores, in search of calmer waters. Unwittingly, a meeting with the enemy in mid-Atlantic had been arranged.

A westbound crossing of the North Atlantic in winter is always something of an ordeal, and in December 1942, with some of the worst storms in living memory raging, it promised to be a long and exhausting battle. But such is a seaman's lot, and when the ships of ONS 154 left Bloody Foreland astern and entered an ocean where the dark, rain-laden clouds turned day into perpetual night and the seas heaved and roared in anger, the grumbles and curses were no louder than usual. The real ire was directed at the heartless ones safe ashore who had seen fit to condemn these men to spend their Christmas in mid-Atlantic, where, given the weather and the threat of the U-boats, any pretence at celebration would be a farce.

Led by Admiral Egerton in the 7,068-ton British steamer *Empire Shackleton*, ONS 154 was made up of 45 ships, escorted by the Canadian Group C1 commanded by Lieutenant-Commander Guy Windeyer in the destroyer *St Laurent*. Windeyer, an experienced and very competent officer, but in command of a group for the first time, had with him the five corvettes *Battleford*, *Chilliwack*, *Napanee*, *Shediac* and *Orillia*. Bad weather had prevented the escorts exercising together before sailing, so C1 lacked that essential element of team experience required for a successful escort group. In support was the fighter catapult ship HMS *Fidelity*, flying the British flag but with a Free French crew, and the rescue ship *Toward*, an ex-River Clyde pleasure steamer of 1,571 tons commanded by Captain G. K. Hudson. The *Toward*'s role was obvious, but the reason for the presence of such a vulnerable ship as the *Fidelity* was not clear.

The defence of ONS 154 against the assaults of the enemy was in good hands, but there was nothing that could shield the convoy from the wrath of the ocean. The ships, most of which were in ballast, fought their way south-westwards in the teeth of a succession of roaring westerly gales, pitching and rolling, sometimes hove-to, their forward progress never exceeding 3 or 4 knots. Seven days out from the North Channel Christmas came and went all but unnoticed as men, exhausted and demoralised by the continual battering they suffered, fought to keep their ships afloat and on course. For those manning the Commodore's ship, *Empire Shackleton*, the strain was doubly hard, for she carried in her holds 1,000 tons of ammunition, replenishment for the magazines of Canada's Navy. As the ship climbed each monstrous wave and slammed into the darkness of the trough, every rivet, plate and frame straining and creaking, there was no escaping the knowledge that each sickening impact might be one too many. One spark caused by steel grating on steel could easily set off the cataclysmic explosion that would vapourise the ship and all 62 souls sailing in her.

Ironically it was *U154*, the southerly outrider of the *Spitz* group, which sighted ONS 154 early on the night of the 26th, when the convoy was some 500 miles to the north-north-east of the Azores. Korvettenkapitän Heinrich Schuch followed standing orders, first reporting the sighting to Dönitz and then beginning to shadow. However, the sight of 45 lightly escorted merchantmen moving at slow speed in the heavy seas proved an irresistible temptation. At 2030 Schuch attempted an attack on the starboard wing column and failed, being driven off by Windeyer's corvettes. No harm was done to either side, but Schuch's premature attack served to warn ONS 154 of the ordeal to come.

The hours ticked by in an uneasy calm, the ships continuing their ceaseless battle with the elements, knowing full well that the wolves were homing in on them. Then, just before midnight, a cold, miserable drizzle set in. It was another burden for those on watch in the open to bear, but the falling visibility gave hope that they might continue to slip through the night unseen. But it was not to be. At 0130 on the 27th, *U356*, with Oberleutnant-zur-See Günther Ruppelt newly in command, more by good luck than good judgement found herself crossing ahead of the convoy. On sighting the lead ships, Ruppelt, with commendable presence of mind, came hard round and ran down between two columns, firing a full spread of four torpedoes from his bow tubes. Two British ships, the 5,952-ton *Empire Union* and the 2,473-ton *Melrose Abbey*, were hit and sank quickly, with heavy loss of life.

The *Toward* dropped back to pick up survivors, and the escorts ran in frantic circles dropping depth charges, but Ruppelt was still inside the convoy, and there he stayed while reloading his tubes. This done, at 0210 he torpedoed the 7,051-ton Dutch steamer *Soekaboemi*, and five minutes later the 24-year-old London ship *King Edward*. The *Soekaboemi*, registered in Batavia and a long way from the blue waters of the Java Sea, did not sink until that evening, when she was finished off by Klaus Hartmann in *U441*.

Günther Ruppelt, on his first patrol in command, had achieved a staggering success, but he paid the ultimate price. When *U356* emerged from within the ranks of the convoy she was sighted by the *St Laurent*. Windeyer went in to the attack, at the same time calling in the corvettes *Chilliwack*, *Battleford* and *Napanee*. *St Laurent* opened up a fierce fire on the U-boat with her 4.7in and Oerlikons, and at least one shell from the big gun went home as Ruppelt dived. Asdic contact was gained, and the four escorts, acting in concert, carried out a systematic depth charge attack which ultimately resulted in the destruction of *U356* and her crew.

When the thunder of the depth charges had subsided, the drizzle closed in around the convoy, and the other U-boats either lost touch or made a discreet withdrawal. The remainder of the night was without incident, and when daylight came again there was a welcome improvement in the weather. The sea continued to go down during the day, and, as some of the corvettes were running short of fuel, Windeyer considered conditions were right for refuelling. At nightfall the tanker *Scottish Heather* dropped eight miles astern and *Orillia*, the corvette in most urgent need, came in under her stern. For over an hour the two ships, attached to each other by hose and lines, rolled awkwardly in the swell while the precious fuel was transferred. Then Oberleutnant-zur-See Wolfgang Leimkühler came on the scene in *U225*. Leimkühler, another commander on his first patrol, went to periscope depth and torpedoed the *Scottish Heather* just as the two ships completed their task and were breaking away. The tanker did not sink and eventually reached the Clyde, but, for the time being at least, Leimkühler put an end to Windeyer's plans for refuelling his ships. This was to have tragic consequences.

Fortunately *U225* was unable to locate the convoy again, and the night once more passed peacefully. The weather improved steadily as the wind dropped, but when daylight approached on the 28th the Atlantic put on its other face. Thick fog rolled in, and station keeping became a nightmare for the 40 merchantmen steaming in close proximity to one another. There were near-collisions but, by the grace of God and the swift reactions of those manning the bridges, disaster was avoided. It is perhaps understandable that, with as many as twenty U-boats forming the *Spitz* and *Ungestüm* groups somewhere in the vicinity, the confidence of those in the Allied ships was misplaced. The morning was not far advanced before *U260* (Kapitänleutnant Hubertus Purkhold) picked up propeller noises on her hydrophones and began to shadow ONS 154. Purkhold signalled for all boats in the area to home in on him.

The fog cleared away in the late afternoon, giving way to warm, sunny weather with light, variable winds and a calm sea. Under any other circumstances these kinder conditions would have been welcomed, offering a chance to walk the decks and feel the kiss of the sun, and to dry out clothes turning mouldy with damp. But as the horizon stretched out to infinity in all directions, so the tension in the convoy rose – not without good reason as it transpired. By this time, in response to *U260*'s call, thirteen U-boats were in sight of ONS 154, which was now 250 miles due north of the Azores.

Windeyer deployed his meagre force as best he could, and during the hours of daylight kept the U-boats at bay, attacking aggressively whenever one appeared on the surface or was detected by asdic. By sunset his men were exhausted, and the U-boats were not long in breaking through the screen to begin their savaging of ONS 154. *Battleford* was first to sight them, her lookouts reporting 'an object on the surface outlined against a break in the cloud on the western horizon'. The corvette altered course to investigate and came upon four surfaced U-boats bearing down on the convoy in line abreast. Two of them dived, and *Battleford* went after the two which remained on the surface, opening rapid fire with her 4in gun. Unfortunately the concussion of the gun put the corvette's radar out of action, and she lost her quarry. *Battleford* then turned to rejoin the convoy, unaware that it had made a large alteration of course after dark. With no radar, and unable to use her radio, she failed to find the other ships until daylight on the 29th.

In the meantime, ONS 154 came under attack. The first victim was the 5,701-ton Norwegian *Norse King*, the second ship of column eleven, hit by a torpedo fired by *U591* (Kapitänleutnant Hansjürgen Zetzsche) at 2004. A few minutes later Wolfgang Leimkühler in *U225* increased his score by putting two torpedoes into the *Melmore Head*, stationed astern of the *Norse King*. She blew up. Leimkühler then found a target for his stern torpedo in the 5,083-ton *Ville de Rouen*, severely damaging her. At 2045 Hubertus Purkhold made his mark by sinking the *Empire Wagtail*. Hermann Kottmann in *U203* was hard on his heels, but his torpedo was a surface runner and skimmed harmlessly through the packed ranks of ships.

There was a lull of about half an hour, then *U406* (Kapitänleutnant Horst Dieterichs), equipped with the new *Flächenabsuchender* (FAT) torpedoes, fired a spread of four and hit and damaged three ships, the *Baron Cochrane*, *Lynton Grange* and *Zarian*. The FATs required aiming only in the general direction of the convoy, and were designed to run in wide circles until they made contact with a target. On this occasion they functioned exactly as their designer had intended, although the explosions they caused were not sufficient to sink the ships they hit. Only one of Dieterich's torpedoes missed.

Wolfgang Leimkühler was next in, firing four single torpedoes. One of these hit the Belgian motor tanker *Président Francqui*, having little effect on the ballasted ship, but two brought the Commodore's ship, *Empire Shackleton*, to a halt and settling by the head. She had been hit in her No. 1 hold, which fortunately did not contain any explosives. However, having lived in fear of their lives for ten days, her crew abandoned ship, and the *Empire Shackleton* slewed out of line, settling by the head. Twelve men were picked up by the steamer *Calgary*, and the remainder by HMS *Fidelity*.

In the space of two hours the U-boats had created havoc in the ranks of ONS 154, torpedoing nine ships, three of which had sunk immediately. Lieutenant Stuart Henderson, in command of the corvette *Napanee*, described the chaos of the night: 'All ships appeared to be firing snowflakes, and tracers crisscrossed in all directions, escorts firing starshells. The sea was dotted with lights from boats and rafts, and two burning wrecks which had hauled out to starboard helped the illumination.'

The U-boats now withdrew, and contented themselves with picking off the abandoned ships drifting astern of the convoy. *U591* sank the *Zarian* with a single torpedo, but missed the *Baron Cochrane*. The latter was sent to the bottom five minutes later by *U123* (Oberleutnant-zur-See Horst von Schroeter), which then fired at but missed the *Lynton Grange*. She went down after another five minutes, sunk by *U628* (Kapitänleutnant Heinrich Hasenschar). Hasenschar, and Siegfried Stretlow in *U435*, then turned on the two corvettes engaged in rescuing survivors from the three merchantmen, but although Hasenschar claimed to have sunk a corvette, all of their torpedoes mercifully missed. Later in the night the crippled *Ville de Rouen* was sunk by *U662* (Korvettenkapitän Wolfgang Hermann), and in the early hours of the 29th Horst von Schroeter and Siegfried Stretlow, using torpedoes and gunfire, finally put an end to the *Empire Shackleton*. Ironically, the Commodore's ship took her 1,000 tons of ammunition to the bottom with her unexploded.

All this time the damaged tanker *Président Francqui* had been limping along well astern of ONS 154, but when daylight came she was spotted by *U336* (Kapitänleutnant Hans Hunger), a latecomer to the battle. Hunger fired a spread of three, but all were duds. The *Président Francqui* continued doggedly on her way until Leimkühler's *U225* stopped her with a torpedo that hit home and exploded deep in her vitals. After two more torpedoes failed to explode, *U336* administered the *coup de grâce* at 0825 on the 29th. The Belgian tanker had proved a tough nut to crack, absorbing eight torpedoes before sinking.

Later in the day the *Norse King*, listing awkwardly but making for the Azores with all the speed her strained bulkheads could withstand, was discovered by *U435* and went the way of all the others who had survived their first torpedoing. The two Royal Navy destroyers HMS *Milne* and *Meteor*, ordered by Western Approaches Command to join ONS 154 from another convoy in a desperate effort to halt the slaughter, arrived too late to save any of them.

The reinforcement of C1 Group caused the U-boats to draw back, but not to go away. They returned to the fray after dark, the object of their attentions being the high-sided fighter catapult ship HMS *Fidelity*. Leimkühler was once more in the van, but in his haste to be first he aimed carelessly and missed. Half an hour later *U615* (Kapitänleutnant Ralph Kapitzky) took her turn and wasted five torpedoes on the same target. The *Fidelity* had AND nets streamed which successfully warded off Kapitzky's torpedoes, although she suffered extensive damage.

The reckoning for the attack on, and the subsequent departure of, the refuelling tanker *Scottish Heather* came next morning, when Windeyer was forced to detach two of his corvettes, *Shediac* and *Battleford*, which were running dangerously short of fuel. At the same time, the newly-joined destroyers *Milne* and *Meteor* signalled that their bunker tanks were almost empty. They too pulled away, leaving only HMCS *St Laurent* and three corvettes to defend the battered convoy. No sooner were the departing escorts over the horizon than Siegfried Stretlow in *U435* found HMS *Fidelity* straggling astern, and sank her with two torpedoes which penetrated her damaged nets. After the ship went down, Stretlow reported seeing between 300 and 400 survivors in the water and drifting on overcrowded rafts. It was later learned that the 37 survivors of the sinking of the *Empire Shackleton*, including Admiral Egerton, her Master and all her deck officers, were lost with the torpedoing of *Fidelity*.

Having been under continual strain and without rest for 72 hours, Lieutenant-Commander Windeyer was now near to breaking point. When, on the morning of the 31st, HMS *Fame* arrived, Commander Heathcote took over as SOE and the exhausted but protesting Canadian was put to bed. Under circumstances which were not in his favour, and in the face of the combined might of the *Spitz* and *Ungestüm* groups, Windeyer had done his best, but it was not enough. When, late that day, the U-boats, their torpedoes expended and fuel low, called off the attack, the action had cost ONS 154 fourteen ships of 74,461 tons and the lives of 486 seamen. For the Germans it was, as Admiral Dönitz remarked, 'a good note on which to end the Battle of the Atlantic for the year'.

# 11

# A Common Enemy

The fourth year of the war, 1943, opened with the wolf packs growing ever stronger. Dönitz now had 400 U-boats in his fleet, and more than 100 of these were at large in the Atlantic at any one time. However, the defence of the Allied convoys was strengthening at a similar rate, with more escort vessels, better radars, and almost constant air cover outside the Greenland Gap. It was in this gap, which some called the 'Black Pit', that Dönitz was now forced to concentrate the main thrust of his attack, but he needed to make haste. With the continued development of the American very-long-range aircraft, the gap was slowly and inexorably closing. Soon the skies above the convoys, from New York to the North Channel, would rarely be without the searching eyes of Allied aeroplanes. The U-boats would have nowhere to hide, except beneath the sea, and, as they were not true submarines, their effectiveness would be severely diminished.

But in the first month of the year Dönitz found himself up against another and far more powerful enemy; the sea itself. January 1943 saw the Atlantic gales of the winter culminating in a frenzy of storms so violent that the U-boats were rendered almost completely impotent. Commanders reported winds in excess of 120 knots, driving rain, sleet and snow, and precipitous seas that made watchkeeping in the conning tower a terrifying ordeal that sapped the will of even the most seasoned hands. Position fixing was impossible, and in the first half of the month the U-boats were so concerned with their own survival that not one Allied convoy was sighted in the North Atlantic.

The big ships fared little better. In fighting their way across the heaving ocean, eight merchantmen foundered, four ran aground and more than 40 suffered serious heavy-weather damage. It was reported that one rescue ship capsized and sank with the weight of ice building up on her decks, while the captain and first lieutenant of the British destroyer *Roxborough* were killed when a giant wave smashed the bridge of their ship. During the course of the month a third of all escort vessels were temporarily taken out of service by the sheer violence of the weather.

As January drew to its tempestuous close at sea, events ashore in Germany were no less stormy. On the 31st Admiral Erich Raeder, under severe criticism from Hitler, resigned, and Karl Dönitz became C-in-C of the German Navy, being promoted to Grossadmiral (Admiral of the Fleet). For Dönitz, at 51, this was the pinnacle of success. He retained executive control over the U-boats but, much against his will, was obliged to move his headquarters to Berlin. There, from the Hotel am Steinplatz in Charlottenberg, he contemplated the situation in the North Atlantic, where he was still convinced Germany's war would be won or lost. The picture was not encouraging, for in January the U-boats had sunk only 27 Allied merchantmen of just under 173,000 tons. Some of this dismal performance could be put down to the atrocious weather prevailing throughout the month, but Dönitz feared that the momentum of his campaign was slackening.

One convoy unfortunate not to escape the attentions of the U-boats was HX 224, the interception of which was to have far-reaching effects. The eastbound convoy HX 224 sailed from New York on 22 January, and was in mid-Atlantic, running before a strong westerly gale, when it was sighted by *U456* (Kapitänleutnant Max-Martin Teichert). Although Teichert was patrolling alone, four other unassociated boats were in the vicinity, but well to the westward. These were ordered to make all speed to *U456*'s assistance. The convoy was heavily defended and the weather made any close approach doubly difficult, but Teichert held on for three days and then, seeing an opening, sank two ships, the 7,177-ton American steamer *Jeremiah van Rensselaer* and the 9,456-ton British tanker *Inverilen*. The other U-boats caught up with the convoy on 3 February, but air cover was now overhead, and HX 224 was saved from further attacks. However, the heavy weather had scattered the convoy, and the British tanker *Cordelia* was now straggling astern. Fate was unkind to the *Cordelia*, for it just so happened that she lay directly in the path of *U632* (Kapitänleutnant Hans Karpf), one of the boats called in by Dönitz. The tanker blew up when Karpf's torpedoes ripped her apart, leaving only one survivor in the water. This man, a British officer, was picked up by *U632*, and for some reason – perhaps he was in shock – volunteered the information to Karpf that the slow convoy SC 118 was following two days astern of HX 224. How the man came to be in possession of such secret information is not clear, but Karpf lost no time in reporting his good luck to U-boat control. Dönitz immediately contacted all boats in the area and formed the *Pfeil* pack. A total of fifteen boats formed a patrol line across the anticipated course of SC 118 and moved slowly westwards, intent on gathering the approaching convoy into its arms. Five boats of the *Haudegen* pack, then 300 miles astern of the convoy, were ordered to close up to assist *Pfeil*.

Convoy SC 118, which had sailed from New York on 24 January, bound for Loch Ewe via the North Channel, consisted of 61 ships, many laden with vital war materials for North Russia. The convoy's escort was Escort Group B2, led by the SOE, Commander F. B. Proudfoot, RN, in the destroyer HMS *Vanessa*, with two other British destroyers, *Vimy* and *Beverley*, the British corvettes *Campanula* and *Abelia*, the Free French corvettes *Lobelia* and *Migonette*, and the US Coastguard cutter *George M. Bibb*. Numerically, B2 was a powerful force, but, apart from its cosmopolitan make-up, it had some serious weaknesses. It was Proudfoot's first appointment as SOE, he was new to the *Vanessa*, and with the exception of *Campanula* and *Migonette* none of the ships had experience of working together as a team. Only *Vanessa* and *George M. Bibb* were equipped with HF/DF, essential for the early detection of U-boats, and the latter's operators lacked experience. However, the rescue ship *Toward*, returning eastwards after her sterling work with the brutally savaged convoy ONS 154, was with B2. She was fitted with HF/DF, and her operators were well experienced in its use. The destroyers also carried the new anti-submarine bomb thrower known as 'Hedgehog'. This was a howitzer-like weapon mounted in the bows which hurled a barrage of 24 66lb bombs, set to land some 230 yards ahead of the ship. The bombs, each containing 30lb of Torpex, entered the water 12ft apart and in a circle about 100ft in diameter. Any U-boat caught in this circle was in for a rough time, although the Hedgehog bombs exploded only on contact, so a direct hit was required.

In January 1943 the German Sixth Army, under Field-Marshal Friederich von Paulus, lay trapped and encircled by the Russian armies at the gates of Stalingrad. Short of food and ammunition, and ill-equipped to withstand the bone-chilling cold, the German troops fought like wild animals at bay, but they were eventually pounded into submission by the huge weight of Russian artillery arrayed against them. On 2 February 90,000 men, all that remained of the 21 divisions von Paulus commanded, surrendered to Marshal Voronov. Hitler's dream of domination of the vast lands of the Union of Soviet Socialist Republics was nearing its end.

On the day that Friederich von Paulus led his men into captivity at Stalingrad, SC 118 was deep into the Atlantic, 500 miles east-north-east of Newfoundland and engaged in a bitter contest with the elements. Storm-force winds and heavy seas had scattered the merchantmen so that the convoy covered an area of almost 50 square miles, making the task of the escorts an immense challenge. The sturdy little corvettes, not one of them of much over 900 tons displacement, were built for heavy weather, but in the tremendous seas running they were barely able to maintain steerage way. The destroyers and the American cutter *George M. Bibb*, slim and fragile, were faring even worse, while a cloudbase down almost to sea level severely restricted air cover. The convoy, with its precious cargoes for the Russian armies, was wide open to attack.

But if the ships of SC 118 were suffering, their immediate enemies, the twenty U-boats of the *Pfeil* pack drawn up in a line across the convoy's course, were faring even worse. Oberleutnant Herbert Werner, First Watch Officer of *U230* (Kapitänleutnant Paul Siegmann), reported winds of up to 150mph and commented:

> On watch, the wind punished us with driving snow, sleet, hail and frozen spray. It beat against our rubber divers' suits, cut our faces like a razor, and threatened to tear away our eye masks; only the steel belts around our waists secured us to the boat and life. Below, inside the bobbing steel cockleshell, the boat's violent up-and-down motions drove us to the floor plates and hurled us straight up and threw us around like puppets.

He also spoke of waves 70m high breaking over the boat, 'forcing us on the bridge to ride for long seconds far below the surface'.

While Herbert Werner's 230ft-high waves may have been somewhat exaggerated, being viewed from the conning tower of a U-boat at sea level, there is little room for doubt that, as Dönitz wrote in his memoirs, 'The elements seemed to rage in uncontrolled fury'. The U-boats, like SC 118's escorts, had a hard fight merely to keep afloat, and it is little wonder that, on the night of 4 February, the convoy sailed through the *Pfeil* patrol line unseen. That would have been that, had it not been for an unfortunate incident. At dawn on the 4th, SC 118 had passed through and was 20 miles to the east of the U-boat line, inching its way to safety, when someone on the bridge of the Norwegian steamer *Vannik* accidentally fired a Snowflake rocket. The brilliant flare, performing as intended, turned the half-light of the grey dawn into brightest day and was seen twenty miles astern, where *U187* lay tossing in the heavy seas. The U-boat lost no time in investigating the source of the light, and by midday had the convoy in sight. Following standing instructions, Oberleutnant-zur-See Ralph Münnich, commanding *U187*, sent off a sighting report, using coded letter groups on short wave. The transmission was brief, lasting no more than twenty seconds, but it was long enough for the *Toward* and USS *Bibb* to obtain a fix with HF/DF. Münnich had by this time overtaken SC 118.

Commander Proudfoot ordered the destroyers *Vimy* and *Beverley* to seek out the enemy, and they soon surprised *U187* on the surface some seven miles ahead of the convoy. Münnich dived as soon as the escorts hove in sight, but his position was marked by smoke floats and *Vimy*, commanded by Lieutenant-Commander Richard Stannard, VC, RN, led the attack. A flurry of well-aimed depth charges and Hedgehog bombs rained down on the submerged submarine, causing major damage. Münnich was obliged to blow tanks, and as soon as *U187*'s conning tower broke the surface, *Vimy* and *Beverley* opened fire with their 4in guns. *Beverley*'s shells fell short, but *Vimy* scored a hit and *U187* took on a heavy list to port, her bows lifted out of the water, and she sank slowly by the stern, her crew spilling out of the conning tower to hurl themselves over the side into the boiling sea. Survivors were picked up by both British destroyers. The *U187*'s first and only war patrol had ended in disaster.

Throughout the remainder of the day *Toward*'s HF/DF operators picked up a series of radio transmissions, indicating a number of U-boats in the area, but although bearings were taken, no further interceptions were made. There were, in fact, five U-boats now in contact with SC 118, including *U609* (Kapitän-leutnant Klaus Rudloff) and *U402*, commanded by Korvettenkapitän Freiherr (Baron) Siegfried von Forstner, both of which had been shadowing the convoy for three days.

On his first war patrol in command of *U402*, in January 1942, von Forstner was 450 miles west-north-west of Cape Finisterre, outward bound from Biscay, when he met up with the 12,053-ton *Llangibby Castle* sailing unescorted. The liner, one of Union Castle's famous fleet sailing out of Southampton for South African ports, had exchanged her lavender hull and white upperworks for drab wartime grey, and had on board 1,500 British troops bound for the threatened island of Singapore. This was a target for which any experienced U-boat commander would have given his eye teeth; to von Forstner she represented a fitting beginning to a career he intended to be successful and spectacular. He took his time and fired a full spread of four torpedoes. The Baron had aimed for the *Llangibby Castle*'s engine room, and if his torpedoes had run true they would have sunk her. But there was a south-westerly gale blowing, and a miscalculation in estimating the liner's speed resulted in the torpedoes hitting right aft, blowing off her stern and rudder but leaving the ship afloat. Twenty-six men had been killed on board and four wounded, but, using her twin screws to steer, the liner's captain escaped into the rain and eventually made the Azores.

Von Forstner moved on towards the US Atlantic coast, where it was said that easy targets were still in abundance, but another three frustrating months were to pass before he claimed his next victim, the 5,249-ton *Empire Progress*. He followed this with the 5,284-ton Russian steamer *Aschabad*, then the US Navy patrol yacht *Cythera*, a mere 602 tons. Then von Forstner was ordered home, and six more months went by before the opportunity came to strike again.

The *U402* left her pen in La Pallice in October 1942, and in November, as part the *Vielchen* pack, sank four Allied ships of nearly 20,000 tons gross. This was the war as von Forstner had imagined it should be. After just twelve months in command he now had 31,000 tons to his credit, and his eye was firmly fixed on a Knight's Cross.

As was the custom in dangerous waters, the convoy commodore ordered a bold alteration of course as soon as darkness closed in, with the aim of confusing and, it was hoped, losing any shadowing U-boats. On this occasion the turn to be made was 45° to starboard, and as U-boats were known to be in the vicinity, the signal for the alteration was to be given by sound only. At the agreed time the Commodore's ship would give a number of blasts on her whistle, to be answered by a single blast by each ship as she turned on to the new course. In theory, the 61 ships of SC 118 should have altered course as one on the Commodore's signal. As it was, conditions were far from ideal for the manoeuvre, with poor visibility, the wind howling in the rigging and waves crashing aboard. It was a miracle that any of the ships heard the Commodore's signal at all on that wild, dark night. However, most of the merchantmen appeared to have done so, or perhaps altered by the clock, but the three port columns and some ships at the rear of the convoy continued on course when the signal was given. Chaos descended on SC 118.

The situation did not become clear until about midnight, when it was discovered that three columns were fifteen miles to port of the main convoy and on a diverging course, with various totally confused ships in between. The corvettes *Lobelia* and *Abelia* were despatched to round up the missing ships, but it was daylight on the 5th before SC 118 was more or less whole again, with only the American ship *West Portal* and the Greek *Polyktor* still unaccounted for. For the time being the convoy was safe, but it had been a near thing. For at least three hours, perhaps longer, as many as twenty merchantmen had been sailing together but completely unescorted. Fortunately the shadowing U-boats were not aware of the situation, so a golden opportunity to inflict heavy casualties was missed. During what remained of the night, attempts were made to penetrate the screen around the main body of the convoy, but these were beaten off by *Vimy*, *Beverley*, *Lobelia*, *Migonette* and *Campanula*, which all made depth charge attacks. Heinz Franke in *U262* claimed a hit on a tanker shortly before 0400, but his torpedoes went wide.

The new day dawned reluctantly, with no perceptible improvement in the weather, and the re-formed convoy, now in mid-ocean, continued its painful advance north-eastwards to the North Channel. At 1030 HMS *Beverley*, sweeping astern, sighted a U-boat fifteen miles on the starboard quarter and carried out a Hedgehog attack, but with no visible result. She continued her box search, and three-quarters of an hour later, when 22 miles from the convoy, sighted a second U-boat on the surface, six miles distant. *Vimy* was called in to assist, but the two destroyers lost contact with the enemy submarine when it dived. *Beverley* and *Vimy* returned to the convoy, but the U-boats were still there on the periphery of SC 118. At 1100 *U413* (Kapitänleutnant Gustav Poel), scouting to the north, found the missing *West Portal* steaming alone, and Poel sank her at his leisure, the American steamer going down with all hands. Some five hours later Kapitänleutnant

Ralf von Jessen in *U266* similarly disposed of the other straggler, the 4,077-ton *Polyktor*.

It is probable that the *Pfeil* boats, now 21 in number, would have made a strong bid to smash the convoy that night, but the odds began to turn against them. Shortly after dark B2 was reinforced by the US Coastguard cutter *Ingham*, and at daybreak on the 6th by the destroyers USS *Babbitt* and *Schenck*, all from Iceland. Proudfoot remained SOE, and disposed his now-considerable force in defensive positions around the merchantmen. *Babbitt* and *Ingham* scouted 5 miles ahead, *Vanessa* and *Beverley* were in the van, *Abelia*, *Vimy* and *Schenck* covered the port side and *Anemone* and *Campanula* were to starboard. Astern, *Migonette* was close up to the rear ships, while *Lobelia* and *George M. Bibb* were sweeping well astern to keep down shadowers. The convoy was steering a course of 053° at 7 1/2 knots and nearing the eastward limit of the Greenland Gap, so air cover was expected soon. The weather continued poor, with the wind blowing force 6/7 from the south-west, but it was showing signs of moderating. Although his group of twelve escorts was multi-national, and had no experience of working together, Proudfoot was confident that the convoy would win through without further loss.

The Commander's optimism seemed well founded, for before sunrise the first Liberators of 120 Squadron arrived overhead from Iceland. On the way out, one of these aircraft, 'X/120', sighted a U-boat on the surface 20 miles ahead of the convoy and forced it to dive. The hunters were about to become the hunted, and for the next eight hours the aircraft were kept busy chasing HF/DF bearings provided by the escorts and *Toward*. Eight U-boat sightings were made during the day, four of these being attacked with depth charges. One of the attacks, by Liberator 'W/120' at 0908, was seen by the cutter *Bibb* as she patrolled astern. She closed the position, picked up a strong asdic contact and carried out a Hedgehog attack, but with negative results.

While the avenging aircraft roared overhead and escorts scurried to and fro hurling depth charges and bombs, the rescue ship *Toward* was involved in a more mundane but no less gripping drama of the sea. Aboard the British steamer *Celtic Star* a seaman had fallen from the mast, sustaining serious injuries, and *Toward* was ordered by the Commodore to render medical assistance. This entailed putting the rescue ship's doctor on board the merchantman and then transferring the injured seaman to *Toward*. In mid-Atlantic, where a big swell is always present, this would have been a considerable feat of seamanship in the best of weather; in the conditions prevailing at the time the transfer called for expertise and bravery of the highest order. The *Toward*'s crew lacked none of this. With one of the corvettes covering him, Captain Hudson brought his ship under the lee of the *Celtic Star* and, dwarfed by the 8ft-high waves, the tiny motor boat battled across the intervening stretch of angry water. The return journey with the casualty was even more hazardous. By the time the operation was completed, the *Toward* and her escort were 21 miles astern of SC 118.

Further east, the wolves continued to snap at the heels of the convoy, but each time they tried to close in on the merchantmen they found themselves under attack, either from the air or from the sea. After dark, with only Proudfoot's escorts defending the convoy, it was inevitable that sooner or later the U-boats would make a breakthrough. This seemed to come at 2005, when Heinz Franke's *U262* sank the small Polish steamer *Zagloba*, but the *Lobelia* was quick to close the gap. Obtaining an asdic contact, the French-manned corvette carried out four attacks which sent *U262* running for cover, leaving oil patches behind on the surface.

The second attempt was made at 2245, and this time the American destroyer *Babbitt* (Lieutenant-Commander S. F. Quarles) was to hand. Her radar detected a U-boat closing the convoy 32 miles on the convoy's port bow, and Quarles gave chase. Unfortunately, *Babbitt* was able to fire only three charges from her port thrower before the U-boat succeeded in getting inside her turning circle. Quarles then called off the hunt owing to the proximity of the convoy.

There was a short lull, and then, a little before midnight, the opportunity for which the *Pfeil* boats had been waiting came. *Campanula*, guarding the starboard quarter of SC 118, had moved up on the flank, allowing Siegfried von Forstner, one of the few experienced commanders on the scene, to bring *U402* in from the south. As he did so *Toward*, returning from her mission of mercy, reached her station at the rear of column twelve. Although *Toward* was a mere 1,500 tons gross, she presented a tempting target to von Forstner, who promptly put a torpedo into her. Hit just forward of the bridge, the rescue ship quickly developed a heavy list, and Captain Hudson gave the order to abandon ship.

Although the *Toward*'s crew were well practised in boat handling, the combination of the ship's heavy list and the rough seas capsized each lifeboat as it hit the water. Only one boat righted itself, and sixteen men sought refuge on board. *Campanula* came to their rescue, but in manoeuvring to pick up the survivors the corvette struck the waterlogged boat, again capsizing it and throwing all the unfortunate occupants into the sea. Only quick action by *Campanula*'s crew saved them. They were the only ones to survive the sinking of the *Toward*, a gallant little ship that had done so much to rescue others. Captain Hudson, 54 of his crew and the luckless casualty from the *Celtic Star* went down with the *Toward*.

The second spread from *U402*, fired five minutes after she hit the *Toward*, found its mark in a more substantial target, the 6,625-ton American tanker

*Robert E. Hopkins*, the rear ship of column eleven. The tanker stayed afloat for twenty minutes, then von Forstner delivered the *coup de grâce*.

Baron von Forstner had shown the way, but in the process had stirred up a hornets' nest, and only one other boat, *U614*, was able to join him inside the escort screen. Both the U-boat and her commander, Kapitänleutnant Wolfgang Sträter, were on their first war patrol and yet to open their score. The 5,730-ton British steamer *Harmala*, homeward bound from Rio de Janeiro and straggling astern of column seven, offered the ideal opportunity for this shortcoming to be rectified, and Sträter took quick advantage. Firing a full spread of four torpedoes, he blasted open the *Harmala*'s thin plates and she went to the bottom, taking 40 of her crew of 64 with her.

Proudfoot's escorts were now racing in to deal with the wolves savaging the stragglers at the rear of the rear of SC 118, but before they arrived von Forstner fired at the 9,272-ton Norwegian motor tanker *Daghild*, the last ship in the starboard wing column. The tanker, carrying the 143-ton tank landing craft *LCT 2335* on her deck, staggered under the force of von Forstner's torpedoes but did not sink. Buoyed up by her cargo tanks, she remained afloat for another 22 hours, and it took two more torpedoes, one each from *U614* and *U608*, to seal her fate. The landing craft went down with her.

Von Forstner and Sträter then prudently withdrew, leaving SC 118 to reform its disorganised ranks in what remained of the night. But von Forstner was back before dawn, creeping up astern to sink the back-marker of column ten, the *Afrika*, an 8,597-ton ex-Danish motor vessel sailing under the British flag. Moving quickly across to port, von Forstner then sank first the American troopship *Henry R. Mallory*, and then the Greek steamer *Kalliopi*. It was a violent end to a violent night, during which Siegfried von Forstner had moved 28,000 tons nearer to his coveted Knight's Cross.

At daylight on the 7th, with the convoy within 600 miles of Iceland, patrolling Liberators again arrived overhead and shattered nerves were calmed. The news that the corvette *Lobelia* had destroyed the convoy's most persistent shadower, *U609*, at dawn with a single depth charge attack gave another boost to morale. Von Forstner, persevering in his efforts to inflict maximum damage, was forced by patrolling aircraft to make no fewer than seven undignified crash dives during the course of the day. Night came with word that a Liberator of 220 Squadron, flying out of Londonderry, had caught *U624* (Kapitänleutnant Graf Ulrich von Soden-Fraunhofen) on the surface 55 miles astern of the convoy and destroyed her with depth bombs. When the British aircraft dropped out of the sky, the Count was engaged in transmitting to base a lengthy report of the previous night's action around SC 118. His urge to chatter cost him dear; there were no survivors from *U624*.

During the night of 7/8th the weather moderated considerably, and the U-boats intensified their attacks on the convoy. The first of these came at 2230 but was thwarted by HMS *Beverley*. Picking up an unidentified radar echo on the starboard quarter of the convoy, the destroyer fired starshell which revealed a U-boat on the surface between herself and the starboard wing column. The U-boat dived and *Beverley* raced in to the attack with Hedgehog bombs, but none found their mark. Five minutes later there was another alarm, which had unintentional but disastrous results. The steamer *Adamas*, out of station somewhere between columns six and seven, sighted a surfaced U-boat to starboard. *Adamas* sheered away from the danger, and in doing so ran across the bows of the *Samuel Huntingdon*, the third ship in column six. The resulting collision was unavoidable, the *Adamas* literally impaling herself on the *Samuel Huntingdon*'s bows. She later sank. The U-boat, perhaps content at sinking an enemy ship without the use of shell or torpedo, made herself scarce before the escorts arrived on the scene.

Later that night, von Forstner returned to claim his seventh victim from the ranks of SC 118. At 2345, fifteen minutes before the change of the watch, when perhaps the convoy's lookouts were flagging, *U402* glided in unseen and torpedoed the British steamer *Newton Ash*, at the rear of column five. The 4,625-ton Newcastle ship, loaded with a full cargo of grain for Hull, went down in a few minutes, leaving only four survivors from a total crew of 43.

Air cover over the convoy was continuous from daylight on the 8th, and the U-boats carried out only two further attacks. One of their number, Sträter's *U614*, was badly damaged on the 9th by an aircraft of 206 Squadron and made for home, cutting short her first war patrol. That evening, Dönitz decided that nothing further could be achieved, and ordered the *Pfeil* group to break off, and so ended the battle for Convoy SC 118. Of the 21 U-boats deployed against the convoy, only five had used their torpedoes during the four-day operation, but these had accounted for thirteen ships with a gross tonnage of nearly 60,000 tons, and another 5,000-tonner, the *Adamas*, had been an indirect casualty. More than half of the total tonnage sunk went to Siegfried von Forstner, who was awarded his Knight's Cross on return to base, but the U-boats had not had it all their own way. Three boats, *U187* (Oberleutnant-zur-See Ralph Münnich), *U609* (Kapitänleutnant Klaus Rudloff) and *U624* (Graf Ulrich von Soden-Fraunhofen) were lost, and four more so seriously damaged by depth charges and Hedgehog bombs that they were forced to withdraw. In all, three-quarters of the U-boats involved were attacked by the ships of Proudfoot's B2 Group, some of whom ran out of depth charges before the action was finished.

Dönitz called it 'the hardest convoy battle of the whole war'. The Admiralty commented grudgingly:

That the ships in the escort were individually efficient is proved by the numbers of encounters that they had with the enemy and the amount of damage they inflicted. Had the escort been equally well trained as a group the encounter might well have been one of the highlights of the U-boat war.

The official inquiry into the action concluded:

> The inability of the escort to fend off the attacks on the convoy on the night of the 6th/7th was due to the fact that it was a scratch team. There were present at this time ten escorts with two more in the vicinity; six of these were destroyers. A force of this size, drilled as a team, understanding the Senior Officer's ideas and intentions, should be ample to compete with such a situation as this. In this case, however, the ships had not worked together previously and were led by a Senior Officer whom they did not know. A further handicap was the fact that a proportion of the force joined after the main escort. There are various criticisms which can be made of the conduct of operations during this period, but the point is that the things which went wrong on this occasion are those which can always be expected to go wrong when escorts are made up of the miscellaneous collection of ships which have had no previous experience of each other.
>
> The main point, of more general interest, which arises is the question of the positioning of the Senior Officer. Undoubtedly in this case, and probably in most cases, he should be astern where he can see what is happening. Had the Senior Officer of this convoy stationed himself astern during the night of the 6th/7th he would have realised at once that ships were being torpedoed and would have had a better idea of the direction of the attack; he would have realised that escorts stationed in the threatened sectors were absenting themselves for long periods, and would thus have been able to reorganise the screen so as to fill the gaps or order them back to the convoy.

Commander Proudfoot may not have emerged from the action with his reputation intact, but he was not solely to blame for the fiasco of SC 118. The convoy had suffered unacceptable losses despite continuous air cover during daylight hours on the 8th and 9th, and a surface escort twice the size normally accompanying a comparable convoy. The lessons to be learned were that no escort group, no matter how big, could function efficiently unless the ships were part of a co-ordinated team, and that air cover at night was essential, which meant fitting all very-long-range aircraft with Leigh Lights.

# 12

# The Turning Point

The five boats of the *Haudegen* pack, called in to assist *Pfeil* in the attack on Convoy SC 118, had reached the end of their endurance when the action was finally called off. They were then ordered home to refuel and rearm, and, it was hoped, to allow their exhausted crews time to regenerate their enthusiasm for the fight. Meanwhile, the winter storms raged unabated and the long-suffering merchant ships continued to ply their trade across the great Atlantic, unchallenged, for the moment, by the latest in their long line of enemies. But the U-boats had not gone away; *Neptun*, *Ritter* and *Knappen*, 60 boats in all, were still on station in the Greenland Gap. These three packs Dönitz now formed into a patrol line on the meridian of 30° West, beginning in 63° North and stretching southwards for 600 miles to 53° North. There were large gaps in the line and, given the appalling weather, it is not surprising that the convoys got through. Over a period of eleven days SC 119, HX 225, ON 164 and HX 226 all slipped through the German net undetected. In fact, during that time only one Allied ship, the American tanker *Atlantic Sun*, was sunk in the North Atlantic. This deep-loaded 11,000-tonner, sailing alone and unescorted, had the great misfortune to cross paths with *U607*, commanded by one of Dönitz's young aces, Ernst Mengersen. The *Atlantic Sun* went to the bottom, taking all her crew with her.

It seemed that the rest of February 1943 might be a singularly unfruitful period for the U-boats, but on the 17th one of the returning *Haudegen* boats sighted a westbound convoy. This was ONS 165, escorted by Escort Group B6, which included the battle-hardened British destroyers *Viscount* and *Fame*. The convoy was on the eastern edge of the Greenland Gap, with 300 miles of ocean to cross without the benefit of air cover, and to Dönitz this seemed a heaven-sent opportunity for *Haudegen* to strike another blow against the Allies before withdrawing. Selecting those boats with torpedoes still in hand, the Admiral formed a new group, *Taifun*, and sent it in pursuit of ONS 165, meanwhile setting up a rendezvous for refuelling from U-tankers after the attack.

The action was slow to be joined, for although the shadowing U-boat held on tenaciously to the convoy, sending regular homing signals, the elements had thrown in their lot with the Allies. Storm-force winds, mountainous seas, strong currents, fog and excessive atmospheric radio interference all combined against the other *Taifun* boats, and for two days they struggled to make contact. When at last they found the convoy, they immediately ran into a hot reception. The escort had been alerted to their coming by HF/DF, and *Viscount* and *Fame* pounced as they approached. *Viscount* dispatched *U69* (Kapitänleutnant Ulrich Gräf), while *Fame* disposed of *U201* (Oberleutnant-zur-See Günther Rosenberg). In return, *U403* (Kapitänleutnant Heinz-Ehlert Clausen) sank the Greek steamer *Zeus*, and *U525* (Kapitänleutnant Hans-Joachim Drewitz) put an end to the long career of the 33-year-old London tramp *Radhurst*. The sinking of two elderly merchantmen carrying no cargo was poor recompense for the loss of two U-boats and their crews. Dönitz commented: 'For us, this engagement, which had resulted in the sinking of two enemy ships and the loss of two U-boats, was depressing'.

While the *Taifun* pack tried in vain to press home the attack on ONS 165, on 18 February, the Luftwaffe's radio intercept service in Paris obtained DF bearings of an aircraft engaged in escorting an Allied convoy. The bearings indicated a position some 300 miles west of the North Channel, and from information already to hand the convoy was identified as either ON 166 or ON 167, both expected westbound. Further bearings taken on the 19th indicated that the convoy was heading to the south-west. *Ritter* and *Knappen*, the two packs best placed, were ordered to intercept.

Six days earlier, the 7,264-ton British cargo liner *Manchester Merchant* had left her home port and transited the 35-mile-long Ship Canal on a typical grey winter's morning. As the steamer made her painfully slow way down the narrow canal, swathes of cold drizzle borne on a keening westerly wind swept across her decks, washing the accumulated grime of the land from her paintwork. Commanded by Captain F. D. Struss and carrying a crew of 67, the three-year-old *Manchester Merchant* reached the estuary of the Mersey in late afternoon and entered the open sea, where the cloud base was down and the heave of the swell ominous. The Atlantic crossing promised to be uncomfortable. Not that this would deter this ship, or those who sailed in her, for they were carrying on a long and unbroken tradition dating back to 1898, when the first Manchester liner set out to reach the St Lawrence and trade with the Canadian ports. Over the years the pattern became established; general cargo outward, grain and apples, and perhaps some live cattle, homewards. But this was 1943 and the war had changed all that. The *Manchester Merchant* was under the control of the Admiralty, and although she would cross the Atlantic, her movements beyond that were at the Admiralty's whim. Captain Struss knew only that his first destination port was New York.

The *Manchester Merchant* reached the North Channel that evening, and there joined the fast westbound convoy ON 166, taking up position at the head of column eleven. Consisting of 63 British, American, Norwegian, Greek and Panamanian merchantmen, ON 166 was escorted by Escort Group A3, an American-dominated group led by Captain Paul R. Heineman, USCG. Heineman, sailing in the Coastguard cutter *Spencer*, had with him the *Campbell*, another Coastguard cutter, the Canadian corvettes *Rosthern*, *Trillium*, *Chilliwack* and *Dauphin*, and the British corvette *Dianthus*. *Spencer* and *Campbell*, Treasury-class cutters of 2,750 tons displacement, were formidable ships, twice the size of a British destroyer and the largest convoy escorts in service in the North Atlantic at that time. Carrying a crew of 243, the cutters were well armed and equipped with HF/DF, but with a top speed of only 22kt were no real substitute for destroyers. However, with the exception of *Chilliwack*, returning to Canada for a long-overdue refit, the members of the group were well used to working together. All of the corvettes were equipped with 271 radar.

Strategically placed at the rear of the convoy, like an ambulance riding station on a line of battle, was the rescue ship *Stockport*, her boats swung out and scrambling nets rigged, ready for action. Built in 1911 for the London & North Eastern Railway's Harwich to the Hook of Holland run, the 1,683-ton *Stockport* was showing some effects of her advanced age but, like all her breed, she was a stout, well-manned ship.

Once clear of the north of Ireland, ON 166 ran into the first of the westerly gales that were to plague it for much of the Atlantic crossing. The convoy adhered to the Admiralty routeing, but at considerable cost, for the ships were ploughing directly into the weather and suffered greatly. For the first four days the average speed was down to less than 5kt, and improved only slightly when, on the 16th, course was altered to the south-west, bringing the wind and sea around on to the bow. By the 20th, the convoy having progressed to only 650 miles west of Fastnet, already nine ships were straggling. Heineman did his utmost to protect the stragglers, but his team, severely hampered by the atrocious weather, was just not large enough.

The seventeen U-boats forming the *Knappen* and *Ritter* groups were also suffering at the hands of the weather as they strove to maintain their extended patrol line along the 30th meridian, through which they hoped ON 166 would pass. From time to time individual boats were granted a respite from the weather when they were allowed to break away to refuel from the U-tankers *U460* and *U462*, then on station some 500 miles north of the Azores. Otherwise, the wait was long and uncomfortable.

The U-tankers, appropriately nicknamed 'milch cows', were broad-beamed Type XIV U-boats of 1,700 tons displacement. They carried no torpedoes for their own use, the space usually taken by these being given over to tanks containing 700 tons of fuel oil. This was sufficient to refuel twelve

Type VIIs, and extend their patrol by four or five weeks. In addition, the tankers, which were commanded by experienced captains and had a doctor on board, were able to supply torpedoes, ammunition, spare parts, food and water, and specialist crew replacements. At the best of times the role of the 'milch cows' was a hazardous one, for their great size made them slow to crash-dive when surprised on the surface. In the weather prevailing in the North Atlantic in the winter of 1943 their task was doubly difficult. However, during the time *U460* and *U462* were on station off the Azores they supplied 27 operational boats with fuel and supplies. This inevitably involved a great deal of wireless traffic, and although their crews, and those of the boats being supplied, lived on a knife-edge of expectancy, their activities were not once interrupted by the Allies. But *U462*'s luck ran out five months later, when she was on her way from Bordeaux, in company with *U461*, to take up station off the Cape Verde Islands. As they crossed the Bay of Biscay the U-tankers were spotted by an American Liberator on patrol, which was then joined by British aircraft. The U-boats attempted to fight it out on the surface, relying on their batteries of anti-aircraft cannon to protect them, but this was a fatal mistake. The *U462* was sunk by a homing torpedo dropped by a Halifax bomber, while *U461* was destroyed by a Sunderland of RAF Coastal Command. The *U460* survived a few months longer, finally succumbing to the depth charges of aircraft from the US Navy carrier *Card* in the North Atlantic. Of the nine U-tankers built, all had been sunk by the middle of 1944. Their role in the Atlantic battle had been a vital one, but their inability to crash-dive quickly brought about their eventual downfall.

Escorts also needed to replenish their bunkers on the long ocean passage, and a feature of ON 166 was that three tankers in the convoy, although empty of cargo, carried fuel oil for the corvettes. Refuelling at sea was an operation only newly introduced. Difficult enough in calm weather, it was a hair-raising experience in anything more than a fresh breeze. The procedure was for the escort to position close astern the tanker, which floated aft a light manilla steadying line. This was picked up by the escort and made fast in the bows of the ship to assist in station keeping while refuelling was in progress, care being taken not to put any weight on the line. A rubber hose was then floated aft from the tanker, hauled aboard with a grappling iron and connected to a fuelling point on the forecastle head of the escort. The pumping of oil then began, a great deal of skilful ship handling being required by both vessels to avoid breaking the steadying line and the hose. During ON 166's 14-day crossing of the Atlantic, escorts were successfully refuelled on no fewer than nine occasions, even in storm-force winds, which says a great deal for the skill and endurance of the men involved.

Sunday 21 February dawned for ON 166 much the same as the previous nine days, with grey, scudding clouds at mast-top height, the great ocean in an angry turmoil, and the interminable westerly wind screaming in the rigging. Having covered almost 1,000 miles without sight or sign of the enemy, and it being Sunday, there was an effort, in the British merchantmen at least, to adhere to normal routine. The weekly treat of bacon and eggs for breakfast was followed by captain's inspection and a roast beef lunch, but this display of apparent indifference to the war was rudely shattered in the early afternoon, when the Admiralty flashed a warning that a U-boat was shadowing the convoy. There was a rush to action stations, the sanctity of the Sabbath being abandoned.

The convoy's shadower was *U225*, commanded by Oberleutnant-zur-See Wolfgang Leimkühler, who, although on his first war patrol, already had a proven record. In an attack on ONS 154 he had sunk two ships and damaged three others, including the 14,919-ton *Président Francqui* and the tanker *Scottish Heather*, which he torpedoed while she was supplying oil to the corvette *Chilliwack*. However, Leimkühler was no match for Captain Paul Heineman, who, on receiving the Admiralty's warning of a shadowing U-boat, took *Spencer* and two of his corvettes to sweep astern of the convoy. The *U225* was sighted eight miles behind the rear ships, and although Leimkühler dived promptly, Spencer's sonar locked on to the U-boat, and in a brief skirmish it was destroyed by depth charges. Wolfgang Leimkühler and his crew perished.

Although *U225* had paid the price for her attempt to hold on to ON 166, she had done her work well, initiating a bitter conflict that, during the next four days, would rage over more than 1,000 miles of ocean. In the dreadful prevailing weather, much of the equipment of both escorts and U-boats was rendered useless, and the fight was reduced to a battle of wits, backed up by raw courage.

In response to Leimkühler's signals, the seventeen boats of the *Knappen* and *Ritter* packs, some of whom were then only 50 miles or so ahead of ON 166, lost no time in closing in on the convoy. The first to arrive were *U332* (Oberleutnant-zur-See Eberhard Hüttemann) and *U603* (Kapitänleutnant Hans-Joachim Bertelsmann). They made contact with ON 166 shortly after noon that day, when *Spencer* and the two corvettes were still nine miles astern and slamming into the heavy seas as they fought to regain station. With only *Campbell*, commanded by Captain T. L. Lewis, USCG, and the three remaining corvettes to cover the convoy, Hüttemann and Bertelsmann had little difficulty in slipping through the screen. For some perverse reason they both then proceeded to attack the same ship, the unfortunate Norwegian motor tanker *Stigstad*. The *U332* fired first, hitting the 5,964-ton ship with one torpedo. Six minutes later *U603* weighed in with two more torpedoes, both of which found their mark. The *Stigstad*, her back broken, sank fifteen minutes later.

When it became apparent that the convoy was under attack, Captain Lewis, commanding the escort in the absence of Heineman, took immediate retaliatory action, but it was too late. Hüttemann and Bertelsmann had already fled the scene. It only remained for the *Stockport* to drop back to pick up the few oil-covered wretches who had survived the sinking of the *Stigstad*. For the rest of the day, ON 166 was left in peace to continue its unending struggle with the elements.

As the hours ticked by, with the ships of ON 166 enjoying what could surely be only a temporary respite, 150 miles astern the next westbound convoy, ONS 167, was in trouble. Outward bound from Biscay on her second war patrol, *U664* (Kapitänleutnant Adolf Graef) made a chance sighting of the slow convoy and radioed the news to base. When Dönitz was informed he ordered Graef to shadow ONS 167 while other outward-bound boats were rounded up to form the *Sturmbock* pack and dispatched to support *U664*. As it happened, the boats called upon were well scattered and failed to make contact with the convoy, or with one another. On the night of the 21st Graef could contain himself no longer and launched a lone attack on ONS 167, sinking with one spread of torpedoes the 4,659-ton American steamer *Rosario* and the Panamanian tanker *H. H. Rogers*, a ship of 8,807 tons. In the furore that followed the sinkings Graef lost contact, and although the *Sturmbock* boats contrived to work around ahead of the convoy, setting up a patrol line in its path on the 23rd, their efforts were thwarted by poor visibility. By the 25th ONS 167 was under the protection of air cover from Newfoundland, and Dönitz was obliged to call off his wolves.

The calm over Convoy ON 166 was shattered when the sun went down, for other U-boats had by then arrived and were eager to attack. But by this time Heineman and his ships had rejoined the escort, and with seven escorts in place around the convoy and the bad weather continuing, approach to the merchantmen was difficult. It was not until after 1900 that the first U-boat penetrated ON 166's defences.

Kapitänleutnant Adolf Oelrich, commanding *U92*, was a man with a mission. On his first war patrol with the *Vorwärts* group in September 1942 he had failed miserably, making three separate attacks on Convoy ON 127 and expending twelve torpedoes at a cost of some 480,000 Reichmarks without registering a single hit. In fact, Oelrich's only success during that uninspiring voyage had been the sinking of the 7,662-ton British steamer *Clan Mactaggart*, which he caught sailing alone near the Straits of Gibraltar. With ON 166 Oelrich intended to remedy his past shortcomings, and he began by lining up his sights on the largest ship in the convoy, the 9,990-ton British steamer *Empire*

*Trader.* This time Oelrich's torpedoes ran true, and the ship staggered and fell out of the convoy, though she did not sink immediately, as Oelrich believed. The *Empire Trader* was an old ship, in her 35th year, but she was strong, and in ballast. Her engines had escaped damage, and later that night she set off for the Azores, escorted by the corvette HMCS *Dauphin.* In detaching *Dauphin* Heineman was taking a grave risk, one he was later to regret bitterly.

Immediately following the torpedoing of the *Empire Trader* the convoy was lit by starshell fired by the escorts, and Oelrich quickly retired into the darkness. He returned again seven hours later, when, just before 0200 on the morning of the 22nd, either by chance or by intent, he singled out the second-largest ship of ON 166, the 9,348-ton Norwegian whale factory ship *N. T. Nielsen Alonso,* bringing up the rear of column two. Oelrich fired a fan of three FAT torpedoes, the first and third of which scored hits. The *Nielsen Alonso* was another survivor from the early days of steam, built in 1900 when Roald Amundsen was still a young man dreaming of conquering the South Pole, and she was not a ship to be sunk easily. She lost speed and straggled astern the convoy, but it was not until three hours later, when *U753* (Korvettenkapitän Alfred Manhardt von Mannstein) put another torpedo into her, that she was abandoned, apparently in a sinking condition.

While Adolf Oelrich had made good his escape after torpedoing the Norwegian whaler, von Mannstein was not so fortunate. It was his bad luck that the British corvette *Dianthus* was close by when he made his attack, and, despite the heavy clutter on the screen caused by the breaking seas, the escort's radar picked up *U753* before she dived. *Dianthus* raced in, firing her Hedgehog with deadly accuracy, and von Mannstein was forced to withdraw. Seriously damaged, *U753* played no further part in the attack on ON 166. As for the *Nielsen Alonso,* the tough old ship stayed afloat for another seven hours before finally being sunk by gunfire from the Polish destroyer *Burza,* on its way to reinforce the convoy's escort.

The *Burza* was one of three Polish Blyskawica-class destroyers that had escaped from the Germans in 1939. She was a ship of 2,144 tons displacement, armed with seven 4.7in guns and six 21in torpedo tubes, and had a top speed of 37kt. Moreover, the *Burza* had a reputation as a ruthless fighting ship. Heineman, aware that the wolves were gathering around his helpless charges, welcomed her with open arms. The appearance of the destroyer also had its effect on the U-boats, which pulled back to await the cover of night.

The first to make contact was *U606,* commanded by Oberleutnant-zur-See Hans Döhler, which came in from the port side. Döhler, who had not sunk a ship since October 1942, when he took part with the *Puma* group in an attack on Convoy HX 212 (ironically also escorted by A3), approached with caution, closing with the leading ships of the convoy. At 1925, one-and-a-half hours after darkness had drawn a kindly cloak over the horrors of the tempest raging around ON 166, Döhler fired all four bow tubes and signalled the beginning of a night of horror. The 6,615-ton Glasgow steamer *Empire Redshank*, in the lead of column one, was first to be hit. Almost simultaneously, Döhler's second torpedo crashed into the side of the 5,687-ton American *Chattanooga City* at the head of column two, and then another American, the 4,959-ton *Expositor* stationed immediately astern of the *Chattanooga City*, staggered as the third shot went home. The *Chattanooga City* went down in nine minutes; the two others lingered on for some hours. The *Empire Redshank* was sunk by the corvette *Trillium*, while the *Expositor* received its *coup de grâce* at the hands of *U303* (Kapitänleutnant Karl-Franz Heine) in the early hours of the 23rd.

The destroyer *Burza*, covering the port beam of ON 166, obtained a firm radar contact soon after the three merchantmen were torpedoed, and hurtled into the attack. HMCS *Chilliwack*, which by then had a visual sighting of *U606*, joined in the fray. Döhler crash-dived and both escorts waded in with depth charges. Slammed by the sustained blast of a rain of 500lb Torpex-filled canisters, *U606* sank like a stone with water pouring in through her conning tower hatch, which had not been properly sealed in the rush to dive. Her terrified crew made frantic efforts to halt her downward plunge, but she reached 750ft – 200ft deeper than her maximum operating depth – with all her compressed air used up in blowing tanks, before she levelled off. Then, over-compensated, she shot to the surface out of control.

By now the Coastguard cutter *Campbell* had joined the fight, and she was nearest to *U606* when she erupted from the depths. *Campbell's* commanding officer, Captain Lewis, showed no hesitation, ringing for full speed and altering course directly for the U-boat. With her guns adding to the hail of shot directed at *U606* by the other escorts, *Campbell* charged, her sturdy bows cleaving through the 30ft seas in a welter of foam and spray. She hit the U-boat squarely abaft the conning tower, all but rolling it completely over. Although *U606* was mortally wounded and began to sink, Lewis found when he backed his ship away that the cutter had also suffered major damage in the encounter. Her bows were completely stove in and she was making water fast. From then on she was out of the fight, and would end up under tow to St John's, Newfoundland. Whether Lewis's action in ramming the U-boat was advisable is a matter for debate, but the end result was the loss to ON 166 of a valuable escort that it could ill afford to be without.

It was reported that, as *Campbell* was backing away, the conning tower hatch of the stricken U-boat flew open and some of her crew came tumbling out. Among them were the First Watch Officer and the Engineer, both of whom appeared to be toasting their misfortune with bottles of champagne. Twelve men were rescued by one of the corvettes, but 38 others went down with the

*U606*, including Hans Döhler, who had a reputation of being one of the most hated commanders in the U-boat service. This might explain the champagne.

With *Campbell* disabled and under tow for St Johns, Heineman recalled the corvette *Dauphin*, ordering her to sink the damaged *Empire Trader*, which she was escorting, and rejoin at all speed. But the *Dauphin* was already 180 miles astern of the convoy and, steaming into the teeth of the storm, she could not hope to be back with the escort group for at least 24 hours. By then she would be too late to help stem the disaster about to overtake ON 166.

The sinking of *U606* gave the convoy a short breathing space, but in the small hours of the 23rd the U-boats were back again, seeking to break through the now thinly stretched screen of escorts. The *U604* (Kapitänleutnant Horst Höltring) claimed the first victim of the new day, and this without risk to herself. Höltring found the rescue ship *Stockport* labouring in heavy seas astern of the convoy, returning to her station after picking up survivors from the *Empire Trader*. The tiny rescue ship, with no one in sight to come to her aid, went to the bottom, taking her crew of 64 and the 91 survivors she had on board with her. There can be no doubt that Höltring was well aware that he had a rescue ship in his sights, for, although they were not marked, these ships were easily identified by their size and construction. In the autumn of 1942 Dönitz had issued the following order to all U-boats:

> There is generally in every convoy a so-called rescue ship, a special ship of up to 3,000 tons appointed to pick up the shipwrecked after U-boat attack. Most of these ships are equipped with aircraft and large motor-boats and are strongly armed and very manoeuvrable, so that they have been described frequently by Commanders as U-boat traps. Their sinking is of great value in regard to the desired destruction of the steamers' crews.

The Admiral had greatly exaggerated the offensive capabilities of the rescue ships; they carried no aircraft and only a few guns for defence, although they did have HF/DF, which they sometimes used to great effect. By and large they were ships of mercy, presenting no threat to the U-boats, but, if one of Dönitz's aims was the killing of Allied merchant seamen, then to him they were legitimate targets.

The loss of the *Stockport* was closely followed by another blow. For a time the weather had been too bad for any refuelling to take place, and early on the 23rd the British corvette *Dianthus* found herself so short of oil that she was forced to break away and make for St John's. She arrived there with her bunker tanks running dry, having made the last few miles burning a mixture of oils scrounged from her paint locker.

With *Dianthus* gone, A3 was reduced to four ships, Heineman's cutter *Spencer*, the Polish destroyer *Burza*, and the two Canadian corvettes *Rosthern* and *Trillium*. This was a force still to be reckoned with, but totally inadequate to defend the 56 merchantmen remaining. The convoy was then 700 miles east of Newfoundland and without air cover.

The wolves resumed their attack soon after the change of the watches at 0400 on the 23rd. By then *U628* (Kapitänleutnant Heinrich Hasenschar) had worked her way deep into the convoy, and was positioned between columns six and seven. Hasenschar had FAT torpedoes on board and used them judiciously, singling out two tankers, the *Winkler*, a Panamanian of 6,097 tons, and the 6,409-ton Norwegian *Glittre*. Both were hit but did not sink, once again illustrating that the longitudinal framing and many watertight bulkheads of the tankers made them extremely difficult to destroy when they were in ballast. The *Winkler* was later sunk by three torpedoes from *U223* (Kapitänleutnant Karl-Jurg Wächter), and Hans-Joachim Bertelsmann in *U603* used another two torpedoes to finish off the *Glittre*, both ships by then straggling astern of ON 166.

There followed a lull as the coming of dawn was awaited, then, at 0735, when the darkness had softened enough for the outlines of the ships to be seen, the peace was again shattered by the crash of torpedoes. Approaching from the starboard side, *U186* (Kapitänleutnant Siegfried Hesemann) fired two torpedoes at the second ship in the wing column, the 5,401-ton American steamer *Hastings*. She sank in seven minutes. Hesemann then turned his sights on the 6,207-ton British tanker *Eulima*. One torpedo went home, but the tanker stayed afloat for another hour before being sunk by *U186*.

*Spencer* was the only escort on the starboard side of the convoy, and Heineman raced in, dropping depth charges, but the enemy had slipped away. The Senior Officer was now faced with a harrowing decision: what was to be done about the men in the water, the survivors from the four torpedoed ships? Hitherto, the *Stockport* had been on station astern, ready to fall back and carry out her rescue work. Now she was no longer there, having paid the supreme price for her dangerous work; those men in the water would soon die unless someone saved them. To deplete the escort further for this work was suicidal, but Heineman was a compassionate man. He detached the corvettes *Rosthern* and *Trillium* to search for survivors, urging their commanders to be quick. All through the rest of that day, while the two corvettes patiently scoured the grey seas astern for survivors, of which there were precious few, *Spencer* and *Burza* nervously patrolled the perimeter of the convoy. Fortunately, the U-boats were either unaware of the opportunity for a massacre being presented to them or they had lost contact, for there were no more attacks on ON 166 that day. It was not until sunset, a purely arbitrary time on a day of heavy overcast and driving rain squalls, that *U621* (Oberleutnant-zur-See Max Kruschka) came creeping in to fire a brace of torpedoes at random. Kruschka claimed a hit, but in reality his torpedoes were lost without trace.

At 2020, *U707* (Oberleutnant-zur-See Günter Gretschel) torpedoed and sank the 7,176-ton American steamer *Jonathan Sturges*, a straggler, but it was not until two hours later that any determined attack developed on the main body of the convoy. Between 2200 and daylight on the 24th, *U653* (Kapitän-leutnant Gerhard Feiler), *U600* (Kapitänleutnant Bernhard Zurmühlen), *U628* and the persistent Adolf Oelrich in *U92* came in one after the other. Feiler fired at and missed the British ship *Delilian*, but hit the 9,382-ton Dutch motor vessel *Madoera*, using in all seven torpedoes. The *Madoera* remained afloat and reached St John's seven days later. Heinrich Hasenschar in *U628* and Bernhard Zurmühlen in *U600* between them used up five torpedoes to sink the 4,391-ton Norwegian *Ingria*, while Oelrich wasted another two in an abortive strike.

In view of the abundance of targets and the dearth of escorts, the night attack had been an expensive failure, and, as it happened, the U-boats' last opportunity to create havoc was thrown away. Soon after dawn on the 24th *Rosthern* and *Trillium* rejoined, and on their heels came the British destroyers *Montgomery* and *Witherington* from the Western Support Force. There were one or two alarms during the day but, by and large, the rest of the 24th passed peacefully. Furthermore, the weather was moderating, and soon aircraft from Newfoundland would be overhead. There were good grounds for believing that ON 166's long ordeal was fast drawing to a close.

During the night the wind fell away to no more than a gentle breeze from the south-east; the swell was still big, but the sting had gone from the waves. Overhead, the clouds drew back to reveal a friendly yellow moon, and for the first time in twelve days the men in the ships felt safe enough to relax. A good night's sleep seemed a distinct possibility. And it was almost so, until, at 0445 on the 25th, *Spencer*, scouting ahead of the convoy, obtained a sharp RDF echo on the starboard bow. Seven minutes later a torpedo track was sighted and *Spencer's* sonar operators reported a firm contact. Heineman attacked at once, but his target, Heinrich Hasenschar's *U628*, escaped.

Captain Struss of the *Manchester Merchant* was one who found it hard to sleep, and was haunting the bridge long before dawn on the 25th. When a lookout reported Hasenschar's torpedo speeding across the liner's bow, Struss hit the alarm bells and reached for his lifejacket. A few minutes later the *Manchester Merchant*, steaming in the lead of column seven and making a satisfying 10kt, was hit simultaneously by two torpedoes. Struss wrote in his report:

> . . . I looked over the fore part of the bridge and saw water pouring over the forecastle head. The ship was settling rapidly by the head, and as she

was obviously doomed I ordered 'abandon ship, every man for himself'. The three lifeboats were lowered, but they capsized, as the ship was still under way. Some of the crew managed to get three rafts away; I managed to knock one clear, but before I could abandon ship on it I was washed off the bridge deck into the sea by the force of water rushing over the ship. I was pulled under by the suction, but rose to the surface quickly, just in time to see the ship slide under the water. She sank by the head, with the propellers still turning, about 90 seconds after being hit.

. . . I could hear men screaming and shouting all around me, and saw lots of small lifebelt lights bobbing about on the swell, but the situation was such that nobody could help anybody else. After about half an hour, the destroyer HMS *Montgomery* came along and rescued fifteen men who were on a raft, but went away leaving the remainder of the survivors in the water. I suppose she had some reason for going away, but when the men in the water saw the destroyer going, their cries were terrible, and from the splashing in the water I imagine they must have tried to follow. It was then I think that most of my crew in the water were drowned, for after the destroyer had gone, I could only hear moans for a while, and then silence.

Two hours later, just as dawn was breaking, the Canadian corvette *Rosthern* came to pick up the men still in the water. I heard her Commanding Officer shout: "Take the men out of the water first", then I saw a small boat approaching. I was pulled out of the water into the boat, then a sailor, Sorensen, and a fireman named Ince, who unfortunately died of exposure before we reached the corvette. Thirteen other men were picked up from upturned boats, and from rafts. I had by this time been in the water about 22 hours, the temperature of which was 47°, and my body was completely numb when I was rescued . . .

The *Manchester Merchant* was the last ship to go down, lost with 37 men 410 miles east-south-east of Cape Race. Her end signalled the culmination of a fierce running battle fought in the most appalling weather conditions over a distance of 1,100 miles. Convoy ON 166 suffered grievously, despite the unstinting efforts of Heineman's escorts, losing fourteen ships of 88,000 tons, including the irreplaceable *Stockport*. Of the 21 U-boats of the *Knappen* and *Ritter* groups involved in the action, two, *U225* and *U606*, fell to Captain Paul Heineman's ships, while *U623* was sunk by a Liberator of 120 Squadron, Coastal Command, as she raced westwards on the surface to join the fight. The scale of the losses was unacceptable for either side, and marked a turning point in the Battle of the Atlantic. The climax was approaching.

# 13

# Death Rides the Storm

When February 1943 drew to its stormy close, the wolf packs had accounted for 63 Allied merchant ships of 359,328 tons in that month alone. In return, twenty U-boats had been sent to the bottom, but for Britain the arithmetic was all wrong. As a direct result of the activities of Dönitz's wolves her imports were down by three-quarters of a million tons, and the situation was going from bad to worse. When it came to food and the necessities of life, the people of the islands were well used to tightening their belts and keeping the upper lip stiff, but in the matter of oil and the tools of war a crisis was at hand. Britain was soon to be the launchpad for the Anglo-American invasion of Europe, and the huge stockpile of arms and transport for this adventure was not growing at the required rate. Far too much was ending up at the bottom of the Atlantic while on passage from America. And things were about to get worse; by this time Dönitz had increased the number of U-boats operational in the North Atlantic to 180, which did not bode at all well for the convoys struggling to get through in the teeth of the winter gales. To make matters worse, American eyes had turned to the Pacific, where a major naval offensive against the Japanese was in preparation. Few US Naval ships could be spared for Atlantic escort duty.

Captain Paul Heineman's A3 Group was still there, but was stretched beyond the limits of prudence. No sooner had the battered ON 166 been handed over to its local escort south of Newfoundland than the eastbound SC 121 was demanding protection for the Atlantic crossing. A convoy of 59 merchantmen loaded with supplies for the Allied invasion force, SC 121 sailed from New York on 23 February and met up with A3 off St John's four days later, on the 27th. Heineman, again sailing in the Coastguard cutter *Spencer*, still had with him the Canadian corvettes *Trillium*, *Rosthern* and *Dauphin*, and the British corvette *Dianthus*. The only new member of the group was the destroyer USS *Greer*, replacing the damaged cutter *Campbell*.

Commanded by Captain Laurence Frost, USN, the USS *Greer* had a unique claim to fame in that she held the distinction of being largely responsible for America entering the war in the North Atlantic. She was an old ship, being of 1918 vintage, but she was a 35-knotter armed with one 3in and four 4in guns, and twelve 21in torpedo tubes. Moreover, she

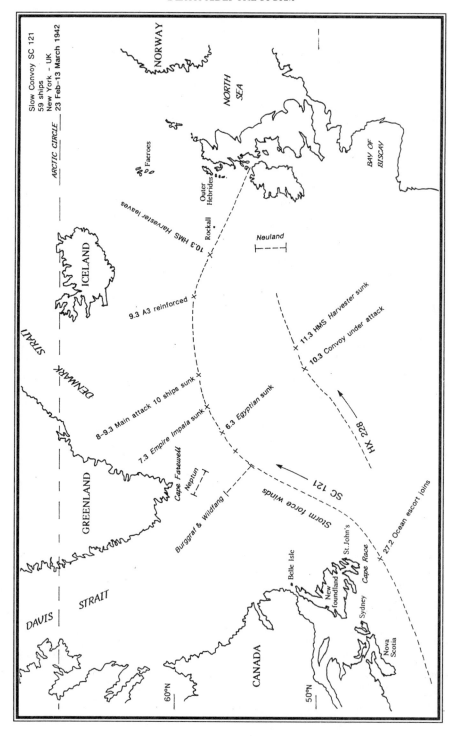

Slow Convoy SC 121
59 ships
New York - UK
23 Feb-13 March 1942

NORWAY

NORTH SEA

BAY OF BISCAY

ARCTIC CIRCLE

Faeroes

Outer Hebrides

Rockall

10.3 HMS Harvester leaves

Neuland

ICELAND

9.3 A3 reinforced

11.3 HMS Harvester sunk

10.3 Convoy under attack

DENMARK STRAIT

8-9.3 Main attack 10 ships sunk

7.3 Empire Impala sunk

6.3 Egyptian sunk

HX 228

Cape Farewell

Neptun

Burggraf & Wildfang

Storm force winds

SC 121

GREENLAND

27.2 Ocean escort joins

Belle Isle

St. John's

New foundland

Cape Race

Sydney

Nova Scotia

DAVIS STRAIT

CANADA

60°N

50°N

and her crew were rested and in the peak of condition, which was more than could be said for the other ships escorting SC 121. Being continuously at sea for two weeks in the most atrocious weather had put an intolerable strain on *Spencer* and the four corvettes. Engines were faltering, half of the group's radar sets were out of action, asdics were unreliable and radio direction finders were acting up. Not least, the escort's crews, tested to the utmost limits by the weather and the enemy, were sorely in need of rest. The prospect of yet another Atlantic crossing, albeit with the wind and sea astern, was not welcome.

When Heineman took over the protection of SC 121 off Newfoundland, the convoy was steaming in fourteen columns, with the Commodore, Captain R. C. Birnie, DSO, RNR (RD), in the Norwegian motor vessel *Bonneville*, leading at the head of column eight. In the rear was the rescue ship *Melrose Abbey*, an ex-coastal passenger ship of 1,908 tons. The *Melrose Abbey*, not to be confused with the steamer of the same name sunk in Convoy ONS 154, in addition to bearing a charmed life, had an impressive record, having covered 42 convoys, in the course of which she had launched her rescue boat on no fewer than 50 occasions.

The loose formation of the convoy – the fourteen columns were advancing on a front seven miles across – worried Heineman, who would have preferred a narrower and tighter order of steaming. Unfortunately, when A3 joined the weather was already so bad as to make any radical change in the formation a hazardous undertaking. For the time being Heineman could do no more than position his six escorts strategically around the convoy, hoping they would be favourably placed to meet an attack from any quarter.

An attack in force was precisely what Admiral Dönitz had in mind for SC 121. As usual he had learned of the sailing of the convoy through the German radio intercept service soon after the ships cleared New York. Initially, Dönitz alerted the *Neuland* pack of thirteen boats, then on station 60 miles south of Cape Farewell. After some consideration he moved the *Neuland* boats further east towards Ireland and formed two more packs, *Burggraf* and *Wildfang*, of seventeen and nine boats respectively. These he deployed across the anticipated path of SC 121 in a long north-west/south-east dog's leg some 450 miles east of Newfoundland. To the north of this, eight boats of a smaller group, *Neptun*, patrolled the waters south of Cape Farewell.

With a total of 34 U-boats strung across the track of SC 121, and another nine acting as backstops in the east, Dönitz's plan for the interception of the convoy seemed foolproof, but nothing is ever certain at sea. Plagued by foul weather, with poor visibility and unreliable communications, the patrol lines had great holes in them. Furthermore, Dönitz had not reckoned with British Intelligence being able to read his signals to the U-boats. Soon after clearing

Newfoundland, Commodore Birnie was ordered to make a substantial diversion to the north, and on 5 March, despite its widespread front, SC 121 sailed through the waiting U-boats unseen. It was only by pure chance that *U405* (Korvettenkapitän Rolf-Heinrich Hopmann), patrolling independently, spotted the convoy when it was 90 miles north-east of the *Burggraf Wildfang* line. Hopmann reported SC 121's position to Dönitz and tucked himself in behind the rear ships.

Being left astern of the convoy they had gathered to ambush, the U-boats were at a distinct disadvantage. Undeterred, Dönitz formed those boats best placed into two new groups, *Westmark* and *Ostmark*, seventeen boats in all, and ordered them to give chase. The *Neuland* group, forming a patrol line 600 miles west of Ireland, he left in place.

By this time SC 121 was sailing through a huge area of low pressure centred over the Denmark Strait, and in the grip of a storm of tremendous proportions. The wind was from the north, full on the beam and blowing force 10, gusting force 11, and carrying blinding squalls of sleet and snow. Regiments of foam-topped, mountainous seas marched in relentlessly from the north and slammed against the unyielding hulls of the deep-laden merchantmen, breaking clean over them and burying their decks in a welter of green, tumbling water. One by one they began to drop out and straggle astern. The escorts, small and fragile in comparison with their charges, suffered a private hell that only those who sailed in the ships could fully describe.

For Captain Paul Heineman, red-eyed and clinging to the bridge rail of the *Spencer* as, beam-on to the steep seas, she sought to roll her masts under, it was ON 166 all over again. The ships he had helped to hold in formation were being slowly scattered to the four points of the compass, romping, straggling, slewing out of line. Heineman's six ships did their utmost to provide a credible defence, but they were out of sight of each other and often out of sight of the convoy itself, and radio communication was at best poor; in the blizzards it was completely ineffective.

At about 2130 on the 6th a moment of panic ensued when *Spencer* sighted two red rockets bursting over the middle of the convoy. Heineman contacted the Commodore and the other escorts, but none had fired the rockets, nor knew who had. Nothing was heard on the distress frequency, 500kcs, so it seemed unlikely that a ship had been torpedoed. Heineman assumed the rockets had been fired in error and the culprit was unwilling to own up. It was a wrong assumption, and was to have serious consequences. The red flares (not rockets) were in fact a signal between two U-boats of the *Westmark* pack, *U566* (Kapitänleutnant Gerhard Remus) and *U230* (Kapitänleutnant Paul Siegmann). These boats had caught up with SC 121 after dark and, radio communication being made impossible by heavy atmospherics, had resorted to visual signals to maintain contact with each other.

Although *U566* lost touch with SC 121 shortly afterwards, Siegmann held on, painstakingly working his way deep into the convoy until, at 2145, he had in his sights the 2,868-ton Liverpool ship *Egyptian*, the leader of column six. The seas were breaking clean over the conning tower of *U230* as she rolled and wallowed in the trough, and although it was the first time Paul Siegmann had used his weapons in earnest in this war, his aim was steady. One of a fan of four torpedoes found its mark in the engine room of the *Egyptian* and she was stopped in her tracks; her head came up into the wind, and she drifted sideways out of the convoy, listing heavily to starboard. From her bridge two rockets climbed skywards and burst in a shower of brilliant white stars, visible only for a fraction of a minute before they were blotted out by a passing squall. The *Egyptian*'s distress rockets were sighted from the bridge of the *Spencer* and also by the corvette *Rosthern*, but negative reports came in from the Commodore and the other escorts. *Rosthern* searched on the starboard quarter of the convoy but found nothing. Heineman took no further action, and the passing of the *Egyptian* went almost unnoticed as, mortally wounded, she drifted astern into the blackness of the storm-filled night. Only the ship next in line astern of her, the 6,116-ton *Empire Impala*, saw her go.

In accordance with convoy standing orders, the *Empire Impala*, a 23-year-old London tramp, should have held her position in the convoy, leaving the better equipped rescue ship *Melrose Abbey* to go to the aid of the *Egyptian*. But, knowing that in the midst of the storm the *Egyptian*'s men did not have long to live, the *Empire Impala*'s master reacted instinctively. He pulled his ship out of line and dropped back to stand by the stricken ship. This decision was prompted by the rigid code of the sea, which demands of all seamen that they put their own lives at stake to save others in distress. Under the prevailing circumstances, with the rescue ship, the Commodore and the SOE unaware that a ship had been torpedoed, perhaps it was a right decision, but the end result was calamitous.

The wolves were gathering around SC 121, among them *U591*, commanded by Kapitänleutnant Hansjürgen Zetsche. Having returned to sea in November 1942 after a long lay-up, *U591* had since made up for her absence, being involved in the attacks on ONS 152, ONS 154 and ON 166. Zetsche's success in these attacks had not been spectacular, but he now had three ships of 13,638 tons to his credit, and had gained a great deal of experience in convoy work. He had also, through his involvement with ON 166, gained a useful addition to his crew. Some time after the Dutch ship

*Madoera* was torpedoed by *U653*, Zetzsche had come across one of the *Madoera's* lifeboats, and had taken from this boat the Dutch ship's chief officer. The prisoner, an experienced navigator, had offered his help in taking sights, and *U591's* position keeping benefited accordingly. Zetzsche was right on target when, at daybreak on the 7th, *U591* came up astern of SC 121. Within a few minutes he had sighted the *Empire Impala* hove-to and attempting to pick up survivors from the *Egyptian*, which had by then sunk. The code of the sea gave way to the exigencies of war, and Zetsche had no compunction in sinking the helpless ship. Of the crews of the *Egyptian* and *Empire Impala*, some 80 men in all, only three survived.

Before he died, the *Empire Impala's* radio officer succeeded in transmitting a distress signal, and this was the first indication Heineman and Birnie had that the rump of their convoy was under attack. For all the good this news did, however, they might as well have remained in ignorance. *Spencer* made an effort to give chase to a U-boat long gone, but the weather had deteriorated even more overnight, and any co-ordinated action was out of the question. Six other merchantmen were straggling astern without protection, but Heineman dare not split his meagre escort force to watch over them. He radioed for help, and was promised that two American and two Canadian escorts would be detached from the westbound Convoy ONS 171. Given the state of the weather, the time of their arrival was a matter for conjecture.

Meanwhile, SC 121 steamed on, the ships labouring in the heavy seas and so widely scattered that the escorts were able to cover only those within visible range, which in the sleet and snow squalls was precious few. Radio communication was erratic, and radar, asdic and RDF were rendered temporarily useless by the fury of the storm. Fortunately for the convoy, the U-boats (there were now twenty in the vicinity) suffered similar problems, perhaps worse, for, sleet and snow apart, breaking waves and flying spray reduced visibility from the conning towers to zero for much of the time. Out of sheer necessity a truce was called on either side.

The action was resumed soon after dawn on the 8th, when the 3,921-ton Hull steamer *Guido*, hopelessly lost and romping ahead ten miles off the starboard bow of the convoy, unfortunately fell in with *U432* (Kapitänleutnant Hermann Eckhardt). Eckhardt had only recently taken command of *U432*, stepping into the shoes of Heinz-Otto Schultze, who in his three voyages in command of the boat had sunk nineteen ships totalling 66,251 tons, earning himself the Knight's Cross. It was a hard example to follow, but Eckhardt was determined to do his utmost. When he sighted the *Guido* making her way to the east, apparently alone, he judged that the gods were on his side. Only one torpedo was required to send the British steamer spiralling to the bottom.

The loss of the *Guido* was witnessed only by her executioner, Hermann Eckhardt, and the rest of the convoy steamed on in ignorance, the men in the ships cursing the weather that made their lives a misery, but at the same time giving thanks that it concealed them from the other enemy lurking somewhere out there in the murk. At noon, in the absence of the sun, dead-reckoning calculations were made of the position, which revealed the convoy to be only 800 miles west-north-west of the North Channel, and soon to come within range of aircraft based in Iceland. It was a cheering prospect.

The noise of the storm and the virtual radio blackout it caused ensured that SC 121's illusion of good fortune continued, even though a few miles astern men were dying unseen and unheard. At 1350 the 5,242-ton *Fort Lamy*, bound from Philadelphia to Liverpool, was hit by a torpedo fired by *U527* (Kapitänleutnant Herbert Uhlig). The *Fort Lamy*, with a huge, 143-ton tank landing craft lashed down on her foredeck, had been experiencing difficulty in the heavy seas for some time, falling further and further astern as her deck cargo threatened to break adrift. When Uhlig found her she had stopped to secure her lifeboats, which were in danger of being swept over the side. One torpedo was enough, for the British ship was carrying a large quantity of ammunition in her holds. She blew up with a roar and a sheet of flame, scattering her remains over the heaving ocean. Of her crew of 49, only three men survived the explosion, and with her passing the Allied invasion force received another setback.

One by one the others were picked off. At 1420 Hansjürgen Zetzsche in *U591* found his second victim, the 27-year-old Yugoslav steamer *Vojvoda Putnik*, hove-to with her steering gear smashed by the seas. Zetzsche's torpedo laid her hull open to the sea, but the *Vojvoda Putnik* was a tough old ship and took more than two hours to sink. The 7,015-ton *Empire Lakeland*, a new ship out of South Shields, went down with all hands at 1858, sunk by *U190* (Kapitänleutnant Max Wintermeyer). She was followed at 2003 by another straggler, the 2,125-ton Newcastle tramp *Leadgate*, torpedoed by *U642* (Kapitänleutnant Herbert Brünning). There were no survivors from the *Leadgate*.

Five brave ships had gone to the bottom unnoticed, and SC 121 steamed on, ignorant of the grave danger closing in on it from all sides. Under the circumstances this was not surprising, for every individual ship, including the escorts, was locked in mortal combat with an ocean gone berserk. The night passed in a cacophony of screaming winds and crashing waves.

The 9th was a day filled with hope and feverish activity. Heineman reported:

During daylight hours on 9th March a number of HF transmissions were DF'd but for various reasons full value in appreciating the U-boat dispositions was not obtained. Chief among these were the endeavours being made at that time to home *Trillium*, one of the escorts who had lost touch, and four escorts joining from Iceland; *Spencer* also experienced difficulty in obtaining the sense of her bearings and it was stated that the performance of *Greer*'s HF/DF was erratic. During this period *Rosthern*, on the starboard beam, expended 44 depth charges in a series of seven promising attacks. A large oil slick was seen with a piece of wood floating in the middle of it.

There was a great sense of relief when, during the day, reinforcements arrived for A3. They were not those ships at first indicated, but the US Coastguard cutters *Bibb* and *Ingham* and the destroyer USS *Babbitt*, despatched from Iceland. The *Babbitt*, fourth-oldest ship in the US Navy and reputed to have been refused when she was offered to the hard-pressed Royal Navy earlier in the war, was nevertheless very experienced in North Atlantic convoy work. The American ships were later joined by the British destroyer *Harvester*, temporarily detached from Convoy HX 228. Commanded by Commander A. A. Tait, HMS *Harvester* was an H-class destroyer of 1,340 tons, having a speed of 35 knots. Built in 1940, she was armed with four 4.7in guns and eight 21in torpedo tubes, making her a powerful addition to A3. In the wake of the warships came British and American long-range aircraft which, despite the low cloud and poor visibility, provided almost constant air cover in the daylight hours, although the scattered nature of the convoy made their task difficult.

It was after darkness closed in and the aircraft had retired to their bases that the U-boats came back. Their attack started with the straggler *Milos*, a Swedish steamer of 3,058 tons, which went down with all hands when *U530* (Kapitänleutnant Kurt Lange) put a torpedo into her. An hour later a U-boat (it may have been Lange) was briefly sighted by the *Raranga* and the *Alcoa Leader*, the rear ships of columns nine and eleven, but little could be done to ward off the attack now to be made on the main body of the convoy. The corvette *Trillium* was still lost somewhere in the storm, and the detection equipment of most of the other escorts had been battered into insensitivity by the weather. Even radio-telephone communication was unreliable.

Twenty-seven U-boats were now gathered around SC 121, and the attack began in earnest. The US steamer *Malantic*, 3,837 tons, second ship of column ten, was the first non-straggler to go, torpedoed and sunk in fifteen minutes by *U409* (Kapitänleutnant Hans-Ferdinand Massmann). She was followed by the Commodore's ship, the Norwegian motor vessel *Bonneville*, leading column eight. The *Bonneville*, also with a tank landing craft on deck, was hit by two torpedoes fired by Rolf-Heinrich in *U405*, and possibly also by one torpedo from *U229* (Oberleutnant-zur-See Robert Schetelig). She went down quickly, taking all on board with her, including the Commodore, Captain Burnie. As the sea was closing over the *Bonneville*, Massmann fired at the 5,989-ton British tanker *Rosewood*, the rear ship of column seven. She broke in two halves, which were later sunk by gunfire from USCG *Bibb*.

With such a vast area to cover, Heineman's ships, most with their radar and asdics out of action, could do little more than rush around firing starshell. The night sky was brilliantly illuminated, but to little effect. *Rosthern*, about 1,000 yards on the starboard quarter, glimpsed a torpedo racing past her stern, and *Dauphin*, three miles on the port quarter, sighted a U-boat, but neither ship made contact with the enemy.

Schetelig struck again a few minutes later, this time at the rear ship of column two. The Cardiff tramp *Nailsea Court*, making a commendable 7 1/2 knots against the heavy seas, was hit in her port side and sank before the boats could be launched. Three men survived the sinking, two of whom were lost when boarding the rescue ship *Melrose Abbey*. Without waiting to see the end of the *Nailsea Court*, Schetelig pushed ahead on the surface to hit the leading ship of column one, the 3,670-ton Glasgow steamer *Coulmore*. She was seriously damaged, but survived to make port under her own steam.

In the midst of the mayhem, HMS *Harvester*, now with 50 survivors on board, was ordered to rejoin HX 228, then some 400 miles to the south of SC 121. Commander Tait was loath to go, but his orders were explicit; all speed to HX 228.

The witching hour of midnight came, and with it the U-boats faded away, but they were back again at daylight on the 10th. Schetelig, having gone deep to reload his tubes during the night, set the ball rolling in the forenoon, firing a spread of two at the Newcastle tramp *Scorton*, the second ship in column five. Both torpedoes missed, and the *Scorton* lived to sail another day.

During the afternoon A3 was further reinforced by the British corvettes *Campion* and *Mallow*, replacing *Harvester*. Coincident with their arrival the weather became even worse, with the wind gusting to hurricane force and virtually paralysing the escort force, for all their energies were devoted to remaining afloat. It was just as well that the U-boats were taking similar punishment, and at times were forced to submerge to escape being swamped. Early on the 11th Dönitz ordered *Westmark* and *Ostmark* to disperse and seek targets in more congenial weather.

Convoy SC 121 was the last North Atlantic convoy in which ships of the US Navy predominated in the escort force, and it had ended in defeat.

Twelve ships of 60,607 tons had gone to the bottom, taking with them nearly 100,000 tons of vital military equipment and several hundred irreplaceable merchant seamen, and this without damage of any sort to the enemy. To be fair to Captain Paul Heineman, he had done his best under the circumstances. The atrocious weather had scattered the convoy over such a wide area that his hard-pressed little ships, with their communications severed and their detection equipment unable to cope with the conditions, had never been in a position to put up a credible defence.

*Harvester* rejoined HX 228 on the afternoon of the 10th, and Commander Tait resumed command of its Anglo-French-Polish escort group B3. This comprised, with *Harvester*, the British destroyer *Escapade*, the Polish destroyers *Garland* and *Burza*, the British corvettes *Narcissus* and *Orchis*, and the three Free French corvettes *Aconit, Roselys* and *Renoncule*. Sailing in support of B3 was the US carrier *Bogue*, with her escorting destroyers *Belknap* and *Osmond-Ingram*. The *Bogue*, a ship of 14,200 tons carrying nine Grumman Wildcat fighters and twelve Grumman Avenger anti-submarine strike aircraft, was the first American aircraft carrier to see service with Atlantic convoys. Her role on this occasion was not notable, for, with force 10 winds prevailing, her aircraft remained in the hangar.

Made up of 60 merchantmen, HX 228 had left New York on 1 March, six days after SC 121, and had been diverted to the south when the attack on the slow convoy began. The Admiralty hoped that the diversion would give HX 228 a clear run, but the new routeing orders were intercepted by *B-Dienst* and Dönitz signalled the *Neuland* pack, then idling 300 miles west of Ireland, to intercept the convoy.

The German attack almost failed to materialise, for by noon on the 10 March HX 228 had all but slipped past the *Neuland* patrol line. It was only by chance that *U336* (Kapitänleutnant Hans Hunger), the southernmost boat of the line, sighted the convoy. The U-boat was in turn herself sighted by a lone aircraft, which with a temporary easing of the wind had managed to take off from the carrier *Bogue*. Unfortunately the aircraft's depth charges jammed in their racks when it attacked, and there was also an unexplained delay in reporting the enemy sighting to the SOE. Meanwhile, *U336* had escaped to signal her sighting to Dönitz. The *U444* (Oberleutnant-zur-See Albert Langfeld) took over from *U336* as shadow, and was later joined by *U221* (Kapitänleutnant Hans Trojer). Hard on the heels of Trojer came *U86* (Kapitänleutnant Walter Schug), *U406* (Kapitänleutnant Horst Dieterichs) and *U757* (Kapitänleutnant Friedrich Deetz). Hunger's *U336* also regained contact.

The attack began soon after dusk, when there was little chance of patrolling aircraft being overhead. Hans Trojer moved in first, and in a swift underwater attack torpedoed the British steamer *Tucurinca* and the American freighters *Andrea F. Luckenbach* and *Lawton B. Evans*. Both the *Tucurinca* and the *Andrea F. Luckenbach* sank, but the torpedo that hit the *Lawton B. Evans* failed to explode.

*Harvester* was first to retaliate. Her asdics picked up *U221* as she crept away, and Tait raced in to drop fourteen depth charges. Contact was lost, but the SOE persisted, first withdrawing to give the impression that he had abandoned the attack, then returning at full speed to drop another pattern of charges. Although *U221* survived, she was so badly damaged that she was forced to break off and make for home.

There was a lull while both sides played a waiting game, and then, at 2032, *U336* made a lone attack. Hans Hunger heard two of his torpedoes detonate and claimed a hit, but no ship was reported sunk or damaged. Oberleutnant Langfeld in *U444*, on the other hand, had better fortune when, after shadowing the convoy since dusk, he found himself in a position to attack. One of his torpedoes hit the 7,197-ton American vessel *William M. Gorgas*, damaging her so severely that her crew abandoned ship. The wreck was disposed of two hours later by *U757*.

Simultaneously with Langfeld's attack on the *William M. Gorgas*, Walter Schug in *U86* and Horst Dieterichs in *U406* both fired pattern-running torpedoes at the 5,464-ton British fruit carrier *Jamaica Producer*. The solid, Clyde-built British ship suffered internal damage but reached port safely. Friedrich Deetz, on his first war patrol, in *U757*, had even worse luck. He was eager to open his score and manoeuvred dangerously close to the Norwegian-flagged *Brant County* before giving the order to fire. The *U757*'s first action almost became her last, for the *Brant County* was loaded with ammunition. The cataclysmic explosion that signalled the end of the Norwegian all but destroyed the U-boat as well. After wasting a torpedo on the wreck of the *William M. Gorgas*, Deetz was then obliged to set course for Biscay. It was four months before *U757* was again ready for sea.

Throughout this latest series of attacks, Tait's escorts fought valiantly to provide cover for the ships in their charge, but, strong as the group was, it ended up running in circles to no good purpose. It was again *Harvester* that made the first contact. She sighted Langfeld's *U444* on the surface and gave chase. Langfeld immediately dived, but Tait had his position, and a well-aimed pattern of depth charges blew the U-boat back to the surface. At a range of only 500 yards Tait opened fire with his 4.7s, at the same time ringing for full speed. The *Harvester* was up to 27 knots when she rammed the damaged U-boat, slicing open her hull. The destroyer's bow was stove in but, more seriously, the half-submerged U-boat became jammed under one of her propeller shafts. After an anxious ten minutes

*U444* slid clear and the two ships drifted apart. In response to Commander Tait's call for help, the French corvette *Aconit*, commanded by Lieutenant de Vaisseau J. M. L. M. Levasseur, arrived on the scene. She caught *U444* in her searchlight as Langfeld was attempting to creep away, and without hesitation Levasseur rammed the U-boat, following up with a pattern of depth charges set to shallow. Only five German survivors were picked up.

The two escorts were now some distance astern of the convoy, and as the damaged *Harvester* could make only 11 knots, Tait sent *Aconit* on ahead. Daylight came, and as *Harvester* limped along on one engine her other propeller shaft collapsed under the strain and she was left drifting engineless in the trough of the waves. This was how Hermann Eckhardt in *U432* found her. Eckhardt went to periscope depth and circled the destroyer warily before firing two torpedoes from close range. *Harvester* broke in two and sank, taking most of her crew with her, including Commander Tait.

Unfortunately for Eckhardt and his crew, who had submerged to 65ft and were celebrating their victory with champagne, *Aconit* was not yet far ahead. The French corvette's lookouts sighted the pall of smoke rising from the sinking destroyer, and Levasseur immediately reversed course and raced back at full speed. A strong asdic contact was obtained as *Aconit* neared the position of the sinking destroyer, and in two attacks Levasseur dropped twenty depth charges and fired 23 bombs from *Aconit*'s Hedgehog. Although *U432* was not badly hit, she lost trim and dived deep. In an effort to halt the dive Eckhardt blew tanks, over-compensated, and the boat shot to the surface, where *Aconit* was waiting. Levasseur opened fire with all of his armament; 4in, 2-pounder and Oerlikons. As the corvette raced towards the U-boat her 4in scored four hits, one in the engine room and three on the conning tower, one of which killed Hermann Eckhardt. The rest of the U-boat's crew were now appearing on deck, and Levasseur slowed down with the intention of putting a boarding party on the submarine, a very difficult feat in the heavy seas running. As might be expected, the corvette rammed *U432* as Levasseur attempted to put her alongside, and the U-boat sank under her. Twenty German survivors were rescued before *Aconit* rejoined the convoy, her bow slightly damaged and her asdic dome smashed.

That night *U440* (Kapitänleutnant Hans Geissler) and *U590* (Kapitänleutnant Müller-Edzards) made a half-hearted attack on a few stragglers at the rear of HX 228, but without success. Next day the weather eased and *Bogue* was able to fly regular patrols, and with aircraft of RAF Coastal Command overhead the *Neuland* boats were called off. Their action would not be greeted with acclaim by Dönitz, for although they had sunk four merchant ships and a destroyer, two of their own number had been lost and two severely damaged. But it was perhaps the Royal Navy that suffered the greatest loss in the sinking of HMS *Harvester* and the death of Commander Tait, a man who would not be easily replaced.

# 14
# The Balance Shifts

The International Load Line Regulations define 'Winter North Atlantic' as running from 1 November to 31 March. It is during these five dismal months that the storms of the Western Ocean reach an awesome climax. The passing of the spring Equinox, when the sun crosses the equator on its journey north, usually signals a return to less-tempestuous times, but in the spring of 1943 it was not so. A foul winter, that had even the most hardened professional seamen wishing for dry land, seemed set to go on and on.

Men in lifeboats apart, the ones who suffered most from the continued onslaughts of the North Atlantic were those who manned Admiral Dönitz's U-boats. When shadowing or attacking a convoy, personal safety and comfort went to the winds, for there was no question of heaving-to or submerging to avoid the worst of the seas. The bridge had to be manned, and, given that a moderate breeze kicked up sufficient spray to interfere with visibility, in a gale waves often crashed down on the conning tower. Personnel on watch wore safety harnesses but, even so, men were washed overboard or injured by the force of the sea. Hubertus Purkhold, in command of *U260*, recorded in his war diary while pursuing an enemy merchantman at the end of March 1943:

> At 2200 I abandoned pursuit. In the attempt to run at high speed before the sea the boat plunged twice. By means of extreme rudders, blowing tanks and reduction of speed I succeeded in getting her to the surface. On the bridge the CO and the watch, after half an hour of this, are nearly drowned. In a very short period five tons of water were shipped through the conning tower hatch, voice pipe and diesel intake.

Although life aboard the big ships was infinitely more comfortable than in the U-boats, they too felt the vindictive power of the sea. The 5,529-ton British motor vessel *Shillong*, commanded by Captain J. H. Hollow, was at sea in the same area and at the same time as *U260*, although their paths did not cross. Hollow reported 60ft waves and severe icing conditions. The *Shillong's* mainmast snapped off above the crosstrees under the weight of accumulated ice, while two of her lifeboats were damaged and two rafts were swept overboard. David Clowe, an apprentice in the *Shillong*, wrote:

The ship carried four lifeboats, but the davits on the port side had been damaged during bad weather just after leaving New York, so that the boats had to be lashed inboard to the boat deck, and could not be launched. It was suggested at the time of the damage that it would be advisable to return to New York for repairs, but as our ship had the reputation of being a 'lucky ship', the Captain considered that it was unlikely that we would be torpedoed, and he therefore thought it unnecessary to return.

Young Clowe had already survived the loss of two ships; the *Trecarrell,* torpedoed in June 1941, and the *Bhutan,* sunk by bombing in June of the following year. On the basis of the 'three-in-a-row' theory, he therefore had serious misgivings about Captain Hollow's decision.

The P & O cargo liner *Shillong,* manned by a crew of 78 and loaded with 9,000 tons of zinc concentrates and 2,000 tons of grain, had left New York on 25 March in the convoy HX 231. Consisting of 61 vessels, 36 British, fourteen American, six Norwegian, three Dutch, one Swede and one Panamanian, HX 231 was a fast convoy carrying 600,000 tons of vital cargo for the United Kingdom. Twenty-two of the ships were oil tankers, and most of the others were first-rate cargo liners like the *Shillong.* The Convoy Commodore was Admiral Sir Charles Ramsey, who flew his flag in the Blue Funnel liner *Tyndareus.*

The ocean escort, Group B7, which took over from the local escort south of Halifax, was led by the dashing Commander Peter Gretton, one of the Royal Navy's most experienced escort group commanders. Gretton was in HMS *Tay,* one of the new 'River'-class frigates, a 20 knots ship of 1,370 tons armed with two 4in guns and six 20mm Oerlikons. With him were the 25-year-old destroyer HMS *Vidette* and the corvettes *Alisma, Pink, Snowflake* and *Loosestrife,* all British. Numerically, B7 was not a particularly strong group to be defending such a large and important convoy, but the ships and the men were all highly-trained and well blooded in action. Under Gretton's experienced hand they had been welded into a first-class team, quick to react and retaliate. There were, however, weaknesses in the group, only one ship, HMS *Tay,* being fitted with HF/DF, and there was no rescue ship attached. In the event of an attack the latter shortcoming would inevitably lead to at least one corvette being occupied in picking up survivors.

In the matter of refuelling his escorts on passage Gretton anticipated no difficulty, given that the weather was not too severe. The convoy had more than the usual complement of loaded tankers, and B7 was well practised in refuelling at sea. The U-boats, on the other hand, had problems. Owing to the increased activity of Allied long-range aircraft and patrols flown from American escort carriers, replenishing bunkers from a U-tanker, which required both boats to lie stopped side-by-side on the surface for some hours, had become an operation fraught with danger. When HX 231 set out to cross the Atlantic, only one U-tanker, *U463*, was at sea, and she had a queue of sixteen U-boats waiting to be topped up. Others had been forced to curtail their patrols and make for home, leaving only the *Löwenherz* pack, comprising fifteen boats, then 400 miles south-east of Cape Farewell, in a position to mount a prolonged attack. By scraping the bottom of his Atlantic barrel, Dönitz succeeded in rounding up another seven boats to reinforce *Löwenherz*, and ordered the enlarged pack to move against HX 231.

When B7 met up with HX 231 off Nova Scotia in the early hours of 30 March, Commander Gretton found the convoy in some disarray, it having run into heavy gales combined with sub-zero temperatures. The signal halyards of all ships were frozen solid, while the signal mast of the Commodore's ship had collapsed under the weight of ice forming on it. Consequently ship-to-ship communication, and in particular the passing of orders by the Commodore, had become virtually impossible. The heavy seas added to the confusion. It took B7 the rest of that day to restore order to the convoy, but by the time darkness fell the stragglers had been rounded up and the 61 merchantmen were steaming in thirteen columns abreast. This presented Gretton with a wide front, almost eight miles across, to cover with his six ships. Although HX 231 was a fast convoy and the U-boats would find it difficult to make contact, there were too many sectors unwatched. Furthermore, with only one ship fitted with HF/DF it would be possible to obtain only a single bearing on any U-boats heard transmitting nearby. Distance off would be a matter of guesswork.

The following three days passed without incident. The wind blew fresh from the north-east, dead ahead in other words, with a rough sea running, but a speed of $10\frac{1}{2}$ knots was maintained. On the afternoon of 3 April, when the convoy was 450 miles due south of Cape Farewell, the first intimation of the presence of the enemy came. *Tay's* W/T operators picked up a transmission from a German shore station which Gretton interpreted as being directed to a U-boat in the vicinity. His fears were somewhat allayed when, two hours later, the Admiralty reported that a convoy to the south of HX 231 had been sighted by U-boats, and would probably soon be under attack. This seemed to suggest that HX 231 might be left alone, but Gretton remained sceptical. He was, therefore, not surprised when, during the night that followed, a stream of coded radio signals was heard from close by, easily recognisable as being from a U-boat. A lone wolf was shadowing them.

An air of nervous expectancy pervaded the convoy for the next 24 hours, word having been passed around the ships that the pack was gathering. All was quiet until the afternoon of the 4th, when HMS *Vidette*, covering the rear of the convoy, sighted a U-boat on the port quarter. The destroyer hurled herself into the attack, causing the U-boat to crash-dive, and then followed up with depth charges. Had Gretton been able to spare another escort to help, the U-boat might well have found herself in trouble, but with 61 ships to protect this was out of the question. As it was, *Vidette* soon had to break off the action to be back on station astern of the convoy before dusk.

Before it was completely dark, both *Tay* and *Alisma* made sightings of U-boats, one on each bow of the convoy. The pack was obviously closing in for a night attack, and there was little Gretton and Admiral Ramsey could do about it. As a last resort Ramsey ordered the merchantmen to zig-zag, a highly dangerous procedure for 61 ships to adopt when steaming in close order in darkness. A signal from the Admiralty informing Gretton that the 4th Escort Group, consisting of the four destroyers *Inglefield, Fury, Eclipse* and *Icarus*, was steaming to his aid was encouraging, but until the destroyers arrived HX 231 was very vulnerable. The wind was in the north-east, blowing a near gale, with the sea heaping up menacingly; overhead the sky was heavily overcast, and although the visibility was excellent the darkness was intense. Gretton was certain the U-boats would attack in force that night, probably coming in from the weather side, and, having checked that all radars and asdics were working, he concentrated his escorts on the port side of the convoy.

Nerves were stretched to breaking point as the night advanced, and there was consternation when an intense white light flared up on the port side of the convoy about an hour after dark. The unwanted illumination came from a flare dropped overboard by nervous hands in a ship in the port wing column. It took some time to extinguish the flare, and meanwhile the convoy was bathed in bright light for all to see. The consequences of this careless accident would follow.

Another hour dragged by, the darkness seeming to intensify as the flare died out, then *Tay's* lookouts sighted a red flash to starboard. At first Gretton put this down to the Northern Lights (the convoy was in 57° North), but he then realised it was too early in the night for the Lights to be seen. Fearing the worst, he waited, then after seven minutes asked all ships to report on their situation by radio telephone. Two minutes later *Alisma* reported that a ship had been torpedoed in column twelve. Knowing it was already too late, but feeling the need to take some action, Gretton ordered all escorts to fire starshell.

At 2215 the *Shillong* was two cables ahead of her assigned position at the head of column twelve and making 10½ knots. No one saw the track of *U635*'s torpedo; the explosion and the severe concussion that followed came out of the black night like a striking thunderbolt. The *Shillong*, struck on the port side in way of her engine room, staggered and all lights went out, creating immediate confusion below decks. On the bridge there was chaos. The concrete armour was blown off, all windows were shattered and, seconds later, the wheelhouse and chartroom, both wooden structures, collapsed. In the radio room, both main and emergency transmitters and receivers were destroyed by the blast, and no distress signal went out. By some miracle no one was killed by the explosion, even in the engine room, where the engineers on watch were able to shut down the engine and escape before the compartment was flooded. The ship took a slight list to port and began to settle lower in the water.

David Clowe, who had been keeping watch on the bridge when the torpedo hit, made an attempt, on his own initiative, to fire the distress rockets, but they failed to ignite. On the orders of Captain Hollow, Clowe then clawed his way through the wreckage to dump the ship's codebooks overboard before making his way to the boat deck. As he hurled the weighted box over the rail the fallacy of the *Shillong*'s 'lucky ship' reputation came home to him forcibly. On this black night in mid-Atlantic, with the wind ratcheting up towards a full gale and the thunder of the waves loud in his ears, Clowe realised not only that the ship was sinking, but that two of her four lifeboats were useless. He later recalled:

It was so dark that I could not see if our two remaining lifeboats had been launched. The ship was settling rapidly, and within seven minutes the main deck was awash, the hull being completely submerged. The 3rd Officer and myself seized a sextant and chronometer, and were making our way down the bridge ladder when a huge wave swept over the deck and carried the 3rd Officer away. I did not see him again. I jumped into the water on the deck, which reached to my waist, struggled to the rail, and dived overboard. Within a few seconds the ship's stern rose into the air, and she slid straight under. . .

The *Shillong* had taken exactly 12 minutes to die.

The furore following the sinking of the *Shillong* caused wide consternation in the convoy, which in turn almost led to a complete break-up of the formation. Three ships of the starboard wing column, the Swedish motor vessel *Vaalaren*, the American tanker *Sunoil* and the Dutch steamer *Blitar*, hared off into the night, never to be seen again. Gretton gave chase in *Tay*, but soon realised he was wasting his time and rejoined the other escorts in the search for the U-boat. By this time, however, Heinz Eckelmann, flushed with the excitement of this success on his first patrol in command, had taken *U635* well out of range.

During the hunt for *U635*, *Tay* came across the *Shillong*'s survivors still fighting for their lives in the icy waters. Gretton had deep misgivings at not being able to help them:

Some were on rafts, some were alone, but no boats had survived and it is my most painful memory of the war that we had to shout encouragement, knowing well that it was unlikely that they would ever be picked up. It was an appalling decision to make as to whether to stop or not, but by leaving her place in the search to do so, the ship would leave a gap through which more attacks could be made and more men drowned. We had to go on. After the search plan had been completed, I sent *Pink* to look for survivors but she failed to find them and after four hours search I had to recall her to her station.

David Clowe later gave a harrowing account of the plight of the men in the water:

Just before leaving the ship I saw a raft some distance away, but as there was a high sea running, it was impossible to reach the raft by swimming. Fortunately, I was carried toward one of the starboard lifeboats, and climbed on board; a few survivors, including the Senior Apprentice, were already in this boat. I discovered later that this was the only lifeboat to be successfully launched, the motor boat had capsized on becoming water-borne, resulting in the loss of the boat's wireless set, which had been placed in it.

The sea was extremely rough, and the wind bitterly cold. I took charge of the boat, as the Senior Apprentice's nerves had given out. I put out the sea anchor and lay head to the sea throughout the night, picking up as many survivors as I could find. At dawn there were 33 survivors in the lifeboat, which was only constructed to carry 32. During the night I came across several dead bodies in their lifejackets. Before dawn, the Senior Radio Operator lost his reason, and became very violent, but after two hours or so he calmed down, sank into a coma, and quietly died.

At dawn I sighted a raft in the distance with some men on it. The sea was too rough for us to row towards it, but at 0900, when the weather moderated a little, I pulled in the sea anchor and rowed towards this raft. Apparently, there had originally been eighteen survivors on this raft, including the Master, who had died. I was told that the raft had capsized several times during the night, resulting in some of the crew being washed away and lost. Others had died from exposure, leaving only one army gunner, one navy gunner, the 3rd Engineer, one apprentice, and a native, alive. I transferred these men to the lifeboat.

As the B7 escorts, having searched in vain for the attacking U-boat, were returning to their stations, the Aurora Borealis was illuminating the northern sky with shimmering curtains of green, red and yellow lights, adding to the drama of the night. It was a spectacular display of nature at play that few were given the opportunity to admire. Oberleutnant-zur-See Werner Winkler, commanding *U630* and, like Eckelmann, on his first war patrol, had by then crept up unseen at the rear of the convoy, which was completely undefended. Slipping between columns three and four, Winkler fired a spread of four torpedoes at two ships, one of which was a tanker. The latter escaped his attentions, but two of his torpedoes slammed into the British ship *Waroonga*.

The 9,365-ton *Waroonga*, a 29-year-old refrigerated ship owned by the British India Steam Navigation Company, was nearing the end of her long voyage from New Zealand via the Panama Canal. She carried 11,000 tons of butter and cheese destined to boost the sparse diet of war-weary British families. Her master, Captain Taylor, was aware of the desperate need for his cargo to get through and, despite the huge hole in the *Waroonga's* side made by Winkler's torpedo, he refused to abandon his ship so long as her watertight bulkheads held. In view of the high seas running, his decision was a wise one; no lifeboat could have survived long in such weather.

Gretton had by now rearranged his screen of escorts around the convoy, preparing to fend off the U-boat attacks he anticipated would come from all sides. However, these did not materialise, and the 56 ships remaining with HX 231 continued to forge north-eastwards, being by then in latitude 58° North and nearing the vertex of their great circle course across the Atlantic. It was bitterly cold and the night seemed endless.

The *Lowenhërz* boats had good reason for leaving the convoy in peace. They had found easier pickings astern, where, out of sight and sound of Gretton's escorts, two of the three ships that had left the convoy in the confusion of the first attack sailed alone. The Swedish motor vessel *Vaalaren*, an innocent neutral caught up in this dirty war of attrition, was first to go. Oberleutnant Robert Schetelig in *U229* had neither the opportunity nor the inclination to question her nationality. One torpedo was sufficient to send the *Vaalaren* and her cargo to the bottom. There were no survivors. A few hours later Götz von Hartmann crippled but did not sink the American tanker *Sunoil*, an easy target limping along on one engine. The *Sunoil* transmitted a distress signal which was picked up in the convoy, and Gretton despatched *Vidette* to investigate.

Daylight on the 5th saw a dramatic change for the better in the weather. The cold was still intense, but the wind which had plagued the convoy since its departure from New York dropped to a mere gentle breeze. Visibility was excellent, and although the long Atlantic swell was only slightly diminished, the waves had subsided into a relative calm. Life in the ships was made bearable again, but the sudden improvement in the weather left HX 231 horribly exposed to the enemy. Gretton remarked: 'The U-boats were chattering like magpies all around the horizon'. *Tay's* HF/DF operators reported a stream of bearings but, no other ships in the convoy being so equipped, the positions of the transmitting U-boats could not be plotted. A little before midday a signal was received that air cover from Iceland was due overhead that afternoon.

The first Liberator of 86 Squadron, RAF Coastal Command, was sighted less than an hour later. It made a dramatic entrance, swooping low to depth-charge a U-boat it had spotted close south of HX 231. Gretton took *Tay* out of the screen at full speed to investigate, but as she sped away, with her bow wave creaming, there was a heavy explosion in the middle of the convoy. Unknown to Gretton, *U707*, commanded by Kapitänleutnant Alexander von Zitzewitz, had evaded *Vidette's* asdic and entered the convoy from astern. Coming to periscope depth, von Zitzewitz fired a spread of two torpedoes, one of which was seen to run across the bows of the *Tyndareus*, Admiral Ramsey's flagship. Before the alarm could be raised, von Zitzewitz's second torpedo hit the 7,124-ton tanker *British Ardour* in her No. 2 cargo tank. The *British Ardour* was fifteen years old, not a great age for a merchant ship, but for many years she had carried kerosene in her cargo tanks, and her bulkheads were corroded thin. The blast of the exploding torpedo ripped through the ship, and her precious cargo of heavy fuel oil gushed into the sea. Fortunately no one on board was injured, and a small fire forward was soon put out, but the tanker was doomed. She sank soon afterwards, leaving a huge black oil slick covering the water, through which her crowded lifeboats glided towards the corvette *Snowflake*, circling close by.

At the time of the sinking of the *British Ardour* there were sixteen members of the *Lowenhërz* pack gathered around HX 231, and others were on the way. Their arrival was ill-timed, however, for more Liberators were now overhead and aggressively attacking any U-boat that dared to show its conning tower. But these aircraft were operating at their maximum range, and the time they were able to spend with the convoy was all too short. By dusk the last one had dipped its wings in salute and roared away to its Icelandic base 500 miles to the north-east. Its going coincided with news from the destroyers of the promised support group that bad weather had delayed their arrival until the next day.

When darkness came on the 5th, HX 231 was in an unenviable position. It was surrounded by U-boats, the air cover had gone, no assistance was at hand and the weather was fast deteriorating. The coming night was not one to be looked forward to, and Gretton was greatly relieved when *Vidette* and *Snowflake* came hurrying up from astern, the latter having the *British Ardour's* survivors on board. *Vidette's* mission had been less fruitful, for after a long and extensive search she had failed to locate the torpedoed *Sunoil*. Ironically, as the destroyer resumed her station astern of HX 231, the American tanker was located, unfortunately by Kurt Lange in *U530*. He put three torpedoes into the helpless *Sunoil*, which blew up and sank. None of her crew survived.

The probing began soon after dark, the first U-boat coming in on the surface from the port side. *Loosestrife's* radar picked up the intruder, and the corvette was quick to act, illuminating the submarine and opening fire with her 4in. The U-boat crash-dived and was seen no more. There was a brief lull, then the battle began in earnest, the wolves coming in singly, one after another, from the starboard side. Had they made a combined effort the outcome might have been different, but, as it was, each separate attack was met and repulsed by *Tay* and the corvettes *Alisma* and *Pink*. The three escorts, working in concert, used starshell and depth charges to great effect, driving off each U-boat as it came in, then racing back to protect the merchantmen. The 7,065-ton Dutch steamer *Blitar*, one of the trio that deserted the convoy when the first torpedoes began to fly on the night of the 3rd, was not so fortunate. Still straggling astern of HX 231, she was beyond the protection of B7 when *U632* (Kapitänleutnant Hans Karpf) came across her. No one lived to tell of the Dutch vessel's end.

During the course of this hectic night, Heinz Eckelmann in *U635* made the mistake of running perilously close across *Tay's* bows in an attempt to break into the convoy. Neither the frigate nor the submarine had previously seen the other, and it is difficult to tell who was the more surprised, but the *Tay's* gunners were first to recover, spraying *U635's* conning tower with 20mm Oerlikon shells before Eckelmann took her under in the fastest crash-dive of his short career in submarines. *Tay* made asdic contact immediately, and one pattern of depth charges was sufficient. There was a great red glow under the water, followed by a heavy explosion that almost rolled the frigate over on her beam ends. So died Heinz Eckelmann and all of his men, with their first war patrol not yet completed. Captain Hollow and the *Shillong* were avenged.

As the night wore on, the intervals between the U-boat attacks increased, until towards dawn they petered out altogether. Gretton and the men of B7 felt justifiably proud, for not only had they beaten off every assault by the U-boats – eleven had been logged – but they had destroyed at least one of them. However, the victory was marred by a tragedy within the convoy. Just before dawn the *Waroonga*, torpedoed on the night of the 4th by *U630*, reported that her watertight bulkheads had given way and she was being abandoned. The weather had been worsening for some hours, and although *Loosestrife* went to their aid, fourteen of the *Waroonga's* crew lost their lives when their lifeboat capsized in the rough seas.

While *Loosestrife* was astern, searching for survivors from the *Waroonga*, *Tay*, zig-zagging ahead of the convoy, detected a U-boat dead ahead and immediately ran in to attack. To Gretton's surprise the U-boat's stern broke the surface for a few seconds almost under *Tay's* bows, just as he was about to give the order to lay a pattern of depth charges. Gretton tried to swing the frigate short round to put her stern to the U-boat, but in the heavy seas she was slow to turn, and when the depth charges rolled down their chutes they were wide of the mark. There was no time for another attempt, for *Tay*, lying across the path of the advancing convoy, was now in danger of being run down. Using both engines on maximum power, Gretton manoeuvred clear then dropped another pattern of charges and marked them with a smoke float, which was the recommended procedure when other ships were near. Unfortunately several merchant ships thought the smoke was a U-boat, and opened fire on it with great enthusiasm, no doubt heightened by the sheer frustration of being under attack for so long without the opportunity to retaliate. The sea around HMS *Tay* erupted in a hail of bursting 4in shells, 20mm cannon shells and 0.303in-calibre bullets, but, by pure good fortune, neither she nor any other ship was hit.

In the midst of this mayhem the first Liberators from Iceland arrived, one of which had surprised *U632* on the surface as she followed in the wake of HX 231. The aircraft's depth charges were well aimed, and *Lowenhërz* lost another member. Soon after the arrival of air cover, B7 was joined by the long-awaited destroyers of the 4th Escort Group, and for HX 231 the battle that had lasted for four days and four nights was over.

For David Clowe and the survivors of the *Shillong* the ordeal was far from finished. Their battered lifeboat lay some 600 miles astern of HX 231, alone on a dark and hostile ocean and without hope of being found. In his report to the Admiralty Clowe wrote:

> Throughout the first two days the weather continued to be exceptionally bad, and by 8 April there were only ten men left alive, one native and nine Europeans. It seemed that it was only sheer determination and the will to live that kept us going, as the 3rd Radio Officer was a perfect specimen of manhood, in good physical condition, and only 22, but soon after he began to suffer from the cold he seemed to lose his will to live, and quietly died. We were all very weak and suffering badly from frostbite.
>
> We had been laying to a sea anchor throughout, but on 8 April the weather moderated slightly, the wind veered to the south-west, so I decided to make sail to the north-east in order to get into the tracks of westbound convoys and aircraft areas. I rigged a sail with a couple of blankets lashed to an oar, and in this way sailed some eighteen miles to the north-east. We also took the opportunity of baling out the lifeboat,

and straightening up the gear. I organised watches, those not on watch sheltered in the after well, with blankets to protect them. It was difficult to persuade some of the men to get up for their watches when it was their turn to take over, but on the whole they were very good, considering the severity of their ordeal. At times the nerves of some of them went to pieces, and I had to coax or bully them to pull themselves together.

On the sixth day [9 April], the weather deteriorated again, so I took down the sail and lay to a sea anchor. This state of affairs continued until the afternoon of the 12 April, when I sighted a Catalina flying boat. I immediately burned two red flares, which the aircraft sighted. I do not think we would have been seen if it had not been for these flares. The aircraft circled the boat and dropped a parcel wrapped in a lifejacket, which fell dead ahead of the lifeboat. It was impossible to row the boat against the high seas, so we just had to watch the parcel float away. The aircraft flew off, but I realised a rescue ship would probably come soon to pick us up. During the day the weather steadily deteriorated, and towards the last hours our lifeboat was several times on the verge of capsizing.

I stood up in the boat, hanging on to the mast, to keep a lookout, and towards the evening a Norwegian destroyer closed the lifeboat. By this time waves about 60ft high were running, and the Captain told us that he could not possibly pick us up in such bad weather. They did, however, make a lee for us, and pumped oil on the water, which did not have much effect. Some two hours later the rescue ship *Zamelek* came into sight, and by magnificent seamanship, and with her improved equipment, was able to take us on board. I got the men to pull towards the rescue ship with their last remaining strength, although by this time everyone was in the last stages of exhaustion. The rescue ship put their bow alongside the boat, thereby making a good lee, and put large baskets over the side. The survivors climbed into the baskets and were hoisted on deck by cranes. I managed to climb up the side net, but collapsed immediately on reaching the deck. We were all on board by 1730 on 12 April.

We were landed at Halifax on 21 April, and taken straight to hospital. I was the only survivor to escape amputation of some kind, all the other survivors having to have fingers, toes or feet amputated. One apprentice has had to lose both legs . . .

Clowe concluded:

I would take this opportunity of paying tribute to the outstandingly gallant behaviour of Cadet G. L. Francis, aged 20. This cadet was more or less responsible for getting the lifeboat away, but refused to board it himself, preferring to leave it for other survivors. He then released a raft, and seeing that this was also overcrowded, he jumped into the sea, and hung on to some wreckage. He eventually climbed on to the raft, but died shortly after from exposure. There is no doubt that his brave and selfless action cost him his life.

I would also like to mention the splendid assistance I received from Apprentice A. B. Moore throughout the whole time we were adrift. This boy, although only 19 years old, behaved stoically throughout, and although he undoubtedly suffered agony, at no time did I hear any complaints from him. I could always rely on his backing and support in whatever decisions I had to make. His magnificent behaviour set a wonderful example to all.

Praise indeed from one who was himself only just out of his teens.

By the time HX 231 arrived off the north coast of Ireland, on 9 April, the threat posed by the U-boats was over, the weather had moderated and it was possible for the first time to make a full assessment of the sacrifices made to get the convoy through. In all, six ships had been lost, three of them stragglers, along with 77,000 tons of cargo and over 200 men. *Lowenhërz*, on the other hand, had lost two U-boats, four others being so badly damaged that they were forced to return to base. The success of the operation had been largely due to Commander Peter Gretton's B7 Group, which in the most severe of weather conditions mounted a magnificent defence of HX 231. Although up to twenty U-boats laid siege to the convoy for four days and four nights, not once did the six escorts give ground. Each time the U-boats came in, the British ships, stretched to the utmost limit to defend this large convoy, hit back and hit back so hard that the *Lowenhërz* boats were never able to mount an attack in force.

The role played by 86 Squadron, Coastal Command, finally tipped the scales in favour of HX 231 and turned what might have been a massacre into victory. Despite weather conditions in which flying would normally have been deemed impossible, the Liberators put an air umbrella over the convoy from dawn to dusk, and beyond, right from the moment their fuel tanks would allow them to reach the ships. They spent so much time overhead that the U-boat commanders came to the conclusion that an aircraft carrier was with HX 231.

# 15

# The Last Great Challenge

It has been said that HX 231 was the turning point in the Battle of the Atlantic. Certainly neither side was able to claim a conclusive victory, but it could not be disputed that Dönitz's 'grey wolves' had for the first time been severely mauled by an experienced and determined escort group working closely with long-range aircraft. Dönitz put the poor showing of the U-boats against this relatively lightly escorted convoy down to a lack of experience on the part of their crews; and he had good reason to do so.

Despite heavy bombing raids on Germany by Allied aircraft, U-boat production had continued to increase, and by mid-April 1943 there were no fewer than 193 boats operational in the Atlantic. On the face of it the wolf packs were in the ascendancy, but Kretschmer, Schepke, Prien and the other 'aces' of the early days of the war were long gone. Dönitz was now forced to crew his boats with inexperienced men, a great number of whom were new to the sea in any form, and in a complex craft like a submarine this was a decided disadvantage. There was no lack of courage or determination, but despite a long and rigorous training programme the experience required to react quickly and instinctively to any given situation was missing. And while the men were away at sea, things were happening on land that did nothing for their morale.

In Russia, Hitler's offensive of the summer of 1942 had gone into reverse. The siege of Stalingrad had been raised, and the German Sixth Army, which in 1940 had swept victorious across Holland and Belgium to the sea, was decimated, 160,000 men being killed and 90,000 taken prisoner. Leningrad had also been relieved, and from the Gulf of Finland to the Black Sea the Wehrmacht was in retreat.

The lot of the Axis forces in North Africa was no better. Mussolini, who saw his Army in danger of being summarily confined to the dustbin of history by the advancing Allies, met Hitler in Salzburg on 7 April to receive reassurance. 'I guarantee you that Africa will be defended,' Hitler told him. 'Verdun stood out against the attack of the best German regiments. I do not see why we should not stand out as well in Africa. With your help, Duce, my troops will make Tunis the Verdun of the Mediterranean.' Three weeks later the remaining German and Italian troops in North Africa were trapped on the Cape Bon peninsula, their air cover shot from the skies and without means of supply or reinforcement. An early surrender was inevitable, and the Allies had already turned their eyes to Sicily, through which in early summer they intended to strike at the soft underbelly of Occupied Europe.

The build-up to the assault on Sicily was already in evidence by the end of April. A long-range Focke-Wulf Kondor, on patrol over the Bay of Biscay, sighted a convoy of fifteen tank landing craft (LCTs) with two escorts, heading south. The Kondor radioed U-boat Command and the *Drossel* pack of ten U-boats, then lying to the north-west of Cape Finisterre, was called in. They sighted the convoy before nightfall, but failed to press home their attack on the grounds that it was thought that torpedoes would pass beneath the shallow-draught landing craft, which rolled and pitched violently in heavy seas. Although only two small escorts were present, no attempt was made by the U-boats to sink the LCTs by gunfire, which could be construed as a lack of determination in the face of the enemy. The *Drossel* boats abandoned pursuit of the convoy, and as they turned away two of their number, *U439* and *U659*, collided and sank with heavy loss of life. Dönitz had good reason to be concerned at the commitment and competence of his new breed of U-boat men. He moved *Drossel* further west into deeper waters, where he hoped the remaining members of the pack would give a better showing.

On 21 April, some days before *Drossel*'s debacle in the Bay of Biscay, the nucleus of Convoy ONS 5 sailed from Liverpool, bound for New York. A rendezvous was made in the Irish Sea with ships from the Bristol Channel, and before nightfall the convoy, 41 ships in all, including two fleet tankers, accompanied by the armed trawlers *Northern Gem* and *Northern Spray*, was heading into the North Channel. With the exception of some of the Bristol Channel contingent, laden with Welsh coal, and the fleet tankers, the majority of the ships were in ballast, and not a man sailing in them was under any illusions as to the long, uncomfortable crossing ahead. As to the trawlers, each a mere 650 tons gross, smaller even than the corvettes, the prospect was a daunting one, although both had already experienced the horrors of the convoys to North Russia.

While ONS 5, formed up in two orderly columns, negotiated the North Channel, the convoy's ocean escort, B7, was raising steam in the sheltered waters of Lough Foyle, on the north coast of Ireland. Commander Peter Gretton's team was preparing to return across the Atlantic only twelve days after bringing in HX 231. Gretton was now in the destroyer HMS *Duncan*, a ship more suited to the SOE. She was a 1,375-ton flotilla leader built between the wars, armed with four 4.7in guns and eight 21in torpedo tubes and having a speed of $35^1/_2$ knots. The frigate *Tay*, now commanded by Lieutenant-Commander R. E. Sherwood, was still with B7, as were the corvettes *Pink*, *Snowflake* and *Loosestrife*. *Alisma* was in dock, and her place had been taken by another Flower-class corvette, HMS *Sunflower*. The second destroyer, *Vidette*, was to join later.

On the morning of the 22nd Gretton held a final meeting with his commanders to discuss tactics for the crossing, then led the way out of the anchorage. The group joined ONS 5 at 1400, as it passed south of the island of Islay. As the *Duncan's* small fuel tanks gave her only a comparatively short range, Gretton was pleased to see two fleet oilers with the convoy. The art of refuelling at sea was now well-practised, and the *British Lady* and her American opposite number, *Argon*, carried ample oil to keep the tanks of all the escorts topped up throughout the passage.

Before sailing, Gretton would have liked a face-to-face meeting with the convoy Commodore, Captain J. K. Brook, RNR, who was in the Norwegian ship *Rena*, but there was no time for this. He had to be content with passing the relevant documents across to the *Rena*, following this with a shouted exchange of ideas with Brook over the loud hailer. By this time ONS 5 had formed up into its steaming order of twelve columns abreast, with the *Rena* leading at the head of column six and the *Northern Gem* and *Northern Spray* bringing up the rear. The primary role of the two trawlers was to act as rescue ships. At the same time, as each was equipped with asdic and armed with a 4in gun, they would be expected to keep an eye open for shadowing U-boats.

At the convoy's designated speed of 7¹/₂ knots, the passage ahead was estimated to take seventeen days, but with Malin Head abeam to port and the first of the long Atlantic swells rolling in, it soon became evident that this prediction might prove wildly optimistic. The weather worsened steadily through the night and all next day, until, on the morning of the 24th, it was blowing a Force 9 gale from the south-west, with a 30ft sea running. The route planned for ONS 5 by the Admiralty would take it into high latitudes, as far as 62° North, so it was unlikely that there would be any improvement.

The first U-boat alarm came at about noon on the 24th, when the convoy was by dead reckoning 90 miles south-west of Rockall. Fortunately nothing came of the alarm, but evidence that the wolves were already gathering was seen in a signal reporting that a B17 Flying Fortress of 206 Squadron, RAF, had attacked and sunk *U710* directly ahead of ONS 5 during the day. At about this time Gretton became concerned about *Duncan's* dwindling fuel supplies, and made his first attempt to top up his tanks from the *British Lady*. The pitching of the two ships in the heavy seas made this a hair-raising experience. When the transfer hose broke, Gretton abandoned the operation and took the destroyer into the middle of the convoy, where she was able to steam at reduced speed and conserve fuel.

Over the next 48 hours the weather worsened further, leading to a nightmare that few who experienced it would ever forget. The laden ships suffered worst, their decks being constantly swept by green seas; those in ballast roller-coasted crazily from crest to trough, their propellers threshing air much of the time. The overall speed of the convoy fell to between 1 and 2 knots, and by the night of the 25th no fewer than eight ships were drifting out of control, having lost all steerage way. Gretton's escorts did their best to hold the convoy together, and succeeded to a remarkable degree, but only at great cost to themselves. In the tiny corvettes, and even tinier trawlers, dwarfed by the mountainous seas, even the most experienced hands were wracked by seasickness and not a corner of the accommodation was dry, but still they kept going.

On the 26th, the thing that everyone feared most in this great assembly of hard-pressed ships happened; two of the merchantmen drifted close to each other and, unable to steer, collided with a resounding crash. One was able to stay with the convoy, but the other ship was so badly damaged that she broke away and made for Iceland at all possible speed. Gretton considered sending a corvette with her, but decided against it. In view of the probable proximity of U-boats, it would have been foolish to weaken the defence of ONS 5 for one ship. She must take her chances with the enemy, as she had done with the sea.

Later that day HMS *Vidette* arrived, and with her three more merchant ships from Iceland. With a second destroyer in his team Gretton began to feel more secure. On the 27th there was a noticeable improvement in the weather, and *Duncan* and *Vidette* were able to refuel from the *British Lady*. It had been hoped to top up both destroyers at the same time by using the second oiler, the American tanker *Argon*, but her canvas hoses, unlike the armoured rubber hoses of the British tanker, proved completely inadequate for the job. The convoy was then some 300 miles south-south-west of Reykjavik, and throughout the day good air cover was provided by RAF Hudsons from that base. Towards evening a signal from Western Approaches Command warned that the eastbound convoy HX 234, passing to the south of ONS 5, was under attack by U-boats. Visibility was now falling, and Gretton dared to hope that his own charges might slip by unobserved while the enemy concentrated on the more attractive loaded ships of HX 234. His hopes were not realised, however, for soon after first light on the 28th HF/DF picked up a U-boat transmitting close by, and directly in the path of the convoy. *Duncan* raced ahead at full speed, but with visibility at only three miles nothing was seen. It seemed certain, though, that the convoy was now being watched.

In addition to ONS 5, four other convoys, SC 127, HX 234, HX 235 and ONS 4, were at sea in the North Atlantic, and the Admiralty was aware that Dönitz had spread a wide net to catch at least one of them. The Admiral had called in four wolf packs for this specific purpose. *Star* was to the south-west of Iceland, *Specht* was covering the north-eastern approaches to Newfoundland, *Amsel* was further south, covering the eastern approaches, and the luck-

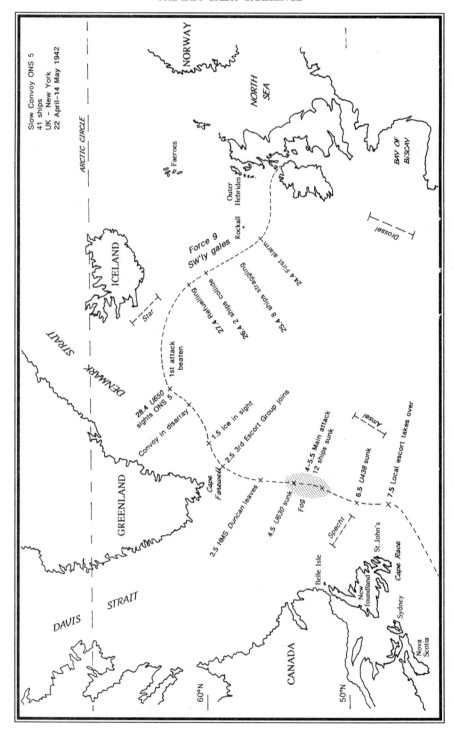

Slow Convoy ONS 5
41 ships
UK – New York
22 April–14 May 1942

NORWAY

NORTH SEA

BAY OF BISCAY

ARCTIC CIRCLE

Faeroes

Outer Hebrides

Rockall

Drossel

ICELAND

Force 9
SW'ly gales

Refuelling

27.4 2 ships collide

26.4 8 ships straggling

25.4 First alarm

DENMARK STRAIT

Star

28.4 U650 sights ONS 5

1st attack beaten

Convoy in disarray

1.5 Ice in sight

2.5 3rd Escort Group joins

4–5.5 Main attack 12 ships sunk

Amsel

6.5 U438 sunk

7.5 Local escort takes over

GREENLAND

Cape Farewell

3.5 HMS Duncan leaves

4.5 U630 sunk

Fog

Specht

Belle Isle

St. John's

New foundland

Cape Race

Sydney

Nova Scotia

DAVIS STRAIT

CANADA

60°N

50°N

less *Drossel* was moving westwards from Biscay to sweep up any ships that evaded the net. In all, 60 U-boats and three U-tankers were involved in this massive German operation.

Dönitz's grand plan almost came to naught, for four of the convoys slipped by, with only one attack reported on ONS 4 by *U404* (Korvettenkapitän Otto von Bülow), which fired a four-torpedo spread at an escorting carrier and missed. The Admiralty was confident that ONS 5, being the most northerly routed of the five convoys at sea, would pass well clear of the *Star* group. This might well have happened, had not *U650* been attacked by US Navy Catalinas and separated from the pack. The attack unintentionally sent the U-boat far enough north to come within 2,000 yards of the leading ships of ONS 5. Her sighting report to Dönitz betrayed her presence, but she had gone deep by the time *Duncan* arrived on the scene.

Dropping back underwater, *U650* surfaced astern of the convoy to begin shadowing. She was soon joined by *U386* and *U378*, while fourteen other boats were on the way in. Gretton and Brook, anticipating that a full-scale attack would not be long delayed, looked to their defences. A substantial alteration of course away from the danger after dark would have been the best move, but the weather had worsened again and it was blowing gale force from the south-west, with a high sea running. It was all that the merchantmen could do to hold their present course. Gretton calculated that, with the wind in the south-west, the U-boats would most probably attack downwind from the port side, and he stationed all of his escorts on this side, with *Duncan* on the port quarter where he could keep an eye on things. This was a high-risk strategy, for it left the starboard side of the convoy completely unprotected; should the U-boats decide to attack from the north, a catastrophe could follow.

Gretton did not have long to wait before his theory was put to the test. Soon after dark the first U-boat came in on the surface, and from the port bow. *Sunflower* was waiting for her, and opened fire with her 4in as she steamed into the teeth of the gale to attack. The U-boat crash-dived, a pattern of depth charges following her down. In accordance with Gretton's orders, *Sunflower* returned to her station without waiting to observe results.

Half an hour passed, then the second U-boat made its move, again approaching from downwind. Luckily, *Duncan's* radar detected the intruder in plenty of time, and Gretton went in at full speed, catching her unawares. *Duncan* was very close when the U-boat dived and Gretton was tempted to ram, but, fearful of major damage to his ship, he held back and then went in with depth charges. He considered the U-boat to be badly shaken, if not sunk, but, mindful of his own orders, he made to rejoin the convoy. As he did so, *Duncan's* radar picked up yet another echo, classified as a submarine, also to port. Gretton turned the destroyer towards the new enemy, increased speed, and her sharp bows began to cleave the heavy seas, creating a welter of foam and spray that advertised her coming. The U-boat escaped, but its attack was frustrated.

In the space of an hour four U-boats had tried to penetrate the defences of ONS 5, and all had been beaten back. It was later learned that two received severe damage from depth-charging; one made port, but the other, *U528*, was surprised on the surface by aircraft of 58 Squadron as she limped home, and sunk by the destroyer HMS *Fleetwood.*

Having been successful in driving off the U-boats at night, Gretton now anticipated a daylight attack, and so was pleased to hear that destroyers of the 3rd Escort Group had been ordered to sail from St John's to come to his aid. But St John's was over 1,000 miles away and, the weather being what it was, the promised help might be a long time coming. Meanwhile, ONS 5 steamed on to meet the new day.

The 29th dawned with the wind easing and the sea flattening out, although the swell was still heavy. While the ships still rolled and pitched drunkenly, their decks were no longer awash. A weak sun broke through the overcast, softening the winter seascape and lifting some of the gloom that hung over the ships. The cold was still intense, for ONS 5 was in latitude 62° North, at the apogee of her long passage and crossing the southern approaches to the Denmark Strait. On the bridge of the 4,586-ton London steamer *Harperley*, third ship of the port wing column, her Chief Officer was planning the day's work on deck with some enthusiasm when *U258* (Kapitänleutnant Wilhelm von Mässenhausen) fired a four-torpedo spread. One torpedo passed across the *Harperley's* bows, missing her by only a few feet.

The *Harperley* had a narrow escape, and so did at least two other ships; the American freighter *McKeesport* was not so fortunate. One of Mässenhausen's torpedoes penetrated deep into the convoy, as far as column four, where the *McKeesport* was second ship. The 6,198-ton steamer staggered as the 800lb warhead exploded forward of her bridge, but except for 2,000 tons of sand ballast she was an empty ship, and stayed afloat and under way. After about half an hour, however, her watertight bulkheads gave way and the sea poured aft, flooding the engine room. At that point the American ship was abandoned, her crew of 68 being taken off by *Northern Gem*. Only one man lost his life, killed by Mässenhausen's torpedo.

While she was engaged in rescuing the *McKeesport's* crew, the *Northern Gem's* asdic detected *U258*, but HF/DF activity indicated that at least four U-boats were close to the convoy, and Gretton decided it was wiser to tighten his screen rather than give chase. His decision proved to be wise, for the sinking of the *McKeesport* signalled another deterioration in the weather, and all ships were soon once more engaged in a fight to keep afloat and on course. At one point the corvette *Sunflower* was swept from end to end by a huge oncoming sea which swamped her bridge and even filled the crow's nest with water.

The first of the 3rd Escort Group's destroyers, HMS *Oribi*, joined that night. She had been escorting the eastbound convoy SC 127 when ordered to reinforce B7, and was already running low on fuel when she arrived. Providentially, dawn on the 30th brought another break in the weather, and Gretton detailed the *British Lady* to fill the *Oribi's* tanks. This proved to be a lengthy operation which took all day, preventing other escorts from topping up. By evening it was blowing a full gale again, and all thought of oiling was abandoned. The U-boats, however, did not give up their efforts to penetrate the screen, *Sunflower* and *Snowflake* in particular being kept busy fending off a series of attacks. The last came a little before midnight, when *U192* broke through to fire a snap shot with a single torpedo before being chased away. The torpedo detonated harmlessly at the end of its run.

The first day of May came, but it brought none of the precursors of summer that might be expected. The wind had risen steadily throughout the night until it was blowing storm force 10, gusting to 11. Ragged black clouds laden with stinging sleet brushed the mast-tops, and the seas were great foam-crested mountains that threatened disaster to any ship that failed to meet them head-on. The convoy began to break up, each ship being left to fight its separate lonely duel with the storm. By mid-morning ONS 5 was scattered all over the ocean, and two ships, unable to take any more punishment, had turned on their heels to run before the storm. They went out of sight within minutes and were not seen again, although they did reach Iceland. As for the U-boats, they were nowhere to be seen, for Dönitz had called them off.

Although the corvette *Pink* had rounded up a number of stragglers and was holding them together and on course, the almost total disarray of the convoy was a huge problem for Gretton. But an even worse complication faced him at noon, when a Liberator of 120 Squadron, RAF, came in under the cloud to report icebergs 30 miles ahead, right in the path of the convoy. Another 20 miles beyond that the aircraft had glimpsed the solid line of the Greenland ice pack. In the prevailing weather conditions the large alteration of course necessary to avoid the danger was impossible. It was fortunate that the progress of the ships was so impeded by the weather that they were all but hove-to.

In the nightmarish 24 hours that followed, ONS 5 gained only 20 miles to the westward. Even so, at daybreak on the 2nd, when the weather had moderated sufficiently to allow manoeuvring, it was a hard task to get the ships rounded up in time to clear the ice ahead. *Pink* and her gaggle of stragglers lay 30 miles astern, and it was only with the help of another Liberator from Iceland that they were brought back into the fold. By the time the round-up had been completed, the Greenland ice pack was visible to starboard, and growlers and dangerous-looking floes were drifting through the columns. *Duncan* was again running short of oil, but the frequent alterations of course necessary to avoid the drifting ice ruled out refuelling from the *British Lady*.

That afternoon the rest of the 3rd Escort Group, the destroyers *Offa*, *Penn*, *Panther* and *Impulsive*, led by Captain J. A. McCoy in HMS *Offa*, arrived from St John's, having experienced great difficulty in finding the convoy. Gretton, who remained SOE, now had at his disposal six destroyers, a frigate, four corvettes and two trawlers, a substantial force by any reckoning. However, this favourable state of affairs for ONS 5 was to be short-lived.

Dönitz, meanwhile, with so many U-boats at sea and so many convoys on passage, and yet with so little to show for his efforts, was becoming frustrated. In desperation he merged *Star* and *Specht* into a new pack of 30 boats code-named *Fink* and, assuming that ONS 5 had slipped through, ordered the pack to attack the next eastbound convoy, SC 128. *Fink* formed up in a north-west to south-east patrol line 300 miles south of Cape Farewell, with eight miles between each boat. At the same time the reinforced *Amsel* group, also numbering 30 boats, had spread out in a wide arc 500 miles east of Cape Race, covering the approaches to Newfoundland. Conditions for an interception were ideal, yet SC 128, by means of a well-executed feint, evaded the net. Dönitz was about to disperse the pack when another unidentified convoy was sighted coming from the north-east, straight into the outspread arms of *Fink*. It was the delayed ONS 5.

On the morning of the 3rd *Duncan*'s tanks had begun to run dry, and Gretton's engineer informed him that the destroyer had just sufficient fuel left to make St John's, and then only at an economical speed. It was imperative that *Duncan* left that morning, and Gretton had no option but to go with her, for rough seas prevented him transferring to another ship by boat or jackstay. He was obliged to hand over command of the group to Lieutenant-Commander Sherwood in *Tay* and set course for St John's. Gretton later commented: 'We were most depressed, feeling we had left the group in the lurch'.

Sherwood was an experienced and competent commander, but he was about to be faced by an immense challenge. During the course of the next day, 4 May, the destroyers *Impulsive*, *Penn* and *Panther* and the trawler *Northern Gem*, all dangerously low on fuel and prevented from oiling at sea by the weather, were obliged to follow Gretton to St John's. Sherwood was left with *Tay*, the two destroyers *Offa* and *Oribi*, the four corvettes *Sunflower*, *Snowflake*, *Loosestrife* and *Pink*, and the armed trawler *Northern Spray*. This was still a large force, but those manning it were worn out by the unrelenting battering they had received at the hands of the weather, exacerbated by long hours at action stations under threat from a ruthless enemy. All ships were running low on fuel, and some were down to their last few depth charges. It had been signalled that the 1st Support Group, commanded by Commander G. N. Brewer and comprising the sloop HMS *Pelican*, the frigates *Wear, Jed* and *Spey*, and the ex-USCG cutter *Sennen*, was leaving St John's that day to join ONS 5, but these ships were 48 hours' hard steaming away. It was perhaps just as well that Sherwood was unaware that up to 60 U-boats were about to be pitted against him.

The first word of the enemy's approach came from the air, when a Catalina of 5 Squadron, Royal Canadian Air Force (RCAF), based at Gander and operating almost at the extremity of its range, sighted a U-boat on the surface astern of ONS 5. Shadowing the convoy, *U438* was caught unawares when the Catalina swept down with her guns blazing. The aircraft made two attacks with depth charges after *U438* crash-dived; the U-boat escaped destruction but suffered enough damage to send her scurrying for home. Less than an hour later *U630*, also shadowing the convoy, was surprised by another Canadian Catalina. As the U-boat dived it was bracketed by four depth charges and ripped apart. A large patch of oil and wreckage marked her last resting place. The real battle for ONS 5 had opened with first blood to the Allies.

By this time the convoy had again been scattered by the appalling weather. The Commodore had a loose formation of 31 ships with him, *Pink* had rounded up five, and six others were straggling well astern and out of sight of the main body. The remaining boats of the *Fink* group were astern of them again, but fast catching up, while the boats of the *Amsel* group lay in ambush off Newfoundland, directly in the convoy's path. *Drossel*, sixteen boats strong, was coming in from the east at maximum speed, hoping to play a part in what promised to be the 'turkey shoot' of the year. Time was of the essence, however, for ONS 5 would soon have continuous air cover from Newfoundland, and Brewer's 1st Support Group was on the way from St John's. Dönitz ordered his U-boats to go in and sink at all costs, and, if attacked by aircraft, to fight it out on the surface with their AA guns. The Admiral desperately needed a decisive victory.

At dusk on the 4th, as the various wolf packs closed in on ONS 5, the weather perversely turned in their favour. The wind fell away to a gentle breeze, the rough seas subsided and the horizon lifted to give unlimited visibility. Conditions were ideal for an attack after dark, although a cold dampness in the air offered the possibility of fog. The battle began far out to the west, first blood going to the RCAF. Two boats of the *Amsel* pack came under attack from the air as they closed in and, in accordance with Dönitz's urging, tried to fight it out on the surface. They were unsuccessful. Werner Winkler's *U630* was sunk by a Catalina of 5 Squadron, and an 86 Squadron Catalina destroyed *U465*.

Two hours after dark the fog, not unexpectedly, came rolling in to set the scene for the ultimate in nightmares. The convoy was already split into three untidy groups and, with visibility from the bridge reduced to less than 50 yards and sound signals forbidden, the merchant ships were steaming blind. On the other hand, the fog gave Sherwood's radar-equipped escorts a devastating advantage over the U-boats.

Fifteen boats were already gathered around the convoy when the fog came down, and one by one they all lost contact as the merchantmen slid into the enveloping gloom. It was not until 2200, when the visibility began to improve again, that contact was re-established, *U125* (Kapitänleutnant Ulrich Folkers) being the first to engage. The dark shape that loomed up ahead of her as she motored at full speed on the surface in pursuit of the convoy turned out to be the British manned ex-French ship *Lorient*. The 22-year-old steamer, her age-ing engines pushed beyond endurance during the storms of the past ten days, had fallen astern and was completely without protection. Folkers put a torpedo into her, but nobody saw her go down. Two days later a US Coastguard cutter found wreckage identified as coming from the *Lorient*, and also her upturned lifeboats. The fate of her crew of 46 was never known.

The 4,635-ton Newcastle tramp *North Britain*, limping along five miles astern of the main body of the convoy, was next to be picked off. She was found by *U707* (Oberleutnant-zur-See Günter Gretschel), and a single tor-pedo broke her back. Thirty-one of her crew of 42 went down with her or per-ished in the freezing waters.

At 2345 the assault on the convoy proper began when Heinrich Hasenschar in *U628* approached from the north, striking deep into the columns before torpedoing the 5,081-ton *Harbury*. The *Harbury*, carrying a full cargo of Welsh anthracite for St John's, New Brunswick, was abandoned, and all but seven of her crew were picked up by the *Northern Spray*. The deserted ship remained afloat for another four hours, finally being sunk by *U264* (Kapitän-leutnant Hartwig Looks).

It was Hartwig Looks, coming in on the port side of ONS 5, who sank the 5,561-ton American steamer *West Maximus* and then the *Harperley*, sis-ter ship to the *Harbury*. Both vessels were hit by two torpedoes, Oskar Curio in *U952* claiming a share of the *West Maximus*. The *Northern Spray*, picking her way carefully through the men and wreckage littering the sea astern of the convoy, rescued all but six of the crew of the *West Maximus* and 39 from the *Harperley*.

Half an hour into the morning of the 5th, *U358* (Kapitänleutnant Rolfe Manke) also came in from the port side to sink the *Bristol City*, lead ship of the port wing column. The 2,864-ton British ship was hit simultaneously by two torpedoes, one striking forward and the other aft of the bridge. Her bulkheads collapsed, her engine room flooded, and she went under in less than ten min-utes. Most of her crew abandoned ship in two lifeboats, but they left behind them fifteen men killed by Manke's torpedoes.

Six minutes later Manke's second spread of torpedoes went deeper into the convoy, one ploughing into the side of the 5,212-ton British steamer *Wentworth*, killing five of her crew and turning the ship into a shambles below decks. But although she had a 12ft-wide hole in her hull at the waterline and her main deck was split right across amidships, the *Wentworth* stayed afloat for another thirteen hours, finally being sunk by Hasenschar in *U628*.

The U-boats lost contact and withdrew at 0400 on the 5th, when the fog returned again with the coming of the dawn, but they left a trail of death and destruction behind them. During one terrifying night ONS 5 had lost seven ships of 32,676 tons and 120 men. More would undoubtedly have lost their lives but for the magnificent work of the rescue trawler *Northern Spray*, which, when the torpedoes were flying thick and fast, snatched men from the water in between depth charging U-boats. The U-boats had by no means had it all their own way, paying a very high price for their efforts. During the course of the night they had made 24 separate attacks on the convoy, each one being met fearlessly by Sherwood's escorts. Fifteen boats were attacked with depth charges, and six were surprised on the surface and came under a hail of shells from the escorts. Seven boats were damaged, and two were lost. *Oribi* rammed and sank *U531* in the fog, while *Vidette* destroyed *U125* in a Hedgehog attack.

Daylight on the 5th brought fine, clear weather, allowing the exhausted escorts to clear their decks and to top up their tanks hurriedly from the *British Lady*. The respite was brief, however, for the wolves were back soon after midday. Having worked around ahead of the convoy undetected, *U638* (Kapitänleutnant Staudinger), torpedoed the Liverpool motor vessel *Dolius*, then in the lead of column two. Staudinger's success was short-lived, for as he was trying to escape on the surface he was spotted by *Loosestrife*. The corvette gave chase, and *U638* was dispatched by depth charges as she dived.

Further astern, *U584* (Oberleutnant-zur-See Joachim Deecke) crept up on the small group of stragglers under escort by the corvette *Pink* and fired a spread of four torpedoes. Three missed and detonated harmlessly at the end of their run, but one hit the 5,565-ton American steamer *West Madaket* and sank her. Deecke got away, but Oberleutnant Happe in *U192*, then making his approach to the group, was detected by *Pink*'s asdics and blown out of the water by depth charges.

Five hours later, with the sun low on the western horizon, the U-boats made their final assault on ONS 5. Sherwood's escorts were by now exhausted, but again they repulsed the enemy with vigour. Only Ralf von Jessen in *U266*, whose only success to date had been against SC 118 when he sank the Greek ship *Polyktor*, managed to break through the screen. Using his bow and stern tubes, von Jessen sank in quick succession two British ships, the 5,136-ton

*Selvistan* and the 5,306-ton *Gharinda* in columns ten and eleven, and then the small Norwegian timber carrier *Bonde* in column eight.

With this last devastating blow the U-boats withdrew. The convoy was then within 450 miles of Newfoundland, and for Dönitz to prolong the pursuit further would have been to risk the destruction of many of his boats by aircraft and warships which were surely on their way to aid the convoy. One of the *Amsel* group, Rudolf Franzius's *U438*, was slow to clear the area, and was surprised by Commander Brewer's 1st Support Group as it homed in on ONS 5. Held in HMS *Pelican*'s radar beam, *U438* was depth-charged to destruction on 6 May.

The loss of *U438* marked the end of ONS 5's seven-day running battle, which had raged over 600 miles of ocean in the most appalling weather conditions. Largely owing to fuelling problems caused by the weather, the cost to the Allies had been heavy; thirteen ships totalling nearly 62,000 tons. For the U-boats it had been catastrophic, with seven boats sunk, five severely damaged and twelve others slightly damaged. Dönitz blamed the fog and the escorts' radars for the U-boat Arm's heavy loss, but there was more to it than that. At long last, after nearly four years of bitter defeat, the balance of power was finally shifting in favour of the Royal Navy.

# 16
# Closing the Gap

On 3 May 1943 the British steamer *Fort Concord* sailed from Halifax, Nova Scotia, bound for the United Kingdom with a cargo of 8,500 tons of grain and 700 tons of military stores, including four aircraft. She was a wartime-built replacement ship, the product of a Canadian shipyard, with a box-like hull having a huge cargo capacity for her size, and accommodation as basic as a 1930s North-East-Coast tramp. Her crew of 55 included eight DEMS gunners who manned her armament of one 4in gun, four 20mm Oerlikons, two twin Marlin machine-guns and two multiple rocket-firing 'Pillar Boxes'. On paper, the *Fort Concord*'s 2,500bhp engine, powered by two oil-fired boilers, gave her a speed of 11 knots, but in reality she could manage only 10 knots, and that with a good following wind. She was, in other words, a typical British merchantman of her day, and it was the dogged determination of those manning such ships, fiercely defended by the Royal Navy and the Royal Canadian Navy, that had at last turned the tide against the wolf packs.

The cost to the U-boat Arm of the battle for Convoy ONS 5, seven U-boats lost in return for thirteen merchantmen sunk, worked out at less than 9,000 tons per boat. Only a year previously the figure had been 100,000 tons for every U-boat sunk, which was then regarded as a fair return. Convoy ONS 5 brought the total of U-boats lost in April to eighteen, and Dönitz now became concerned for the success of his campaign in the Atlantic. He put much of the blame for the high losses on British 10cm radar, with which most convoy escorts and many long-range aircraft were now fitted. Search receivers carried by the U-boats were unable to detect the short-wave transmissions of 10cm radar, and in consequence boats were being caught on the surface and attacked without warning, all too often with fatal results.

The efficiency of the British radar in locating surfaced U-boats played a great part in their defeat, but it was only part of the story. Two years earlier, on 9 May 1941, Kapitänleutnant Fritz-Julius Lemp, commanding *U110*, was involved in an attack on the westbound convoy OB 318 south of the Denmark Strait. At that time Allied convoys were poorly protected and the U-boats were riding on the crest of a wave of unprecedented success. Lemp, operating on the surface in daylight, sank two British merchantmen and was going for a third when the corvette HMS *Aubretia* suddenly swept into view, obviously intent on ramming. Lemp crash-dived, but *Aubretia's* depth charges so damaged *U110* that she could not escape when the destroyers *Bulldog* and *Broadway* appeared on the scene. The combined depth charges of the two destroyers and the corvette blew *U110* to the surface. Lemp was killed, and a boarding party from *Bulldog* captured the submarine, and with it her Enigma coding/decoding machine and associated documents.

The acquisition of the Enigma machine from *U110* was largely responsible for the cracking of the U-boat code by cipher experts at Bletchley Park. More importantly, the Germans were not aware of the loss. The *U110* sank while she was being towed into port, and so well was the secret of the captured Enigma machine guarded that Dönitz assumed it had gone down with the submarine. Meanwhile, the code-breakers at Bletchley Park were effortlessly reading the majority of radio traffic between the U-boats and their bases. It may well have been that radar detected the wolf packs as they closed in on a convoy, but more often than not the Admiralty had been aware of their presence, and their intentions, many days in advance through the radio waves. Even as late as 1959, when Dönitz published his memoirs, he was still convinced that his U-boat code had not been compromised. The Admiralty saw no reason to disillusion him, and in fact did not release the story of *U110* and the capture of the Enigma machine until 1966, 21 years after the end of the war.

Allied air power over the Atlantic also reached a new peak in the spring of 1943. Very-long-range Liberator IIIs of the RCAF, based in Newfoundland, had at last closed the Greenland Gap, the terrifying 'black hole' that had for so long been the killing ground of the wolf packs. On the sea, the first British aircraft carrier specifically designed for convoy escort work had made its appearance. HMS *Biter*, commanded by Captain Conolly Abel Smith, was a converted merchant ship of 8,000 tons, armed with three 4in guns and fifteen 20mm AA cannon and carrying a squadron of fifteen Fairey Swordfish aircraft. The Swordfish, a fabric-covered, single-engined biplane with a top speed of 90 knots, had an exceptionally low stalling speed and was therefore ideal for carrier work. Unfortunately, *Biter* herself was so slow and vulnerable that she required three destroyers to protect her wherever she went. Her career was almost ended prematurely on 2 April, when she was sailing in support of ONS 4. In the grey light of dawn, Otto von Bülow in *U404* found the carrier in his sights and fired a full spread of four torpedoes. When he observed four detonations von Bülow claimed to have sunk the carrier. The truth was that all of von Bülow's torpedoes exploded short of their target, and *Biter* was unharmed. This was *U404's* swan song; four months later she was caught on the surface in the Bay of Biscay by Allied aircraft and sunk.

Surprise attacks by aircraft on U-boats as they crossed the Bay of Biscay on their way to or from their bases was, in the opinion of the Admiralty, partly responsible for an 'incipient decline in morale amongst at least some U-boat crews'. Hitherto, the U-boats had crossed the Bay homeward and outward on the surface at full speed, confident in the knowledge that they had ample time to dive when an enemy aircraft was sighted. The advent of the 10cm radar and the Leigh Light changed that, and avenging Liberators now swooped out of the clouds day or night without warning. The toll of boats caught on the surface by aircraft and blasted out of the water began to rise alarmingly, and Dönitz ordered all commanders to submerge at the first sign of enemy radar transmission and stay submerged for at least half an hour. Unfortunately for the U-boats, their search radars were ineffective against the 10cm radar, and the element of surprise remained with the Allied aircraft. Later in the year Dönitz would mount more anti-aircraft guns on the U-boats, send them out in pairs and order them to fight it out on the surface, but for the time being they were forced to spend long hours crawling along underwater when they should have been running free on the surface. This additional hardship did nothing for the already uneasy U-boat men.

Furthermore, the danger did not end with the completion of a patrol, for Allied bombers had turned their attention to the U-boat bases of the French Biscay coast. Docked in their pens with 16ft of reinforced concrete over them, the U-boats and their crews were safe, but the incessant rain of high explosives, which reduced the areas around the pens to rubble, posed a serious problem. Routine repairs, storing and refuelling became difficult operations fraught with danger, and a run ashore to the nearest *estaminet* (if one could be found still standing) involved a high risk of being blown into small pieces. For men who had endured several months at sea in a cramped iron coffin besieged by bombs and depth charges, this was the final indignity. Many walked down the gangway never to return.

The *Fort Concord* joined up with Convoy HX 237 late on 3 May as it passed Halifax, two days out of New York, taking up position as lead ship of column three. Although the convoy was not large, comprising only 46 merchantmen in all, it was well escorted. Lieutenant-Commander E. H. Chevasse, RN, led Escort Group C2 in the destroyer HMS *Broadway*, and had with him the frigate HMS *Lagan*, the British corvette *Primrose* and the RCN corvettes *Morden*, *Chambly* and *Drumheller*, the last two being old hands at convoy escort duties. In support of C2 was the merchant carrier HMS *Biter* and her three Home Fleet destroyers. Liberators of the RCAF were overhead, and *Biter's* Swordfish stood ready to take off as soon as the U-boats threatened.

The equinoctial gales had blown themselves out, and with all ships making 10 knots the crossing promised to be fast and uneventful; if Dönitz's roaming wolf packs could be avoided. But trouble was not long in coming to HX 237. On the night of the 4th the convoy ran into dense fog as it approached the

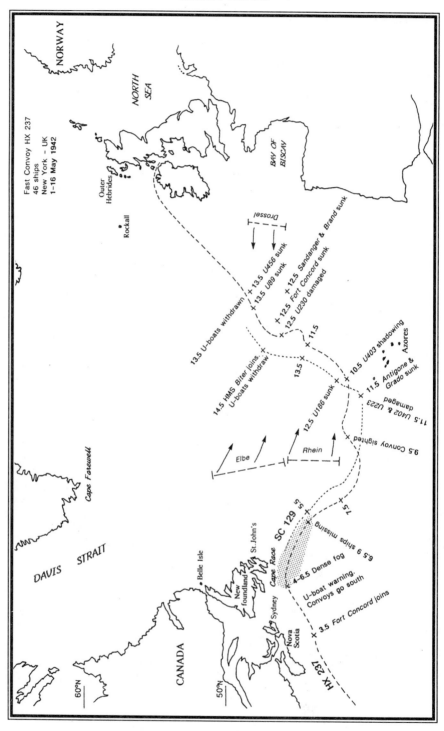

Fast Convoy HX 237
46 ships
New York – UK
1–16 May 1942

Grand Banks of Newfoundland, and order descended into confusion as the radarless merchantmen steamed blind within easy collision distance of each other. The fog continued for the next 48 hours, and the speed of the convoy dropped to a crawl, but miraculously – and largely due to keen eyes and ears – there was no clash of ships. However, when the visibility began to improve on the morning of the 6th, nine ships were missing, including the *Fort Concord*.

While HX 237 was preoccupied in feeling its way through the dense fog of the Grand Banks, *B-Dienst*, the German naval intelligence service, passed to Dönitz two Admiralty signals it had decrypted. One gave the sailing details of the slow eastbound convoy SC 129, and the other gave similar information on HX 237. Convoy SC 129 had sailed from Sydney, Cape Breton, a few days before HX 237, but would obviously be overhauled by the faster convoy either in the vicinity of Cape Race or a little further east. Accordingly, Dönitz decided to set an ambush into which he hoped at least one, and perhaps both convoys, would sail. From the survivors of the attack on ONS 5 and others just arriving in the area he formed two new packs, *Elbe* and *Rhein*, and stationed them 520 miles east of Cape Race in a 600-mile-long dog-leg patrol line stretching from 51° North to 43° North.

Weather conditions east of Cape Race were favourable, and it seems likely that Dönitz's net would have gathered in both convoys but for Bletchley Park. The Enigma decoders read the Admiral's signals to *Elbe* and *Rhein* within 24 hours of them being sent, and the Admiralty advised SC 129 and HX 237 to take immediate evasive action. The convoys were then some 400 miles east of Cape Race, within 60 miles of each other and on north-easterly courses. On receipt of the warning, both turned through 90° and headed south-easterly to pass around the southern extremity of the *Elbe/Rhein* patrol line. When Dönitz learned of the diversion he commented:

> Once again we must question how it was possible for the enemy to learn of our dispositions . . . It is just possible that he knew these through his airborne radar, but we can hardly accept this. Moreover, it seems improbable that he has broken into our cipher system, unless, of course, one of our boats has been captured intact.

Unknown to the Admiral, this was exactly what had taken place two years earlier.

As soon as it became clear that the two Allied convoys were skirting around the trap set by Dönitz, the *Rhein* pack, 36 boats strong, was instructed to head south-east at full speed. Its orders were to assume a new patrol line some 200 miles further east, and in the path of HX 237's new course. The *Elbe* boats, which were further to the north and had no hope of making contact with HX

237, went south-east to block the escape of SC 129. The *Drossel* pack, which, following the attack on ONS 5, had been sent east to intercept the Freetown–UK convoy SL 128, was ordered to return to the west at all speed to assist *Rhein*.

One of the *Rhein* boats sighted HX 237 on the 9th, but visibility was falling and she lost contact again. Next morning, *U403* (Kapitänleutnant Heinz-Ehlert Clausen) sighted an ocean-going tug heading east at speed. Deducing that the convoy must be in the vicinity, Clausen followed on the surface, and the tug led him to HX 237 that afternoon. By that time, however, the convoy, which was making 10 knots, was 90 miles to the east of the *Rhein* patrol line, and there was no hope of a successful pack attack by *Rhein*. Dönitz ordered Clausen to continue shadowing HX 237 while the six boats of the *Drossel* pack, still to the east, homed in on the fast convoy.

The *Rhein* and *Elbe* packs were then sent in pursuit of the slower SC 129, which they came up with on the afternoon of the 11th. The convoy was escorted by Captain Donald Macintyre's battle-hardened B2 Escort Group, and the action that followed was a brutal and salutary lesson for the U-boats. Before dark, Baron von Forstner in *U402* succeeded in penetrating the destroyer screen and fired a four-torpedo spread. The Baron had aimed well, for two of his torpedoes hit simultaneously the 4,545-ton British steamer *Antigone* and the *Grado*, a Norwegian steamer of 3,082 tons. The rescue ship *Melrose Abbey*, following in the rear of SC 129, picked up survivors from both ships, only two men being lost.

Although *U402* made off underwater, she was so badly damaged by depth charges that she dropped out of the fight. However, for Macintyre, flying his flag in the destroyer *Hesperus*, the loss of the two merchantmen, in daylight, was like a personal affront. In the previous nine months B2 had not lost a single ship to the enemy. When Oberleutnant Peter Gerlach in *U223* attempted an attack from astern after dark, he caught the full might of Macintyre's wrath. *Hesperus* attacked *U223* with depth charges, shelled and rammed her when she resurfaced, and followed her with depth charges set deep as she plunged to 700ft to escape. Twelve days later *U223* limped into St Nazaire with her conning tower riddled with holes, her pressure hull leaking and her engine room awash. Two of her crew had lost their lives and several others were injured. It was many months before the boat was again fit for sea.

Over the next 36 hours B2 fought a fierce action, holding at bay at least a dozen U-boats intent on savaging SC 129. They came in on the surface and underwater, keeping Macintyre's destroyers and corvettes constantly chasing from side to side and from one end of the convoy to the other. At one point Macintyre spotted the wake of a periscope moving across the bows of the *Hesperus*. He went in again and again with depth charges set shallow, until bubbles of oil and tell-tale scraps of wreckage and human flesh came to the surface.

Siegfried Hesemann's *U186*, one of the victors of the ON 166 action, was later posted missing, believed lost with all hands.

The U-boats lost contact with SC 129 following the sinking of *U186*, but regained it next day, when no fewer than eleven attackers were driven off by Macintyre's ships. Some of the escorts were now running short of depth charges and their crews were tired, but the timely arrival of HMS *Biter*, detached from HX 237, tipped the scales. The carrier immediately put her aircraft into the air and the U-boats, realising the odds were stacked against them, withdrew. Convoy SC 129 reached port with no further loss and, with one U-boat sunk and two heavily damaged, the victory was once again with Donald Macintyre and B2.

Having wandered away from HX 237 in fog in the early hours of the 6th, the *Fort Concord* had proceeded independently, intending to meet up with the convoy again on the 7th. Chief Officer J. B. Tunbridge reported:

We endeavoured to make the rendezvous for the 7th using dead reckoning as the visibility was too bad and we were unable to obtain sights. At 1200 on the 7th we sighted a destroyer who gave us the bearing and distance from the convoy, but I think the officer responsible reversed the bearing, because, instead of dropping astern to where the convoy was, we proceeded on a bearing which took us well ahead of it, and consequently failed to contact the convoy. On the 8th May we received a signal from the Admiralty giving us rendezvous for the 8th, 9th, 10th and 11th May. The fog lifted during the night of 8/9 May, so on the morning of the 9th we were able to take sights and succeeded in making the rendezvous for the 10 May. We found only four other merchant ships at the rendezvous, but there was no sign of the main part of the convoy or any escort vessels.

We continued in company with these four other vessels, making the rendezvous for the 11 May. The convoy was still not in sight and as we did not see any escort vessels or aircraft, we opened our sealed orders and proceeded independently at full speed. During this day we intercepted distress messages from two ships astern of us. We did not know submarines were in our immediate vicinity and received no diversionary signals.

The distress messages picked up by the *Fort Concord*'s radio operator must have emanated from the *Antigone* and *Grado* with SC 129, torpedoed some 400 miles astern. But distance cannot be measured by radio signals received by a single station, and the British ship's Chief Officer might be forgiven for imagining the enemy to be close at hand.

The *Fort Concord's* turn was not to come until nearly eight hours later. At 0040 on the 12th, having left the other ships behind, she was 720 miles west-north-west of Cape Finisterre and making 10¼ knots on a north-easterly course. The weather was fine and clear, with good visibility and a fresh south-westerly wind; a fine, early summer's night in the North Atlantic. Not another ship was in sight on the broad horizon, and the war seemed a million miles away. But for her arsenal of guns and drab grey camouflage, the *Fort Concord* could well have been any British merchantman on her homeward run three days out from the Channel. Indeed, among those keeping the sombre middle watch, from midnight to 0400, there was an unusual air of anticipation, and all the talk was of home and family, of good times past and those yet to come. It may well have been because of this relaxed atmosphere that no one saw the torpedo streaking in from the port side.

Kapitänleutnant Max-Martin Teichert, in *U456*, had been stalking the *Fort Concord* for some hours, and by midnight had moved into a position close on the unsuspecting merchantman's port quarter. His torpedo struck her in the after part of her engine room, causing a massive explosion that all but threw the ship on her side. When she righted herself, the sea poured in through the smoking gash in her hull and she began to settle bodily.

Chief Officer Tunbridge, off watch and sleeping at the time, was rudely awoken, but reacted instinctively. Grabbing his lifejacket as he left the cabin, he made a dash for the bridge, reaching it in time to hear the order to abandon ship. He then made his way aft to the boat deck, where he met a scene of utter devastation. Through the smoke and flames he saw that the engineers' accommodation, directly over the engine room, had collapsed like a pack of cards, and that the port after lifeboat – the only motor-powered boat – had been blown away. As Tunbridge struggled with others to clear away another lifeboat, the sea was already lapping over the boat deck. Less than a minute after the loaded boat cleared the ship's side the *Fort Concord* sagged amidships, broke her back, and sank with her bow and stern in the air. It is believed that 40 of her crew went down with her, most of them trapped in the accommodation. The lifeboat containing Tunbridge and fourteen others was sighted by a Swordfish from *Biter* during the afternoon of the 12th, the survivors being picked up by the corvette *Drumheller* before dark.

The *Fort Concord* was the first of the ships sailing independently to be lost. She was followed by the 9,432-ton Norwegian motor tanker *Sandanger*, sunk by Hans Trojer in *U221*, and another Norwegian motorship, the *Brand*, sunk by Oberleutnant Rudolf Baltz in *U603*. These unfortunate ships had sailed right into the patrol line being set up by the *Drossel* pack to catch HX 237.

Clausen in *U403* had held on to the convoy for 24 hours, until, constantly attacked by surface escorts and aircraft, he had been forced to break off contact. However, he had done what was required of him, shadowing the convoy until the *Drossel* boats had set up their ambush. Of these, it was *U230* (Kapitänleutnant Paul Siegmann) that, at 0615 on the 12th, made the first sighting of the HX 237. Oberleutnant Herbert Werner, Siegmann's first-watch officer, was astounded by what came over the horizon:

> I saw an amazing panorama. The entire horizon, as far and wide as I could see, was covered with vessels, their funnels and masts as thick as a forest. At least a dozen fast destroyers cut the choppy sea with elegance. As many as two dozen corvettes flitted around the edges of the convoy.

Despite Werner's overestimation of the strength of HX 237's escort, *U230* surfaced at 0915 and made her sighting signal to Dönitz and the rest of the *Drossel* boats. She then remained on the surface, intending to move closer before diving to attack. However, neither Siegmann nor Werner had noticed an aircraft carrier with the convoy, and at 0955 a small aircraft 'dropped out of the sun' on the surfaced submarine. Siegmann crash-dived with a hail of depth bombs following him down and severely shaking the boat. This was the beginning of six terror-filled hours for *U230*. Every time Siegmann surfaced, determined to get a shot at the convoy, he found an aircraft overhead, waiting for him, and was forced to dive deep again. In the course of the day the U-boat received a constant pummelling that would have sent most boats running for home, but Siegmann would not give up. Finally, at 1638, *U230* was at last in position for a submerged shot at a merchantman, but Siegmann raised his periscope only to find the lens filled with the flaring bows of a destroyer speeding in to ram. With engines racing full ahead, hydroplanes hard down and water flooding into her main ballast tanks, *U230* plunged into the depths. Oberleutnant Werner described what happened next:

> As the boat descended swiftly, the harrowing sound of the destroyer's engines and propellers hit the steel of our hull. An ear-shattering boom ruptured the sea. A spread of six charges lifted the boat, tossed her out of the water, and left her on the surface at the mercy of four British destroyers . . . For seconds there was silence . . . After a whole eternity our bow dipped and the boat sank – and sank. A new series of exploding charges lifted our stern with a mighty force. Our boat, entirely out of control, was catapulted towards the bottom five miles below. Tilted at an angle of 60°, *U230* tumbled to 250m before Friedrich [*U230*'s chief engineer] was able to reverse her fall.

Chevasse's ships had the measure of *U230*, and once they had put her down they had no intention of letting her rise again. For the next two hours the submarine was subjected to an incessant bombardment by depth charges and Hedgehog bombs as ship after ship made its run over her. While one escort dropped its charges, others held the U-boat in their asdic beams, making it impossible for Siegmann to escape by using his engines. He allowed the boat to sink deeper and deeper, until she eventually reached the incredible depth of 280m (915ft). There they waited, gasping for breath, with the air becoming fouler by the minute and water spurting from joints and valves as the tremendous outside pressure threatened to crush the boat's flimsy hull. Above, the charges continued to rain down, but, as the maximum setting for a depth charge was 500ft, they did little damage beyond striking terror into the hearts of *U230*'s crew. It was 0430 on the 13th before Chevasse finally called off his escorts and Siegmann was able to bring *U230* slowly to the surface. After enduring 36 hours of almost non-stop attack, both boat and crew were in very poor shape, but they eventually reached home.

Dawn was breaking as *U230* crept away, and in the same early light Teichert's *U456* was surprised on the surface by a Liberator of 86 Squadron circling ahead of HX 237. Teichert dived at once and it seemed that *U456* would escape without damage, and this might well have been so if the Liberator had not been carrying a new American weapon, the Mark 24 Mine or 'Fido'. This, in effect, was an airborne 'homing' torpedo, which, when dropped near a submerged submarine, homed in on her propeller noise. At this stage of its development 'Fido' had the reputation of being erratic, but in this case it went straight to the target. However, although *U456* was badly damaged and forced to surface, it was not attacked further because the Liberator was running short of fuel. Next day she was still on the surface when an aircraft of 423 Squadron, RCAF, found her. The frigate *Lagan* and the corvette *Drumheller* were called up, and although Teichert was able to dive he could not go deep. The escorts attacked with their Hedgehogs and the crippled U-boat went down for the last time.

Soon after the destruction of Teichert's boat, *U89* (Korvettenkapitän Dietrich Lohmann) took advantage of the diversion to make a stealthy approach to the convoy on the surface. This was Lohmann's final mistake, for the trimmed-down boat was spotted by the sharp-eyed observer of one of *Biter*'s Swordfish, then slowly circling the convoy. The aircraft attacked and called in the destroyer *Broadway*. *Lagan* was nearby, and between them the two ships depth-charged *U89* to destruction.

Late on the 13th, with HX 237 only 450 miles south-west of Ireland, Dönitz called off the remains of the *Drossel* pack, commenting:

Right from the first day carrier-borne aircraft were sighted and later the carrier herself. These and other land-based aircraft greatly hampered operations, which finally had to be broken off because the air support was too powerful.

Three days later HX 237 arrived safely in British coastal waters, having lost only three ships of 21,389 tons, and these would probably have been still afloat if they had not become lost in the fog off the Grand Banks and romped ahead of the convoy. *Drossel*, on the other hand, had suffered grievously, losing *U89*, *U186* and *U456*, while *U402* and *U223* were so badly knocked about that they were obliged to run for home. Nor was the account closed. On the 15th, while returning east, *U753* (Korvettenkapitän Alfred Manhardt von Mannstein) was sunk by a British joint air/sea action. The wolf pack *Drossel* had been decimated, and for precious little return.

News of the British victory crossed the Atlantic, and when Convoy SC 130 sailed from Sydney, Nova Scotia, escorted by Commander Peter Gretton's powerful B7 Group, a safe passage was anticipated. The convoy was composed of 39 ships, including the escort oiler *Bente Maersk*. Apart from this vessel the merchantmen were all ageing coal burners, typical tramps of the day, with their Plimsoll marks barely visible and making volumes of black smoke as they fought to maintain a convoy speed of $7^1/2$ knots. Gretton, again in the destroyer *Duncan*, had with him the destroyer *Vidette*, the frigate *Tay*, the corvettes *Sunflower*, *Kitchener*, *Snowflake*, *Pink* and *Loosestrife*, the trawler *Northern Spray* and the rescue ship *Zamalek*. An RCAF B-17 Flying Fortress from Newfoundland provided air cover.

As was to be expected in early summer, the convoy ran into dense fog when nearing the Grand Banks, causing the usual confusion. One ship left during the night to return to St John's, but otherwise all went well until *Vidette*, scouting in the van, picked up a large iceberg on her radar. The iceberg lay right across the convoy's path and, with no time to pass the word for an alteration of course, it seemed that one or more collisions of *Titanic* proportions were inevitable. *Vidette's* captain saved the day by putting his ship between the iceberg and the convoy, warning off the oncoming ships by using his searchlight and continuously sounding the international code letter 'U' ('You are standing into danger') on his siren.

The fog cleared next morning, but another danger loomed on the horizon for SC 130. *B-Dienst* had warned Dönitz of the convoy's coming, and the Admiral gathered together 33 U-boats, which he formed into two packs, *Iller* and *Donau*. A line of ambush was set up to the east of Cape Farewell.

The Admiralty signalled news of the wolf packs, but the first hard evidence the convoy had of the threat came on the night of 18 May, when U-boats were heard transmitting close by. It was a clear, calm night with bright moonlight, but when the escorts investigated they found nothing. At 0100 on the 19th more transmissions were heard, and an HF/DF fix pinpointed the U-boat responsible as being four miles on the port bow. *Duncan* gave chase, but the excellent visibility favoured both sides. The U-boat dived and escaped before the destroyer approached within three miles.

Before dawn, the Commodore took the convoy through an emergency turn of 90° to starboard with the object of throwing off shadowers, but to no avail. When, at first light, Liberators of 120 Squadron from Iceland arrived overhead, they reported sightings of U-boats all around the convoy. Gretton had the advantage of having three ships equipped with HF/DF, and any U-boat transmitting was immediately plotted and found itself the target of both escorts and aircraft. Throughout the following twelve hours, try as they might, the U-boats were unable to break through the tight defensive screen around SC 130. Baron Wilhelm-Heinrich von Pückler und Limpurg's *U381*, which had last seen action against Convoy SC 107, tried once too often and went down under a hail of Hedgehog bombs from *Duncan* and *Snowflake*, never to resurface.

That night, after a day of frenzied activity, an exhausted B7 was joined by the 1st Escort Group, made up of the ex-USCG cutter *Sennen* and the three frigates *Wear*, *Jed* and *Spey*. The reinforcements were a welcome sight around SC 130, but in no way did they deter the U-boats, which continued their efforts to break through the screen over the next 36 hours. Their endeavours were fruitless, for every time they made the approach their way was barred by warships and aircraft intent on their destruction. On the 19th, *U954* (Kapitän-leutnant Odo Loewe) followed in the wake of *U381*, being sunk by a Liberator of 120 Squadron, and then *U209* (Kapitänleutnant Heinrich Brodda) went under to the depth charges of *Jed* and *Sennen*, and a Hudson of 269 Squadron sank *U273*. Next day a Liberator of 120 Squadron caught *U258* on the surface and put an end to the careers of Wilhelm von Mässenhausen and his crew.

In the early hours of the 21st Dönitz called off his wolves, who by then had lost five of their number, not one of which had been given the opportunity to fire a single torpedo, let alone sink an enemy ship. It was a humiliating defeat for the *Iller* and *Donau* groups, and Dönitz himself had suffered a great personal tragedy as a result of the action. When *U954* went down on this, her first war patrol, she took with her 21-year-old Peter Dönitz, the Admiral's son.

These were bitter days for Grossadmiral Karl Dönitz, whose 'grey wolves' had once threatened to sweep Allied ships from the seas. His private grief he kept to himself; of operational matters, he wrote in his memoirs:

Radar, and particularly radar location by aircraft, had to all practical purposes robbed the U-boats of their power to fight on the surface. Wolf pack operations against convoys in the North Atlantic, the main theatre of operations and at the same time the theatre in which air cover was strongest, were no longer possible. They could only be resumed if we succeeded in radically increasing the fighting power of the U-boats. This was the logical conclusion to which I came, and I accordingly withdrew the boats from the North Atlantic. On 24 May I ordered them to proceed, using the utmost caution, to the area south-west of the Azores.

When the account for the months of April and May 1943 was presented, it became clear that the day of the U-boat in the North Atlantic was over for the time being at least, if not for ever. The total of Allied ships sunk in the two months, 106 ships of 593,000 tons, was still heavy, but nowhere near as bad as the 200 ships of over a million tons for the same months in the previous year. The really significant feature of the spring of 1943 was the unsustainable loss of 61 U-boats in two months. Dönitz blamed radar and increased Allied air cover, and to some extent he was right, but the root cause of the defeat lay with the U-boat crews. Hounded relentlessly while they were at sea, terrorised by bombs in their Biscay bases, and with the knowledge that the reign of the Third Reich was fast coming to an end, they had lost heart.

# 17

# A Last Throw of the Dice

When Dönitz withdrew his wolf packs from the North Atlantic, the retreat was an opportune one for the Allies, allowing the convoys laden with guns, tanks, aircraft and ammunition for the planned invasion of France to cross virtually unmolested. The few U-boats that had been left behind, mainly for weather reporting and to confuse the enemy with their radio transmissions, were all but impotent in the face of the improved defence of the convoys. By the end of August 1943 they had accounted for only four ships of just over 20,000 tons.

Meanwhile, Germany's Götterdämmerung drew nearer. In the East, where Field Marshall von Manstein's demoralised armies faced the hell of another Russian winter, a terrible bloodbath was in progress as Soviet tanks and men, in overwhelming numbers, flung themselves against the retreating German lines. Allied bombers, flying around the clock, saturated the cities of the Third Reich with fire bombs, inflicting enormous civilian casualties. In one night alone 42,000 had died in a raid on Hamburg, the industrial heart of the Ruhr lay in ruins, and even the capital, Berlin, cowered under a nightly rain of bombs. On 3 September General Montgomery's troops crossed the Straits of Messina from Sicily and landed on the toe of Italy, near Reggio. American forces followed them six days later, and the fate of Italy was sealed.

The U-boats, mostly operating independently in the Mediterranean and the Indian Ocean, continued to have some success, but at a price. In the three summer months of June, July and August they sank only 82 Allied merchantmen, while losing 79 of their own number. Dönitz almost faced a one-for-one situation, and at the end of August, with only 40 boats available for deep-sea operations, he accepted that they must be used in a last bid to turn the war in Germany's favour. This could only be done by savaging the enemy's North Atlantic convoys. The wolves must return to their traditional hunting ground.

In sending the U-boats back into the North Atlantic, Dönitz did not intend to let them go disadvantaged, and ordered that they be equipped with the best means of attack and defence that German technology could provide. At that stage the greatest threat came from Allied aircraft, which at the end of August patrolled the skies over the great ocean day and night from Biscay to the Gulf of Maine in ever-increasing numbers. These aircraft, Liberators, Catalinas, Sunderlands and Flying Fortresses, were all radar-equipped and could spot a U-boat on the surface long before visual contact was made. In the field of radar, German scientists were a long way behind their Allied counterparts, and had still not produced a set suitable for U-boats. They had, however, come up with the *Wanze* radar detector and the *Aphrodite* radar decoy, which gave a U-boat being tracked by radar some warning of the danger and a chance to escape. Past experience showed that a U-boat caught on the surface by an enemy aircraft could best survive by remaining surfaced, running at full speed and fighting off its assailant with AA guns. To this end, a semi-automatic 3.7cm and two four-barrelled 2cm cannon were fitted on deck. This enhanced armament was capable of throwing up a hail of shells lethal to any aircraft approaching too close.

The greatest moment of danger faced by a U-boat when attacking a convoy was in penetrating the escort screen, but it was hoped to overcome this risk by the use the new *Zaunkönig* torpedo. The *Zaunkönig*, or T5, was similar to the Allied airborne Fido in that it homed in on the propeller noise of the target. In addition to conventional torpedoes, a U-boat operating against a convoy was to be provided with three or four T5s, the theory being that she would use these to blast her way through the escort screen before falling on the hopefully defenceless merchantmen.

In early September, to spearhead the return of Dönitz's 'grey wolves' to the North Atlantic, the *Leuthen* pack put to sea. It comprised 22 boats from the Biscay bases and six from the North Sea, accompanied by the supply tanker *U460*. All of the attack boats were equipped with *Wanze* detectors, *Aphrodite* decoys, extra anti-aircraft cannon and T5 torpedoes. *Leuthen*, the best-equipped wolf pack ever seen in the Atlantic, had specific orders from Dönitz to target escorts rather than merchant ships. This was to be the last throw of the dice; a last desperate bid by a desperate man to regain supremacy in the North Atlantic.

*B-Dienst* had passed the word that a slow westbound convoy was due to sail from the UK in the second week of September, and it was assumed that it would take the shortest route, for this had been the practice since the withdrawal of the wolf packs in May. Dönitz therefore proposed to position his boats in a line across the great-circle track in longitude 25° west, which it was calculated the convoy would reach some time on the 21st. In view of the threat from patrolling Allied aircraft, the *Leuthen* boats were ordered to proceed submerged by day, advice which was evidently not followed by *U341*. She was sunk by a Liberator of 10 Squadron, RCAF, on the morning of the 19th, and not even her four-barrelled pom-poms were able to save her. Other boats dropped out for various reasons, and when it took up its position 400 miles south-south-west of Iceland on the 20th, *Leuthen* consisted of 22 boats. Their presence was as yet unknown to the Admiralty.

On this, their long-awaited return to the North Atlantic, the U-boats were in luck, for not just one, but two westbound Allied convoys were at sea. The slow convoy ONS 18, made up of 27 ships, had sailed on the 13th, while ON 202, a fast convoy of 38 merchantmen, left the UK two days later, on the 15th. Both were taking the short northerly route, and would at some time be in very close proximity to each other. Convoy ONS 18 was escorted by Escort Group B2, with the SOE, Commander M. J. Evans, in the destroyer HMS *Keppel.* Evans had with him the destroyer HMS *Escapade*, the frigate HMS *Towy*, the British corvettes *Narcissus* and *Orchis*, the Free French corvettes *Lobelia*, *Roselys* and *Renoncule*, the trawler *Northern Foam* and the merchant aircraft carrier *Empire MacAlpine*. The *Empire MacAlpine* was one of six bulk grain carriers taken over on the stocks and converted to carry four Swordfish. She sailed under the Red Ensign, was crewed by merchant seamen and carried a substantial cargo in her holds. Inevitably, being essentially a loaded merchant ship, she was handicapped by lack of speed and manoeuvrability, but she was, nevertheless, a powerful addition to B2. Given suitable weather for the Swordfish to take off from her short flight deck, the *Empire MacAlpine* would give Commander Evans a considerable advantage over the U-boats.

Convoy ON 202's escort, led by Commander P. W. Burnett in the Canadian destroyer *Gatineau*, was Escort Group C2, comprising, in addition to *Gatineau*, the destroyer HMS *Icarus*, the frigate HMS *Lagan*, the Canadian corvettes *Drumheller* and *Kamloops*, and the British corvette *Polyanthus*. In support was the rescue ship *Rathlin*, and air cover was provided for both convoys by very-long-range Liberators of 120 Squadron from Iceland. It was these aircraft that warned of U-boats concentrating in mid-Atlantic, which led to the Canadian 9th Support Group being sent to follow in the wake of the two convoys. This consisted of the destroyers *St Croix* and *St Francis*, the frigate HMS *Itchen* and the corvettes *Chambly*, *Sackville* and *Morden.*

Being some 3kt faster than ONS 18, ON 202 began to overtake the slower convoy, and on the morning of the 19th the two were within 90 miles of each other and in latitude 57° North, 600 miles out from the North Channel. The ships were in a state of maximum alert, and it was probably the increasing tension as the day wore on that caused an accidental firing of *Escapade's* Hedgehog. The bombs exploded on board, causing considerable damage, and it was necessary for the destroyer to turn back, leaving B3 considerably weakened.

The *Leuthen* boats were still forming their patrol line and not yet expecting a convoy when, late on the 19th, ONS 18 was sighted. The U-boats attacked persistently from midnight onwards, but were driven off by B2, which claimed to have damaged one of their number. At about 0200 on the 20th Paul-Friedrich Otto in *U270*, who had yet to claim an enemy ship, ran into the leading ships of ON 202. Unknown to Otto, *U270* had already been detected by HF/DF and HMS *Lagan* was racing in to investigate. *Lagan* had the U-boat on her radar screen, but Otto dived when the range came down to 3,000 yards. The frigate came on, oblivious to the danger, and when she was within 1,200 yards Otto fired a *Zaunkönig* from his stern tube. The T5, fired for the first time at an enemy ship, functioned perfectly, homing in on *Lagan's* propellers and blowing off 30ft of her stern. Twenty-nine of the frigate's crew were killed and, although she later reached port under tow, she was eventually written off as a total loss.

By dawn four U-boats were in contact with ON 202, and although the escorts kept them at bay, they held on to the convoy. At 0630 *U238* (Kapitän-leutnant Horst Hepp) broke through the screen and with one spread torpe-doed two 7,000-ton American Liberty ships, the *Theodore Dwight Weld* and the *Frederick Douglass*. The *Theodore Weld* sank immediately, but the other ship, although abandoned by her crew, remained afloat until sunk that night by *U645* (Oberleutnant-zur-See Otto Ferro). Survivors from both ships were picked up by the rescue ship *Rathlin*.

During the day, in falling visibility, the U-boats lost touch, and while they were out of contact ONS 18 and ON 202, then only 30 miles apart, were ordered to merge and form one convoy. Escort Groups B2 and C2 were joined by the 9th Support Group, and by late afternoon the combined convoy of 64 merchantmen was surrounded by a screen of five destroyers, three frigates, eleven corvettes, one trawler and one merchant aircraft carrier. Overhead, Lib-erators of 120 Squadron kept a constant vigil. When, at dusk, the visibility improved and five of the *Leuthen* boats regained contact, they found the sea covered with ships as far as the eye could see.

Manfred Kinzel, viewing the awesome spectacle from the conning tower of *U338*, was momentarily stunned, but recovered quickly and went in to attack while there was still daylight. As he approached the convoy on the surface, a Liberator swooped down and began to circle the boat. In a situation like this Dönitz's orders were to remain on the surface, call in other boats in the vicin-ity and fight back with the improved AA guns, hoping that the massed fire-power of several boats would bring down or at least deter the attacking aircraft. Kinzel signalled the other U-boats to join him but none complied, leaving *U338* to defend herself. As it turned out, it was not necessary for the attacking aircraft to approach within range of Kinzel's guns; the Liberator car-ried a 600lb 'Fido' acoustic torpedo, and *U338* went to the bottom with her stern blown off.

The *U386* (Oberleutnant-zur-See Fritz Albrecht) eluded the Liberators and approached the convoy, only to be chased off by *Keppel* and *Roselys* when Albrecht sent in a sighting report. Hubertus Purkhold in *U260*, hard on

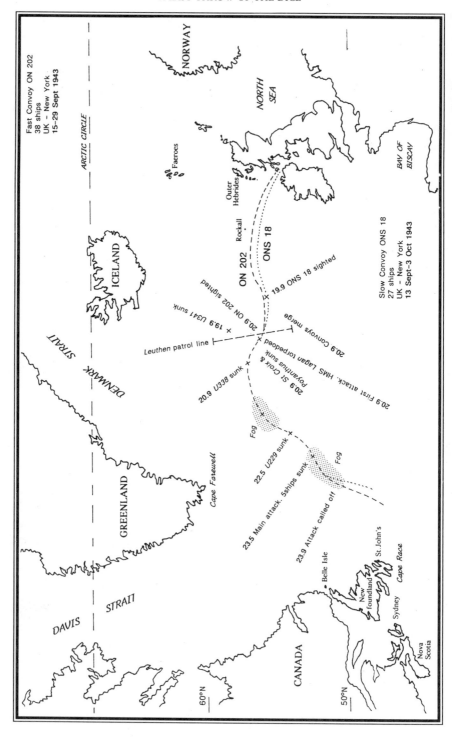

Albrecht's heels, loosed off a full spread at the massed ships, but all of his torpedoes failed to explode.

The sun was just disappearing below the western horizon when the U-boats, at least twelve of whom were ringing the convoy, switched their attention to the escorts. The first one in, *U305* (Kapitänleutnant Rudolf Bahr), was picked up by *St Croix's* asdics, and the Canadian destroyer raced in with depth charges. Bahr slewed around stern-on to the escort and fired a T5. The torpedo homed in on *St Croix's* propeller noise and exploded under her stern with devastating results.

HMS *Itchen* raced in to the crippled destroyer's aid and narrowly missed destruction herself when Bahr fired a second T5. The torpedo exploded in the frigate's wash, fortunately far enough astern not to cause serious damage. Some time later Rudolf Barr again fired at the *St Croix*, and this time the destroyer broke her back and sank. The British corvette *Polyanthus*, moving in to pick up survivors, was on the receiving end of a T5 fired by Oskar Curio in *U952* and also went down. These two very gallant ships, the old four-stacker *St Croix* and the product of a new war, *Polyanthus*, both veterans of many North Atlantic convoy battles, sank within sight of each other. Only one man of the corvette's crew survived, but most of the destroyer's crew were left clinging to rafts in the freezing water.

The night was filled with alarm as U-boat after U-boat darted in to fire their acoustic torpedoes and then retreat at full speed. Robert Schetelig in *U229*, Horst Rendtel in *U641*, Gerhard Kluth in *U377*, Paul-Friedrich Otto in *U270* and Joachim Deecke in *U584* all claimed hits on the twisting and turning escorts, but none penetrated the screen. In his second attack Schetelig became careless and was sighted by the destroyer *Keppel*. In his report of the action Commander Evans wrote: 'Only when the range had closed to 800 yards did the U-boat become aware of the presence of *Keppel* and turn abruptly away. *Keppel* fired a couple of rounds and then rammed just abaft the conning tower.' As she passed over the U-boat the destroyer dropped ten depth charges, and these must literally have torn *U229* apart, for all that came to the surface was oil and wreckage. The force of the collision stove in the *Keppel's* bows almost back to the fo'c'sle mess deck, but she carried on, still a credible fighting unit.

Fog came down in the early hours of the 21st, putting an end to *Leuthen's* determined attack on the escorts. The U-boats maintained contact with their hydrophones, but without radar they were blind and dared not risk blundering into the convoy screen on the surface. They kept their distance, perhaps resting on their laurels, for, in all, they had made fifteen attacks with T5s that night, and reported to Dönitz the sinking of seven destroyers and three more probably sunk. No doubt the Admiral treated these claims with caution, but it did seem that, even allowing for the loss of *U229*, the first action using the *Zaunkönig* torpedo had succeeded beyond his wildest dreams.

In reality, Convoy ONS 18/ON 202 had lost two valuable escorts, plus one other damaged beyond repair, and two merchantmen had gone down. This was a grievous loss in ships and men, but represented only a fraction of the convoy and its escort. The rest pressed on to the west, using the cover of the fog to make a diversion to the southward.

In the early afternoon of the 21st the fog thinned sufficiently for the carrier *Empire MacAlpine* to fly off one of her Swordfish, but the clearance was only very temporary and the aircraft was forced to return to the carrier after only a short flight. By nightfall, because of the danger of collision in the fog, the convoy was spread out over a front of nearly ten miles. The visibility improved somewhat after dark, and at about 2100 the U-boats attacked again. The escorts responded, *Chambly* damaging *U584* with gunfire after Deecke missed with a T5, and Curio's *U952* was rammed and severely damaged when the trawler *Northern Foam* exacted vengeance for the sinking of the *Polyanthus*. During the night at least eight *Leuthen* boats were in touch, and they persisted in their efforts to break through to the convoy, but they were repeatedly beaten back. Only the dense fog which returned at dawn on the 22nd put an end to their activities.

It was again early afternoon before the fog cleared enough to allow air cover, and then Liberators of 10 Squadron, RCAF, arrived overhead from Newfoundland. They found a number of U-boats on the surface around the convoy and fierce air/sea battles developed, the U-boats using their increased firepower to great effect. They did not escape unscathed, however. Paul-Friedrich Otto's *U270*, which had earlier crippled HMS *Lagan*, was so badly damaged that she turned away and made for home; Gerhard Kluth, the commander of *U377*, was seriously wounded, and his boat also withdrew.

That night, with the convoy 400 miles south of Cape Farewell and making a south-westerly course for Cape Race, the attacks continued, the U-boats coming in singly or in pairs from all directions. At about midnight the frigate *Itchen* was scouting ahead of the convoy in company with the Canadian corvette *Morden* when a surfaced U-boat was detected close by. *Itchen* switched on a small searchlight before attacking and *U666* was caught in the beam, but her commander, Herbert Engel, acted swiftly, firing two T5 torpedoes before diving. One torpedo exploded harmlessly in the wake of *Morden*, but the other went home in the stern of *Itchen*, and the frigate exploded with a blinding flash as her main magazine went up. Debris was hurled so high in the air that some of it landed on the conning tower of *U666*. Tragically, *Itchen* had on board the 85 survivors of the sinking of the *St Croix* and the only man saved from the corvette *Polyanthus*. Of the more than 200 aboard the *Itchen*, only three men were picked up by an American merchantman which came to their rescue. They were one man of the frigate's crew, one from *St Croix* and the sole survivor of the *Polyanthus*, who by then must surely have come to believe in miracles.

The next two hours passed peacefully, then at 0020 on the 23rd *U238* broke through the screen again. Horst Hepp fired a spread of five torpedoes, three of which found their mark. The 3,642-ton Norwegian motor vessel *Oregon Express*, the 7,134-ton British steamer *Fort Jemseg* and another Norwegian, the 5,096-ton steamer *Skjelbred*, all went to the bottom. Twenty minutes later Oskar Curio also broke through and fired four torpedoes; two sank the 6,198-ton American steamer *Steel Voyager*, one missed, and one hit another US freighter, the *James Gordon Bennett*, but failed to explode.

So, with the muffled clang of a dud torpedo striking the all-welded hull of an American Liberty ship, the battle for Convoy ONS 18/ON 202 came to an end, and the U-boats of the *Leuthen* pack withdrew. They claimed fifteen destroyers sunk by the new T5 torpedoes and nine merchantmen sunk by conventional torpedoes, for the loss of two U-boats. The actual figures were three escorts sunk, one severely damaged and six merchant ships lost, while three U-boats were sunk and three damaged. The honours went to the Allied warships and aircraft, but the *Zaunkönig* torpedo had proved to be a deadly new weapon. This prompted swift countermeasures from the Admiralty, and within weeks decoys imitating propeller noise were being towed behind all North Atlantic escorts.

The year 1943 had not been a good one for the U-boats. Ousted from the North Atlantic in the spring by the growing might of the Allied convoy escort forces, they had returned with new weapons but had failed to make a substantial impression. A return to the heady days of 1942, when fat merchantmen fell to their torpedoes at the rate of 100 a month – which was what was required – seemed most unlikely. Dönitz still had faith in his 'grey wolves', but as Commander in Chief of all German naval forces he decided to play another card in his shrinking hand.

On 22 December Convoy JW 55B, consisting of nineteen merchant ships with a close escort of British destroyers, was passing south of Spitzbergen, bound for Archangel, when it was sighted by a German reconnaissance aircraft. Word was passed to Dönitz, who ordered the battleship *Scharnhorst*, then in Alten Fiord, to prepare for sea to intercept and destroy the convoy. The 32,300-ton *Scharnhorst*, the only big German ship remaining operational, mounted nine radar-controlled 11in guns with an effective range of 25 miles, and was not expected to have any difficulty dealing with JW 55B's escort.

Accompanied by five destroyers, and with Konteradmiral Bey on board, *Scharnhorst* sailed from Alten Fjord in the evening of Christmas Day, 1943.

The Admiral's intention was to intercept and attack JW 55B, then being shadowed by a U-boat, the next day, when the convoy was about 50 miles south of Bear Island. The weather was in its customary foul winter mood; gale-force winds with sleet and snow, but it was hoped that this would prevent detection of the attacking force. Unknown to Admiral Bey, news of *Scharnhorst's* sailing had been flashed to the Admiralty, who took immediate action. Convoy JW 55B's escort was increased to fourteen destroyers, with a covering force of three cruisers, while the battleship *Duke of York*, then on station to the south-west of Bear Island with the cruiser *Jamaica* and four destroyers, was ordered to close in. The hunter was about to become the hunted.

There can have been precious little Christmas cheer in any of the ships on either side as, in three isolated groups, they ploughed through the heavy seas and driving snow towards their preordained rendezvous off the desolate Bear Island. The wind howled, spray froze in the rigging, and the cold was so intense that it seemed to penetrate into the very marrow of the bones of those unfortunate enough to be on watch above decks.

In these high latitudes the sun does not rise above the horizon in December, and it was still dark when, at about midday on the 26th, *Scharnhorst* sighted the ships of JW 55B. The German battleship was immediately attacked by the convoy's escorting destroyers and cruisers. In a brief engagement both *Scharnhorst* and the cruiser HMS *Norfolk* were hit, then the German ship withdrew to the south, shadowed by the escort cruisers. Meanwhile, HMS *Duke of York*, guided in by the cruisers, fought her way through the heavy seas until, at 1600, her radar detected *Scharnhorst* at a range of 23 miles. *Scharnhorst's* escorting destroyers had become lost in the gloom of the Arctic twilight, and the German battleship was unaware of her danger until, at 1650, starshell burst over her and the *Duke of York* opened fire with her big guns at 12,000 yards. At the same time the British destroyers raced in with torpedoes. *Scharnhorst* fled to the east, and in a running fight she was hit several times. Her speed dropped, and at 1900 the pursuing destroyers closed in, scoring hits with four torpedoes. The *Duke of York* then regained contact, opening up a devastating fire at 10,000 yards, and very soon it was all over. The mighty *Scharnhorst*, the last of Germany's big ships, sank, taking all but 36 of her complement of 1,970 officers and men with her.

Dönitz's attempt to hit the convoys with big guns had ended in catastrophic failure, and he now had to fall back on the U-boats. But little time remained, for German backs were now well and truly to the wall. On the Eastern Front, Field Marshall von Manstein's forces, retreating in disorder, were only eighteen miles from the pre-war Polish border and would soon be defending German-held territory. In Italy, Allied troops were held up at Cassino, but plans were already in hand for a landing at Anzio, less than 40 miles south of Rome. And the terrible, morale-destroying air raids continued, Lancasters of the RAF bombing by night and US Army Air Force Flying Fortresses by day. Over all this hung the threat of impending invasion.

When the new year of 1944 was ushered in, Dönitz had 436 U-boats in commission, of which 168 were operational. Most of these, however, were Type VIIs and Type IXs, now old and no longer able to run rings around Allied escorts as they had once done. Dönitz's hopes were pinned on the new Type XXI boats, with which he believed he could cut the supply lines stretching across the Atlantic and so either thwart Allied invasion plans or, at the very least, delay the landings. The Type XXI U-boat was a true submersible. With the aid of the *Schnorkel* tube, which supplied air for the diesel engines, it was capable, in theory, of staying submerged indefinitely. It had a range of 22,000 miles, an underwater speed 17kt and was equipped with sensitive listening devices capable of detecting enemy ships up to 50 miles away. In addition to conventional torpedoes, the Type XXI also carried *Zaunkönig* acoustic torpedoes.

Although 40 of the new U-boats were building, they were overtaken by the course of events. When, in the spring of 1944, it became evident that Allied troops would soon cross the Channel, only a few Type XXIs were ready, and Dönitz had no option but to fall back on the older boats. His revised plan was to station a chain of U-boats to keep watch in the North Sea, the English Channel and the Bay of Biscay, while other boats stood by in Norwegian and French ports, ready to put to sea and cause havoc among the Allied invasion fleet when it was sighted. In May he addressed a message to all U-boat commanders:

Gentlemen, as you know, the Allied invasion is expected momentarily. You must be in position to sail at any hour. Because our intelligence has not been able to discover the exact date and location of the landing, I have only general instructions for you. We shall be prepared to counter the blow wherever it falls. In Norway we have 21 boats on alert. The Biscay ports of Lorient, Saint Nazaire, La Pallice and Bordeaux are staffed with another 21 boats. Most likely, however, the invasion will simply cross the Channel and try to land some 20 to 50 miles from England. This is where you gentlemen step in. Headquarters' directive is short and precise: ATTACK AND SINK INVASION FLEET WITH THE FINAL OBJECTIVE OF DESTROYING ENEMY SHIPS BY RAMMING.

At about this time fate dealt Karl Dönitz another sickening blow with the news that his remaining son, Leutnant-zur-See Klaus Dönitz, had lost his life aboard an E-boat when attacking landing craft assembling off the Isle of Wight. The Admiral had now given both of his sons for a cause that even he had come to recognise as lost.

On the night of 5/6 June 1944 a huge armada of 6,100 ships, carrying 150,000 Allied troops, their arms, ammunition and equipment, left ports on the south coast of England, its objective the beaches of the Bay de Seine in Normandy. Operation *Overlord*, which was to end in the humiliating defeat of the forces of the Third Reich, had begun. Grossadmiral Karl Dönitz, who, in common with most of Germany's leaders, had been reluctant to accept that the day of reckoning was so near, was taken by surprise. The U-boats he had assigned to anti-invasion duties were still in port. Eventually, on the 6th, while Allied troops were swarming ashore on the beaches of Normandy, some 35 boats put to sea from the Biscay ports; only nine were Type XXIs fitted with *Schnorkels*. These nine headed for the waters around the Isle of Wight, where supply convoys were assembling, seven others went further west to lie off Plymouth, and the eighteen boats remaining formed a defensive line in the Bay of Biscay. It was too little, too late, and throughout the rest of 1944, while the waters of the English Channel and its approaches were thick with supply convoys, the U-boats sank only 60 ships.

By the end of the year most of the bases on the Biscay coast of France had been liberated and the U-boats had returned to the German ports in the North Sea and Baltic, from whence they had come four years earlier. In December they put to sea again in force, moving into British coastal waters to deliver what Dönitz thought could be a decisive blow against Allied shipping. By the end of January 1945 they had sunk only nine merchantmen and had lost seven of their own number. In February they mounted an attack on the Allied convoys pouring arms into North Russia, sinking fifteen merchant ships and losing fourteen U-boats. Finally, in March, the end of the road was reached when eighteen U-boats were lost for twelve merchant ships sunk. Sixteen other boats were destroyed by air attacks while in port. Karl Dönitz's great campaign to sweep Allied shipping from the seas was no longer sustainable, yet the U-boats fought on right until the last hours of the war. The final torpedoes were fired in the North Sea late on 7 May 1945 by Kapitänleutnant Emil Klusmeyer in *U2336*, sinking the Norwegian steamer *Sneland I* of 1,791 tons and the 2,878-ton British steamer *Avondale Park*. The war in Europe ended a few hours later.

It had been a close-run thing, the U-boats in their unrelenting campaign sinking with ruthless efficiency 2,759 Allied and neutral merchant ships and 148 warships, and killing almost 60,000 men. Only the skill and daring of the largely British and Canadian escort ships, the grim determination of the merchant seamen, and the huge capacity of American shipyards to turn out replacement ships decided the issue in the end. Not surprisingly, the price paid by the U-boat arm for this near-victory was enormous. Of the 1,170 U-boats built, 863 became operational in the war, and of these 753 were lost. With them went 28,728 men, all young, dedicated to their cause and unquestionably brave.

The submarine has always been regarded by professional seamen as an unethical weapon to send against a merchant ship, and its indiscriminate use in the Second World War put an end to all pretence of civilised warfare at sea. Yet those who served in the U-boats believed themselves blameless for the atrocities they visited on innocent seamen. One of the survivors, Oberleutnant Herbert A. Werner, wrote:

> Very much to the point, duty was the first and last word in the lexicon of the U-boat men; and, remarks to the contrary notwithstanding, we did our duty with a correct gallantry unsurpassed in any branch of the service on either side. We were soldiers and patriots, no more and no less, and in our great dedication to our lost cause we died in appalling numbers. But the great tragedy of the U-boat Force was not merely that so many good men perished; it was also that so many of our lives were squandered on inadequate equipment and by the unconscionable policies of U-boat Headquarters.

It is unlikely that any of those who, in the dead of a storm-filled Atlantic night found their ship blown from under them, and died alone and unseen in the icy waters, would have agreed with Herbert Werner. To die facing an enemy was one thing, perhaps honourable, but to fall to an assassin who hid under the sea was a cruel and undeserved fate.

There can be no doubt, however, that, although the U-boat men may claim to have acted honourably, their integrity was stained with the blood of innocent men. In 1942, when the unparalleled productivity of the American shipyards became evident, Hitler said:

> Merchant shipping will be sunk without warning with the intention of killing as many of the crew as possible. Once it gets around that most of the seamen are lost in the sinkings, the Americans will have great difficulty in enlisting new people. The training of seagoing personnel takes a long time. We are fighting for our existence and cannot therefore take a humanitarian viewpoint. For this reason I must give the order that since foreign seamen cannot be taken prisoner, and in most cases this is not possible in the open sea, the U-boats are to surface after torpedoing and shoot up the lifeboats.

Whether or not Dönitz agreed with Hitler's edict is not recorded, but on 17 September 1942 he issued the following order:

To all Commanders.

1) All attempts to rescue members of ships sunk, therefore also fishing out swimmers and putting them into lifeboats, righting capsized lifeboats, handing out provisions and water, have to cease. Rescue contradicts the most fundamental demands of war for the annihilation of enemy ships and crews.
2) Orders for bringing back Captains and Chief Engineers remain in force.
3) Only save shipwrecked survivors if statements are of importance to the boat.
4) Be hard. Think of the fact that the enemy in his bombing attacks on German towns has no regard for women and children.

In effect, Dönitz was putting an end to the humanitarian gestures some of his U-boat commanders had been in the habit of making towards men they had condemned to the water or lifeboats. There was no direct instruction to dispose of Allied crews, but the mere mention of the bombing of women and children implied that a Nelsonian eye might be turned on the over-zealous commander.

Dönitz was charged with war crimes at the Nuremberg trials in May 1946, and might well have joined the other Nazi leaders in the death cell had it not been for evidence given by Admiral Chester Nimitz, C-in-C of the US Pacific Fleet. Nimitz stated, somewhat naively, that on the orders of the Naval Chief of Staff US submarines had waged unrestricted warfare against Japanese ships throughout the war in the East; in other words, they were no better than the U-boats. On the strength of this admission Dönitz escaped the death penalty and was sentenced to serve ten years in prison.

Karl Dönitz died at Aumühle, near Hamburg, on Christmas Eve 1980. He was buried with full military honours on a cold, crisp January morning in 1981, his funeral attended by many of the men who had served his bidding in the U-boats. In his address, the Pastor who conducted the funeral said of the Admiral: 'He was, for me, one of the most devout Christians I have ever met'. This praise for the man who had once called Adolf Hitler 'one of the greatest heroes of German history', and was responsible for the deaths of tens of thousands of largely innocent seamen, is surely hard to justify. But, then, to this day Dönitz is still regarded by a generation of Germans as the man who, with his 'grey wolves', came so very close to ensuring that the Third Reich lived on for a thousand years.

# Bibliography

Beaver, Paul, *U-boats in the Atlantic*, Patrick Stephens, 1979.

Bucheim, Lothar-Günther, *U-boat War*, Collins, 1978.

Churchill, Winston S., *The Second World War*, Cassell, 1950.

Collier, Richard, *1941: Armageddon*, Hamish Hamilton, 1981.

Crane, Jonathan, *Submarine*, BBC, 1984.

Dönitz, Grand Admiral Karl, *Memoirs - Ten Years and Twenty Days*, Greenhill Books. 1990.

Gretton, Sir Peter, *Convoy Escort Commander*, Cassell, 1964.

Haldane, R. A., *The Hidden War*, Robert Hale, 1978.

HMSO, *British Vessels Lost at Sea 1914–18 and 1939–45*, Patrick Stephens, 1988.

HMSO, *The Battle of the Atlantic*, HMSO, 1946.

Hoyt, Edwin P., *The U-boat Wars*, Robert Hale, 1985.

Jones, Geoffrey, *Defeat of the Wolf Packs*, William Kimber, 1986.

Lamb, James B., *The Corvette Navy*, Macmillan of Canada, 19??.

Martienssen, Anthony, *Hitler and his Admirals*, Secker & Warburg, 1948.

Mason, David, *U-boat - The Secret Menace*, Macdonald, 1968.

Milner, Marc, *North Atlantic Run*, University of Toronto Press, 1985.

Ministry of Defence (Navy), *German Naval History. The U-boat War in the Atlantic*, HMSO, 19??.

Padfield, Peter, *Dönitz – The Last Führer*, Victor Gollancz, 1984.

Poolman, Kenneth, *Periscope Depth*, William Kimber, 1981.

Robertson, Terence, *The Golden Horseshoe*, Evans Brothers, 1955.

— *Walker RN*, Evans Brothers, 1956.

Rohwer, Jürgen, *Axis Submarine Successes 1939-1945*, Patrick Stephens, 1983.

Roskill, S. W., *The War at Sea*, HMSO, 1954-61.

Showell, J. P. Mallmann, *U-boats Under the Swastika*, Ian Allen, 1987.

Slader, John, *The Fourth Service*, Robert Hale, 1994.

Terraine, John, *Business in Great Waters*, Leo Cooper, 1989.

Thomas, David A., *The Atlantic Star 1939–45*, W. H. Allan, 1990.

Van de Vat, Dan, *The Atlantic Campaign*, Hodder & Stoughton, 1988.

Werner, Herbert A., *Iron Coffins*, Mandarin, 1990.

Whitehouse, Arch, *Subs and Submariners*, Doubleday, 1961.

# Index